Audrey K, Judd gave these to me and Sarah M on Wed, Aug. 15, 2015 ♡

Praise for *You're Already A[mazing]*

"I am honored to endorse this book for my friend Holley Gerth. Not only is she a fabulous, relatable writer, but she is a gift to everyone who has had the opportunity to share a corner of life with her.... In *You're Already Amazing*, Holley invites you to settle in with her, to hear the words of Christ, and to walk away changed. I have a feeling you'll be calling her your friend by the time you finish the first chapter, and I also have the sense that you'll feel a peace in knowing what the Lover of your soul longs for you to embrace as reality. He created you just as you are, for purposes that will bless and honor him. We can all use that reminder!"

Angie Smith, Women of Faith speaker and author of
I Will Carry You and *What Women Fear*

"Simply put, this is a book for every woman. Every woman who feels a crack line somewhere in her heart. Every woman who needs to find her way back to hope, Jesus, and everything she was made to be in Christ. Holley Gerth is a fresh voice for every woman—she echoes the voice of our Father."

Ann Voskamp, New York Times bestselling author of
One Thousand Gifts

"Stepping out to be who God's called us to be is a faith dare. We can't make this journey alone, and because of Holley's book, we don't have to. Holley's words strike that beautiful balance of trusted confidante, biblical counselor, and encouraging BFF. *You're Already Amazing* gives our hearts permission to be at home with who we are and to receive God's love down deep where we crave it most."

Bonnie Gray, www.FaithBarista.com

"Holley Gerth turns words like a poet. Warm and personal, *You're Already Amazing* is a biblical, practical handbook for every woman's heart. I would love to read this again with a small group of women or high school girls."

Emily P. Freeman, author of *Grace for the Good Girl*

"Reading this book is like sitting down for a conversation with Holley—and trust me, that's a real treat. You'll get all her attentive compassion and empowering wisdom. Best of all, you'll end up believing the truth of her God-given message: You are amazing!"

Heather Gemmen Wilson, bestselling author and international speaker

"Holley has an amazing way of speaking to and captivating the heart of a woman. This inspirational book is a must read for any woman needing a huge dose of encouragement and new perspective on how amazing she really is!"

Janet Daughtry, co-founder, Biblical Coaching Alliance

"*You're Already Amazing* offers women a dare they can't refuse. In Holley's gentle, loving way, she challenges us to dismiss the lie we think about ourselves—the one that insists we aren't enough. And then she offers us the tools we need in order to believe that we are already amazing. I found freedom in her words."

Kristen Welch, author of *Don't Make Me Come Up There!*
and founder of Mercy House ministry

"When you're wondering who you are and why you are, this book is like the good friend who takes you out to coffee to help figure it out. Holley Gerth understands all the expectations we heap on ourselves and shows us how to lay them down one by one in favor of the relationship God is inviting us into. This book and its message are the most wonderful, encouraging, and comforting relief."

Lisa-Jo Baker, social media manager for DaySpring
and community manager for www.incourage.me

"I so appreciated Holley Gerth's heart as I read *You're Already Amazing*—a work full of encouragement, joy, and extremely helpful prompts that helped me overcome obstacles in my own heart. This book is a perfect addition to the library of any woman who wants to see genuine life change and experience it with joy alongside."

Mary DeMuth, author of *Beautiful Battle*

Praise for *You're Made for a God-Sized Dream*

"Holley held my hand as I helped launch one of the biggest, scariest, most beautiful God-sized dreams I've ever been a part of. It impacted thousands of women from over twenty countries. This book is the blueprint that helped me make it through. I lived Holley's words throughout all the speed bumps, pitfalls, and loud voices of fear pummeling the inside of my head and the pit of my stomach. Holley's encouragement is practical, grounded in experience, and laced with grace, gospel, grit, and enough experience to convince you not to quit when the fear gets the loudest but to press on and into the God who gave you the dream in the first place. Everyone needs a guide when they're on a God-sized journey. With a sense of humor and a side of cheerleading, Holley is the one I'd recommend with two thumbs up."

—**Lisa-Jo Baker**, social media manager for DaySpring, community manager for the website (in)courage, and visionary for the (in)RL conference

"God has a dream for you. Yes, *you* have a God-sized dream, even if you don't know what it is yet. Holley will show you how to tap into your dream and thrive in it. You'll feel like you have a personal guide to help you overcome your fears, define your dream, and understand how to pursue it with confidence. Holley is the encouraging friend you'll need for the exciting adventure into your God-sized dream."

—**Stephanie S. Bryant**, cofounder of (in)courage and creative mastermind at S. Bryant Social Marketing

"I can't remember the last time I turned the pages of a book so eagerly. Holley's words have revolutionized my way of thinking with such a simple concept: that my dreams can't be bigger than God. If he's in my soul-planted dreams—and I think he is—then why wouldn't he also craft my life to fulfill those very same dreams? Holley is remarkably gifted at explaining universal heart truths to those of us in different seasons of life and then equipping each of us with the motivation to make those truths a reality. I thank God for my friend, this gifted writer Holley."

—**Tsh Oxenreider**, author of *Organized Simplicity*, blogger behind SimpleMom.net, and creative director of SimpleLivingMedia.com

"Reading this book is like having your own personal cheerleader by your side as you pursue your God-sized dream. Holley will challenge you to overcome your fear and stop sabotaging yourself, all the while reminding you that you're amazing and perfectly designed for turning your dream into reality."

—**Mary Carver**, author of the blog *Giving Up on Perfect* and monthly columnist at (in)courage

"Reading *You're Made for a God-Sized Dream* isn't like reading at all; it's more like a visit with a trusted friend, the one who speaks truth and wisdom into your life and helps you to see yourself the way God sees you. I have no idea how Holley accomplishes this (does every reader feel like they've found a new best friend?), but she does! God used this dream of Holley's to help me believe in the dreams he's seeded in *my* soul—those urgings that won't go away, the things that hide in secret places but are clawing for escape. Sifting through Holley's insights, I feel almost like I have *permission* to dream now; I didn't realize how much I swept those hopes to the corners of my heart."

—**Robin Dance**, author of the blog *Pensieve*

"Holley Gerth is a cheerleader for women with God-sized dreams of all shapes and sizes. She'll encourage and equip you to pursue the dream God planted in your heart."

—**Dawn Camp**, writer, photographer, and author of the blog *My Home Sweet Home Online*

"Holley is every woman's sister and a profound writer whose words touch the farthest corners of a woman's heart. Relational and personal, *You're Made for a God-Sized Dream* will show you how to give wings to your dreams as you fly straight to the heart of God."

—**Kristen Strong**, writer and author of the blog *Chasing Blue Skies*

"I used to think God-sized dreams were only for people with perfect faith, powerhouse social media platforms, or personalities that thrive in a high-stakes environment. Then I met Holley Gerth, and little by little she helped me realize that God-sized dreams are for everyone, including me. Including you. Combining her rock-solid wisdom as a certified life coach with her sincerely encouraging heart, Holley invites you to take a peek at the God-sized dreams designed specifically for you."

—**Deidra Riggs**, owner and writer of *Jumping Tandem*, managing editor for TheHighCalling.org, and contributing writer for (in)courage

You're Already
Amazing

You're Made
for a
God-Sized
Dream

You're Already Amazing

Embracing Who You Are, Becoming All God Created You to Be

Holley Gerth   2 in 1

You're Made *for a* God-Sized Dream

Opening the Door to All God Has for You

Revell

a division of Baker Publishing Group
Grand Rapids, Michigan

© 2012, 2013 by Holley Gerth

Published by Revell
a division of Baker Publishing Group
P.O. Box 6287, Grand Rapids, MI 49516-6287
www.revellbooks.com

Combined edition published 2015
ISBN 978-0-8007-2668-3

Previously published in two separate volumes:
You're Already Amazing © 2012
You're Made for a God-Sized Dream © 2013

Printed in the United States of America

Unless otherwise indicated, Scripture quotations are from the Holy Bible, New International Version®. NIV®. Copyright © 1973, 1978, 1984, 2011 by Biblica, Inc.™ Used by permission of Zondervan. All rights reserved worldwide. www.zondervan.com

Scripture quotations labeled ESV are from The Holy Bible, English Standard Version® (ESV®), copyright © 2001 by Crossway, a publishing ministry of Good News Publishers. Used by permission. All rights reserved. ESV Text Edition: 2007

Scripture quotations labeled KJV are from the King James Version of the Bible.

Scripture quotations labeled NIV 1984 are from the Holy Bible, New International Version®. NIV®. Copyright © 1973, 1978, 1984 by Biblica, Inc.™ Used by permission of Zondervan. All rights reserved worldwide. www.zondervan.com

Scripture quotations labeled NKJV are from the New King James Version. Copyright © 1982 by Thomas Nelson, Inc. Used by permission. All rights reserved.

Scripture quotations labeled NLT are from the *Holy Bible*, New Living Translation, copyright © 1996, 2004, 2007 by Tyndale House Foundation. Used by permission of Tyndale House Publishers, Inc., Carol Stream, Illinois 60188. All rights reserved.

15   16   17   18   19   20   21   7   6   5   4   3   2   1

In keeping with biblical principles of creation stewardship, Baker Publishing Group advocates the responsible use of our natural resources. As a member of the Green Press Initiative, our company uses recycled paper when possible. The text paper of this book is composed in part of post-consumer waste.

green press INITIATIVE

Contents

You're Made for a God-Sized Dream   223

You're Already Amazing

Embracing Who You Are,
Becoming All God Created You to Be

For amazing you

and the God who made you that way

Introduction

The Dare

Pssst... pull up a chair and I'll tell you a secret. You'd better lean in close for this one.

Ready?

You don't have to *do* more, *be* more, *have* more.

I'm sure there are security alarms going off somewhere. You should probably hide this book when your in-laws come over. And this could be the makings of a Sunday morning scandal.

But it's true.

It's the kind of true that will change your life, set you free, and make you wake up smiling for the first time in a long time. I know because that's what it did for me (and believe me, for this non-morning girl that's nothing short of miraculous). I've seen it happen to a lot of other women too. I've read it in their words through thousands of comments on my blog. I've seen it in their faces as they sit on the couch in my counseling office. I've heard it in a new kind of laughter over coffee with friends.

So watch out, sister. If you keep reading, you just might be next.

Even if we've never met, I know this about you: you're a daughter of God, a holy princess, a woman created with strengths you've yet to fully grasp and a story that's still being written by the divine

Author himself. And if you really take hold of who you are and what you're called to do, there will be no stopping you. That's because there's no stopping him *in you*—and he's got bigger plans for your life than you've even imagined.

Okay, you've been warned.

If you're feeling brave, I dare you to read on . . .

A **Heart-to-Heart** Talk

My friend sits across the table at lunch. She's lovely, wonderful, a bringer of joy to my heart. Yet today there's little light in her eyes. She talks of endless juggling—kids, work, church, marriage, sex, groceries, and God.

She whispers, "Sometimes I don't even like my life. And I feel so guilty because I'm so blessed."

She speaks of reading books, doing studies, and listening to sermons that say she needs to give more, have more quiet time, find more friends.

"I try," she says. "I try so hard and I just fall further behind."

She describes her spirituality as a treadmill that keeps having the speed turned up. She runs faster and faster, only to become more exhausted.

As she shares, I think not of where she is going but of the One who is pursuing her heart. He stands just behind her, but she can hardly hear his voice above the whir of the track.

"Dear daughter," he whispers. "Come to me. You are weary and burdened. I will give you rest. You're already pleasing to me."

I tell her this and she pauses, sighs, leans into that truth for a moment. I watch the treadmill slow and then stop as she rests instead in the arms of grace.

A woman settles onto the couch in my counseling office. I can tell she's got something hard to say this week. She shifts back and forth. I see the words rolling around in her mind and finally making their way to her lips. She tells of abuse from those who should have protected her. Rejection instead of love. Names called in the privacy of her home and the public of the playground. Sticks and stones could break her bones, but it's words that have broken her heart. She finally comes up for air, and as the tears run a river down her cheeks, it seems a single lie follows their tracks.

"You could never be enough."

If it were audible it would be said with a hiss—the same one that has haunted Eve's daughters since the Garden. And within me I feel the response rising from a more Tender Voice.

"Tell her the truth."

So I do, and the rivers of tears become torrents, buckets of loss and fear poured out in that office. Empty and full, she looks up and smiles.

It's the first time I've ever seen her do so.

She writes me an email from across the world. I've never seen her face or even visited her continent. But we are more alike than different.

She tells me of feeling meaningless and wondering if she has anything at all to offer. She types, "Everyone else matters but me. Everyone else has something to offer but me. God must be so disappointed."

As I read her words I feel a physical ache in my chest, a longing for her to see what I can see in just a few sentences—that she has kindness, creativity, gifts, and strengths. She is brave, compassionate, and valuable.

I think of God placing his hand over hers as she types those sentences, wanting with all of his heart to replace those wounding words with new ones that reflect his love for her.

I type back, "Yes, you matter. No one can take your place. God made just one *you*, and this world needs you just as you are."

I hit "Send" and pray the truth will make its way straight to her heart.

Wherever I connect with women, it seems the same hurt is there. I recognize it well because I've felt it too.

I know what it's like to stare at the ceiling in the middle of the night and ask hard questions with few answers. I know what it's like to hide in the corner of the room, hoping no one will notice me, wondering if I'll ever be wanted. I know what it's like to wrestle with insecurity, guilt, and impossible standards of my own making. *I know.*

Yet there also came a point when my heart began knowing something deeper as well. In my desperation, I started asking God what he really wanted for his daughters. I searched the Scriptures, talked to women, pondered and prayed. I'm still trying to understand all of it and, quite clumsily, to fully live it. But what I discovered just may be the best news you'll ever hear.

So let's talk.

Would You Like to Have Coffee?

Imagine I ask you to have coffee with me—which is exactly what I do with my dearest friends. There's just something about sitting across a table from someone you truly care about that really gets a conversation going. (And if you're not a coffee drinker, then tea or a yummy dessert are perfectly acceptable substitutes.)

I call, text, or email: "Can we get together? There's something I'd really like to tell you."

We pick your favorite spot. I meet you at the door. We settle into a quiet corner. Order our favorite drinks. Swap small talk over mochas or tea.

Sip by sip we go deeper, until we land at the level of the heart...that place where it's hard to go in the middle of the busy and the broken.

I clear my throat, lean back, look you in the eyes, and say:

~ *"It's time you knew you're amazing."* ~

You smile, laugh awkwardly, glance at the ceiling. "I know, I know," you reply. "So kind of you to say."

I respond, looking at you more intently.

"I mean it's time you *really* knew. And there's more:

- You're not only amazing.
- You're enough.
- You're beautiful.
- You're wanted.
- You're chosen.
- You're called.
- You've got what it takes ... not just to survive but to change the world."

By this time your fingers are wrapped around your cup. You stare down at the bottom of it, focused on the emptiness, wondering why these words are so hard to hear.

Finally, you ask, "Who told you that?"

And I respond, "The only One who really knows—Someone who loves you."

You're God's "It Girl"

There's a pause in our conversation, and you point to a frame on the wall. It's a portrait of a woman taken by a professional photographer. The image makes it clear that she's the kind of girl who makes heads turn and smiles appear out of thin air. She looks entirely serene and effortlessly chic. We speculate that even grande mochas don't go to her hips.

"Okay," you laugh, "I could understand if you told her she's amazing. But me? I've got a lot of work to do. I'm not exactly the 'it girl.'"

"Good thing you're not," I casually respond.

You're a bit surprised. "What did you just say?"

"I said it's a good thing you're not the 'it girl.'" And with a twinkle in my eye, I lean in to tell you why.

Our culture is obsessed with the "it girl." She's defined as a woman who has it all together—whatever "it" is <u>at the moment</u>. We want to be like her and do what she does. We can't imagine anyone feeling the same way about us. Life becomes a competition to see who can be the prettiest, trendiest, and most stylish. In the corporate world, it's who can climb highest, fastest, farthest. In the church (don't think we're exempt) it's who can be the sweetest, godliest, most servant-hearted. Depending on the day or year, who that woman is changes. It's an endless game of "tag—you're it" that <u>exhausts us</u> all and makes us competitors rather than sisters.

I compare myself to others

But when we look at the kingdom of God, it's a different story. There aren't "it girls" (or guys). There are only "*is* girls." God looks at you and says, "<u>She *is* loved, accepted, and valued. She *is* created just the way I wanted her to be.</u>"

Our biblical buddy Paul wrote letters to some of the first churches. He told early Christians that we're a body. Someone is a hand. Another person is a foot. <u>There's no competition—only complementing and completion.</u> Part of the beauty of that is how different we are from each other. As my friend Jennifer Leep says, "God creates each of us to be uniquely who we are—just like each part of the body is unique. We don't need more than one of a given body part. Nor would we want more than one. Sure, we have two hands and two feet. But not two *right* hands or two *left* feet. Each part of the body has a purpose that only it can fulfill. The same is true for us. That's a truth that's easy to understand *and easy to forget*."

Most People Don't

In my life, forgetting the truth we just talked about often starts with one phrase: "Most people don't . . ."

Those three words *ping, ping* in my mind over and over like pebbles against a glass window. When they do, I pause and consider, "It's true. Most people don't spend so much time sitting in front of a laptop and writing." And then it comes: "What's the matter with you? Why can't you relax and be more like most people?"

You've had these words thrown like stones at you too, haven't you?

Most people don't . . . wear themselves out in the kitchen because they believe a meal feeds hearts and fills bellies.

Most people don't . . . throw off their entire schedule because they take time to listen to the stranger in the grocery store who's having a hard day.

Most people don't . . . pore over spreadsheets until their eyes are red because they see numbers as a sort of art and a way of bringing order to a chaotic world.

It's true. Most people don't do what you do, love what you love, feel the kind of passion you feel about that thing.

I started thinking about this recently, and I realized we're in pretty good company if we feel like we're not like most people. After all:

- Most people don't . . . build an ark.
- Most people don't . . . lead people through the desert to the Promised Land.
- Most people don't . . . die on a cross to save the world.

But aren't we glad one person did each of these things?

If most people don't do what you do, and you're passionately pursuing Jesus with your life, then it's probably not just a human plan. The heartbeat of God is probably somewhere within it. We need you, just you, to fulfill that purpose, complete that project, bring that gift to the world in a way no one else can.

Most people don't ... but you do.

In your own wonderful way, you're God's "is girl."

And that's amazing.

Putting the Pieces Together

Back at our corner table, a waitress stops by and asks if we need anything else. She lifts an empty cup from the table, revealing more of the surface beneath. It's a mosaic, hundreds of broken pieces placed together again to make a vibrant pattern.

I run my hand over the roughness and reflect, "This has been the hardest part for me."

You tilt your head and pull your brows together, a look of concern crossing your face. "What do you mean?"

"The brokenness in my life has sometimes made it difficult for me to believe I could ever be amazing."

I can relate to those scattered pieces on the tabletop because my life is made of much the same. Bits of hurt tossed here and there, dreams shattered. This has especially been true in the last five years or so. My husband and I have struggled with infertility all that time (and we still do). That kind of brokenness isn't a loss you mourn once and move on from; it stays.

As I drove home from work one day, the pain I felt seemed especially pointless, and in turn, my life did too. "God," I whispered, "how can you use me when I'm so broken?"

A song came on the radio that repeated a verse from Isaiah over and over again:

> He was pierced for our transgressions,
> he was crushed for our iniquities;
> the punishment that brought us peace was on him,
> and by his wounds we are healed. (Isa. 53:5)

I started singing along with the words. As I did it seemed God whispered to my soul, "You think you have to take what's broken and make it perfect in order to be used by me. But I think in a completely different way. I took what was perfect, my Son, and made him broken so that you could be whole. And because you belong to him, your brokenness can bring healing to others too."

love!

I touch the mosaic again. "It's a crazy, upside-down way of thinking. But it's true. God has used my brokenness in ways I never expected. It's become part of who I am, a surprisingly beautiful part."

My friend and fellow writer Angie Smith can also relate to broken pieces. She shared a story on her blog *Bring the Rain* about smashing a pitcher and then piecing it back together again after the loss of her daughter:

> I began to realize that this pitcher was my life, and every piece was part of a story that God had chosen to put together. I started crying, and remembering things I thought I had forgotten. It took a long time to finish, but it was time well spent. Every nook and cranny whispered to me, until at last it stood in all its imperfection.
>
> *Here you are, Angie.*
>
> *You are mended. You are filled with my Spirit, and I am asking you to pour yourself out.*
>
> The image of my life as a broken pitcher was beautiful to me, but at the same time, it was hard to look at all of the cracks.
>
> I ran my fingers along them and told him I wish it had been different. How I wished I had always loved him, always obeyed him, always sought him the way I should. I was mad at the imperfections, years wasted, gaping holes where it should be smooth.
>
> But God, my ever-gracious God, was gentle and yet convicting as he explained.
>
> *My dearest Angie. How do you think the world has seen me? If it wasn't for the cracks, I couldn't seep out the way I do. I chose the pitcher. I chose you, just as you are.*[1]

God has put my heart together again too. It's not the same as before—but it's good. He's filled those empty spaces with his grace and, surprisingly, joy. Oh, sure, there are still days when I try to tear the table apart again and make it into something else I think I'd like better. But those days are fewer and farther in between.

I touch the seams between the pieces in the table again and say, "It's a good thing God can put us back together again. I'm totally craft challenged. I'm not even allowed to use a hot glue gun!"

We both laugh and then sigh, lost in our thoughts, wondering at the way God works. He doesn't just restore; he transforms. Beauty from ashes—or brokenness.

The End (and the Beginning)

By this time the coffee shop is almost empty. We take one last sip and make plans to get together again soon.

"Remember," I say as we walk toward the door, "it's true—you're already amazing."

You laugh, "Okay, I'll try to believe it. But you might need to say it a few more times."

"I will. I promise."

We step into early evening. The lights outside are just starting to really shine.

And maybe, just maybe, the ones inside are too.

2

Who Am I, *Really?*

Who am I?

It's a question we ask throughout our lives. Oh, maybe we don't use those exact words. But we're looking for the answer from the time we awkwardly enter the middle school cafeteria and hope for a table where we belong. It can drive us to fix our hair a certain way, date that boy, break that rule, join that club, or pursue that degree, and it can ultimately take us to the life we have now. Even as grown women, we still ask it. We just trade the junior high cafeteria for a women's retreat, corporate boardroom, or playgroup. No matter how many years go by, we still ask, "Who am I, *really?*"

And until we can answer that question, it's impossible to believe we're amazing.

I believe the desire to know who we really are has been placed within us by the heart of heaven itself. God wants us to understand who he created us to be so that we can fulfill the purpose he has for our lives. Sometimes we feel guilty for wishing we knew more about ourselves. After all, we're not supposed to focus on ourselves, right? I often hear women say, "That's selfish." But it's not the question that matters—it's what we do with the answer.

If you want to understand yourself just so that you can do whatever you'd like for your personal gain, then it's self-centered. If your intent is to love God, others, and yourself more, then knowing who you are is one of the most unselfish things you can do. And I have a feeling that second option is why you're reading this book. Yes? So push that guilt aside and give yourself permission to explore who God made you to be.

Once we decide we want to know who we are, we still wonder, "But how can I know who I am?" This chapter is designed to give you tools to help answer that question. The following pages are broken into sections that will give you an overview of three different parts of who you are: your strengths, your skills, and your "who." Each section includes an interactive tool that will help you apply what you've read specifically to you.

A little disclaimer: All the chapters in this book have interactive tools and exercises, and you have full freedom to use them in whatever way works best for you—whether that's doing them as you go, waiting until the end, or even (gasp!) skipping them completely. For a printable version of the tools and exercises, go to www.holleygerth.com/books. And if you're interested in going deeper, check out the guide in the back of the book. You can use it on your own, with a few friends, or in a group.

Your Strengths

I always find these q's kind of awkward

When new clients come to me for counseling, I ask them to fill out a form. In one place it asks, "What is one of your strengths?" There are far more personal questions on the page, but that's the one that's most often left blank. Women walk through the door and apologize,

"I couldn't think of anything to put for that question." Whatever else we may talk about in our sessions, we always work on finding strengths. It's like mining for diamonds. I know those strengths are in there—we've just got to find them and bring them into the light.

It's the same way with you. Like I said before, I wish we could have coffee together so that I could find those strengths with you in person. You've got them. I know it. God does too. After all, he's the One who placed them within you.

So what exactly is a strength? *A strength is a personal characteristic that can be used on behalf of God in service to others.* Usually strengths are present throughout our lives but can be enhanced through experience or training. Strengths are part of *who we are* while skills are more about *what we do*.

· · · · · · · · · **Find Your Strengths: 5 Minutes** · · · · · · · · ·

Circle three strengths that apply to you.

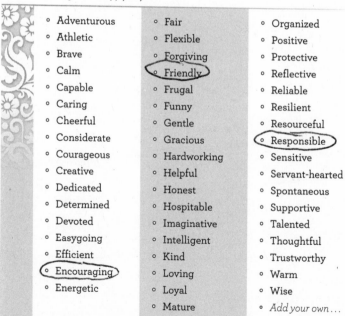

○ Adventurous	○ Fair	○ Organized
○ Athletic	○ Flexible	○ Positive
○ Brave	○ Forgiving	○ Protective
○ Calm	○ Friendly	○ Reflective
○ Capable	○ Frugal	○ Reliable
○ Caring	○ Funny	○ Resilient
○ Cheerful	○ Gentle	○ Resourceful
○ Considerate	○ Gracious	○ Responsible
○ Courageous	○ Hardworking	○ Sensitive
○ Creative	○ Helpful	○ Servant-hearted
○ Dedicated	○ Honest	○ Spontaneous
○ Determined	○ Hospitable	○ Supportive
○ Devoted	○ Imaginative	○ Talented
○ Easygoing	○ Intelligent	○ Thoughtful
○ Efficient	○ Kind	○ Trustworthy
○ Encouraging	○ Loving	○ Warm
○ Energetic	○ Loyal	○ Wise
	○ Mature	○ *Add your own . . .*

If you're still wondering if the words you circled are strengths, then you can put them through the STRENGTH test:

Service	*Does it help me serve God and others?*
Time	*Has it been present throughout much of my life?*
Relationships	*Do others see this?*
Energy	*Do I feel energized when I'm living this way?*
Natural	*Does this come naturally to me most of the time? Or do I know God has intentionally developed this in me even though it doesn't?*
Glory	*Does God ultimately get the glory from it?*
Trials	*Even in hard times, does it usually come through somehow?*
Heart	*Does this really feel like a core part of who I am?*

The Source of Your Strengths

How did you get your strengths? God created you with them. You are "fearfully and wonderfully made" (Ps. 139:14). Then he allows life experiences to develop your strengths even more.

For example, I love words. *Always have.* I don't like numbers. *Never have.* Are you nodding your head with me? Shaking it back and forth in disagreement? Marcus Buckingham and Donald O. Clifton, authors of *Now, Discover Your Strengths*, say there's a reason for your particular response. They explain that our brains are actually wired to approach life in certain ways: "By the age of three each of your hundred billion neurons have formed fifteen thousand synaptic connections with other neurons.... Your pattern of threads, extensive, intricate and unique, is woven."[1]

Pretty amazing, huh? Marcus and Donald go on to say that by age sixteen, half of these connections are lost. "Oh, no!" I thought when I first read that. But it's actually a great big, "Oh, yes!" to who God created you to be. The connections dropped allow you to focus intensely on the remaining ones, your strengths. As Marcus and Donald say,

> Your smartness and your effectiveness depend on how well you capitalize on your strongest connections. Nature forces you to shut down billions of connections precisely so that you can be freed up to exploit the ones remaining. Losing connections isn't something to be concerned about. Losing connections is the point.[2]

In essence, the most vibrant connections become our strengths, and those that fade away become our weaknesses. I love this because there are parts of me I wish I could change. (I'm sure no one else feels that way.) I don't have many decorating, details, or dinner-making connections in my brain. No, ma'am!

But it turns out that God has physically wired me with strengths that let me fulfill his purpose for my life. And he helps me do so by strategically creating certain weaknesses too. It gives "power made perfect in weakness" (see 2 Cor. 12:9) a whole new meaning. *Our divinely created strengths (fueled by God's power) are actually supported by our weaknesses, because if we were good at everything, we wouldn't focus on much of anything.*

Sigh of relief. Maybe no one else struggles with this, but it was some of the best news I've heard in a long time. For my husband's sake, I'm still going to try to keep those weaknesses a little in check. (Who made coffee without a filter last week because she's not so good at details? *Ahem.*) But I'm also going to celebrate who I am and who you are—fearfully and wonderfully made, strengths and weaknesses woven together just right.

Living in Your Strengths

Once we know our strengths, we can begin to feel a lot of pressure to maintain a certain standard. We tell ourselves, "I have to *always* be friendly." Or "I should *never* miss an opportunity to be kind." Then when we miss the mark, we're quick to condemn ourselves. But even in our areas of strength, we'll mess up. We'll fall short. We'll make mistakes. That's why there's grace.

And we don't have to muster up the power to live in our strengths ourselves. Philippians 4:13 says, "I can do all things through Christ who strengthens me" (NKJV). Jesus is the source of our strengths, and he's also the One who enables us to live in them each day. We don't have to force ourselves to be "on" all the time. Instead our focus can be on remaining "in" Christ. Just ask him to use your strengths to glorify him and serve others. And if you mess up, ask forgiveness and keep on going.

Also, be gentle with yourself. When we're tired, hungry, lonely, or afraid, our strengths can quickly flip to the other extreme. Passion becomes irritability. Sensitivity turns into worry. If you find yourself having a reaction that's not helpful, just stop and take a deep breath. Think about what you're feeling and what you need.

Rather than wishing you were different, stop and say, "I'm getting away from my strengths right now." Then ask yourself, "What do I need to do to change this reaction and respond out of one of my strengths instead?" Ask God for help, and then take action. *When you attack yourself, you side with the enemy.* God is always for you—that means you can be too. We'll all slip out of our strengths at times. The key is just getting back into them as quickly as possible. Receiving God's grace and giving it to ourselves speeds up that process.

The goal is not perfection. It's simply to be in an intimate relationship with Christ each day, fully embrace who he created us to be, and seek to fulfill the purpose he has for us. He is our greatest strength—and the One who enables us to live out all the other strengths he's placed within us.

> Hey, you . . .
> The one wondering if you've got strengths.
> *You do.*
> The one questioning if God really even wants to use you.
> *He does.*
> You've got gifts to offer the world.
> Things that are good and right and true.
> No one else can make a difference like you can.
> *Like you already are.*
> Dare to believe it.
> Dare to receive it.
> Stand tall, be strong, just go out there and be *you*
> in your own wonderful way.
> Today.

Your Skills

Now that you know your strengths, what do you do with them? Chances are, you're already doing something. Strengths are made to be expressed. We call those expressions *skills. A skill is a strength expressed in a specific way that builds up others and benefits the kingdom.*

Skills can get overlooked. Besides being made fun of in the movie *Napoleon Dynamite* (okay, that was pretty hilarious), they can sometimes seem less than spiritual.

For example, you might wonder, "How does something like cooking help the kingdom?" (Besides potlucks, which are just about the best kind of goodness this side of heaven.) In the DaySpring Cards creative area where I worked, this verse stayed on the wall for many years:

> I have filled him with the Spirit of God, with skill, ability
> and knowledge in all kinds of crafts. (Exod. 31:3 NIV 1984)

This verse reveals that God's hand is in our skills, in the ordinary things we do. *And they matter.* A lot. We don't all have the same skills. For example, the "all kinds of crafts" part doesn't quite fit me. If the word *craft* appears in my life, it starts with a "K" and ends with me making macaroni and cheese.

To help us figure out our skills, I've got another list. Take a look and find yours.

· · · · · · · · · · *Find Your Skills: 5 Minutes* · · · · · · · · · ·

Circle three skills that apply to you.

○ Acting	○ Decorating	○ Persevering
○ Adapting	○ Empathizing	○ Persuading
○ Administering	○ Encouraging	○ Planning
○ Advising	○ Evaluating	○ Prioritizing
○ Analyzing	○ Expressing	○ Problem-solving
○ Appreciating	○ Growing	○ Protecting
○ Assembling	○ Guiding	○ Relating
○ Believing	○ Helping	○ Responding
○ Building	○ Imagining	○ Risk taking
○ Challenging	○ Influencing	○ Serving
○ Cleaning	○ Initiating	○ Sharing
○ Collaborating	○ Leading	○ Speaking
○ Cooking	○ Listening	○ Supporting
○ Communicating	○ Maintaining	○ Teaching
○ Connecting	○ Managing	○ Training
○ Constructing	○ Motivating	○ Writing
○ Coordinating	○ Negotiating	○ *Add your own …*
○ Counseling	○ Nurturing	
○ Creating	○ Organizing	

Connecting Strengths and Skills

Skills Circles can be a fun way to connect strengths with skills. Draw a circle and write one of your strengths in the middle. Then draw small circles around the edge and write related skills in them. Here's a personal example:

The size of each circle is related to how much I express that strength through the skill. For example, I write a lot more than I speak.

Have fun with this! Doodle, put these in your journal, write them on napkins next time you're stuck on a plane. This isn't meant to be a big project—just a little tool.

We usually express the same core strength in many different ways. That reveals a lot about who we are and what God has called us to do in our lives.

Watch out, world! We've got skills and we're not afraid to use them. (Except for the hot glue gun. I'm still not going there. You fabulously talented crafty people handle that one for me, okay?)

Skills for Different Seasons

A few years ago I had the opportunity to help women go through a study called The Significant Woman: Pursuing God and His Unique Design for Your Life. During the study, many of the women confided things like, "I know one of my strengths is being creative. But right now I don't even have time to take a shower because I have a new baby! I feel guilty for not doing what God wants me to do."

While strengths stay consistent throughout our lives, the skills that display them vary depending on the season we're in and the specific assignment God has given us. For example, when I asked those women questions, I found that they were still being creative! They told stories to their toddlers as they tucked them in, came up with new games to play, or just found interesting solutions to the everyday issues that come with having little ones. That strength was still coming through loud and clear—it just looked different than before, so it was harder for them to recognize. If you're in a season of life where you're not getting to use a particular skill, ask yourself, "What is the strength behind this skill?" Then see if there's another way you're already expressing this strength or one you'd like to try.

While what we do may change, the reason we do it stays the same. "Whatever you do, do it all for the glory of God" (1 Cor. 10:31). King David had the skill of shepherding. He did that first with sheep and then as a ruler of God's people. Peter had the skill of fishing—first with actual fish and then with hearts. God will use you in a lot of different ways throughout your life.

Here's a little confession: I can tend to focus too much on my skills, especially in the busy times of my life. I spin my wheels, wear myself out, and try to do everything at once. When I finally slow down enough to hear God's voice, it seems what he often whispers to my heart is, *"Holley, I want your heart more than your hands."*

Yes, our skills matter. Yes, they are important to God's purpose for our lives. But in the end, what he wants most is simply *us*. Our hearts. Our dreams. Our days. Then what we do with our skills is just a natural response—and ordinary activities such as cooking or cleaning become just as sacred as leading a church or going on a mission trip.

I've been thinking of you right there in the middle of
*   the ordinary . . .*
changing diapers, writing reports,
driving, cleaning, fixing, blessing.
Ordinary is hard for me.
Is it ever hard for you?
I like the new.
The exciting.
And yet it seems God has been whispering
that I need to look at the ordinary with new eyes.
All that seems small can be really BIG.
And what we do every day
matters more than we know,
more than we see.
You are making a difference.
You deserve to be applauded—
for just digging in, doing what you do,
keeping at it no matter what.
So from the bottom of my heart . . .
THANK YOU
for all you do.
(I've got a feeling it brings joy to God too.)

Your "Who"

Our strengths and skills aren't meant just for us. So the next step is to take some time to consider who shares our lives and stories. Before we do so, I'd like to bust the myth among women that goes something like this: "Everyone else has lots of relationships, but not me."

Facebook, Twitter, and all the other social media sites out there can make it seem as if the whole world is one big party and we're not invited. The enemy can use that to lie to us and make us feel alone. But it's not true.

According to an article in *USA Today*, 25 percent of Americans do not have even one friend they can confide in. Including family, the average number of close relationships is still only two.[3] What I want to highlight here is this: *you are doing okay in your relationships.*

That being said, let's take a closer look at the relationships in your life. I've created a little diagram to help us out.

Your Social Circles: 5 Minutes

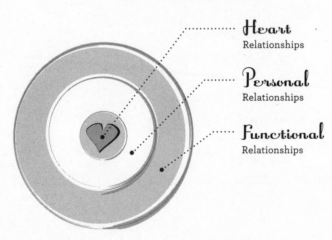

Heart
Relationships

Personal
Relationships

Functional
Relationships

◦ **Heart Relationships**
This is your inner circle, those with whom you can truly share who you are, the ups and downs. Some family members and your close friends would be here.

◦ **Personal Relationships**
These people share your life in your neighborhood, church, work, family, and so on. You care about each other, but they are more casual relationships than the first group.

◦ **Functional Relationships**
These connections are very casual, and interactions have a practical purpose. You might call them acquaintances.

Think about names that would be in each of the circles above and write them there if you'd like. You don't have to include everyone you know—just enough to give you a broad overview of who's in your life and how you're connecting to others.

When we look at the life of Jesus, we see he had different types of relationships just like those in the previous chart. He had three disciples who were closest to him, then the twelve, the forty, and the multitudes.

Like our skills, our relationships will vary with the seasons and stages of our lives. When my husband and I first got married, we moved to a new town. I'd had several close friends in college but now suddenly found myself alone. It took several years of trying to connect with people (and a lot of praying!) before I formed new bonds where I now lived. So if you find yourself in a season of fewer relationships, give yourself grace and know it's most likely not about you. If you find you're intentionally holding back or avoiding people, talk to a counselor or someone you trust so your heart can heal and you can reach out again.

Connections to others impact our lives now and our legacies forever. As DaySpring cofounder Dean Kerns once said, "All we take with us into eternity are our relationships with God and each other."

Who You're Called to Serve

After you know your strengths (who you are) and skills (what you do) as well as understanding the relationships in your life, then you're ready to explore who you're specifically called to serve.

Yes, we're all called to love each other. And yet there's usually a group of people that has a special place in your heart. You might love working with kids, women, older adults, or inner-city youth. Knowing your *who* can help you make strategic choices about which opportunities to pursue and which to pass up.

Lisa-Jo Baker (who blogs at www.thegypsymama.com) is an amazing woman who has found her *who*. Raised in South Africa, she's done humanitarian work all over the world. Right in the middle of that journey, she discovered that she felt deeply called to serve moms with young kids. She sent me this email:

> I am at an incredible leadership conference in the Pacific Northwest. There are primarily men here, and they are discussing some groundbreaking work their organizations have done to bring justice to the poor and afflicted. For many years that is the kind of work I have been involved in also.
>
> But I have consistently felt this call on my heart to speak into the lives of women. Young mothers and wives who feel that what they do isn't important. So I blog. I write my heart out to this beautiful audience who need to be encouraged as I wish someone had done for me. Because young mothers and struggling women have great needs too. And it is my delight to be used by God to be part of the plan for meeting them.[4]

A few months after writing this email, Lisa-Jo became the social media manager for www.incourage.me, a website for the hearts of women. One of the other cofounders and I had been praying about who would be the right person to step into that role. In one of those rare moments, it seemed God almost audibly put Lisa-Jo's name on my heart. Without knowing anything, Lisa-Jo sent me another email saying she was resigning from her current position and asking us to keep her in mind if anything ever became available with (in)courage. When we called Lisa-Jo and shared that we had already been thinking of her, the "yes!" she responded with came easily because she knew (in)courage reached the exact group of people she felt called to serve.

While it seemed to happen quickly, Lisa-Jo found her *who* through a journey that took years. The same is often true of us. And yet there are usually glimpses along the way. Our heart is drawn to a particular group. We get excited when we know we'll be around a certain type of people. We feel at home with kids and out of place with teens. We love serving seniors but would rather skip out on nursery duty. We feel drawn to families rather than individual women. There are clues that lead us to who God wants us to serve.

· · · · · · · · · · **Find Your Who: 5 Minutes** · · · · · · · · · ·

◦ I feel especially drawn to:

Matt, Sarah, Annye / teenagers (in need / struggling)

◦ I'm at my best when I'm with:

my small group ... (crying can be a "best", right? lol)

◦ God has given me a tender spot in my heart for:

Matt, Sarah / people who love the Lord or need encouragement

◦ My strengths and skills seem to help:

people who are going thru tough times; people I don't know that well

What you wrote might be very general (for example, "my family" or "women"), or it might be very specific ("children with special needs under the age of five"). Either way is okay.

Also, your *who* may change throughout your life. Right now you might be focused on toddlers because you've got three of them! Later on, you might shift your focus to mentoring college students.

It's also okay if you don't find a specific *who* right now. As mentioned before, we're all called to love each other. So if nothing comes to mind here, just serve whoever is in your life right now!

When an opportunity that seems to fit with your strengths, skills, and *who* comes along, you can use the tools in this chapter as filters to see if it's really in the center of what you're created to do. If it is, you can be fairly sure God is giving you the green light! If not, ask him if he specifically wants you to accept it as a special assignment that's outside of what you're called to do most of the time.

> your strengths + your skills + who you're called to serve
> = you making a difference in the world in your own
> amazing way

God's Heart for Who You Really Are

Even when we know our strengths, skills, and how we best connect with others, it can still be intimidating to think about living all of that out. That's especially true if we're a bit on the insecure side (I am).

Here comes a confession: *I'm intimidated by you.* And by you, I mean women. Put me in a room of my peers, and it won't be long before my hands are sweaty and I'm shaking in my boots (yes, the cute ones I bought from TJ Maxx in the hopes they'd somehow hypnotize everyone into liking me—you know what I'm talking about).

It got so bad I even took drastic measures a few summers ago. Disclaimer: There is some serious dorkiness coming in the next few sentences. If you're offended by that, you should stop reading now.

I went to the library and checked out all the social skills books. The ones like *How to Have Friends and Influence People without Relying on Your TJ Maxx Boots.* And I read *all* of them. I know—don't say I didn't warn you.

Through my ambitious pursuit of coolness, I discovered that my insecurities came from a much deeper place than an inability to make coherent small talk at times. What I thought might be some sort of social ailment turned out to be a spiritual one.

Inside a voice whispered, "You're not enough." Depending on the day, an extra word might be thrown into that sentence:

- You're not *pretty* enough.
- You're not *outgoing* enough.
- You're not *likeable* enough.

SAME!

So I kept spinning my wheels on an endless treadmill. I'd make progress in one area, only to realize I had miles to go in another. Exhausted, I finally began pondering and praying.

"Lord," I asked, "why do women feel as if we're not enough?"

It seemed I heard a whisper in response: *"Because they're not."*

For a moment I thought I had some holy static happening.

"Excuse me, God, it sounded like you said we're not enough. Could you repeat that, pretty please?"

Again, gently and firmly, "You are not enough."

By then I started thinking perhaps my heart had dialed the wrong number and the devil was on the line. But in that pause it seemed God finished the sentence: "You are not enough . . . *in me you are so much more.*"

BUT

- We are *much more* than pretty . . . we are wonderfully made.
- We are *much more* than likeable . . . we are deeply loved.
- We are *much more* than okay . . . we are daughters of the King.

I think the enemy tricks us into believing we are not enough because he knows if we discover the truth, we'll be unstoppable.

If you've embraced that lie like I did, then together we can start trading it for the truth. We are chosen, cherished, created women who have all we need to fulfill God's plans for our lives. He has made us just as he wants us to be. We have something to offer that no one else can bring . . . and the world is waiting.

Girls, let's stop shaking in our boots and instead start standing tall for him together.

Let's use our strengths, skills, and relationships to make a difference.

Let's be who we are, *really*.

I can't do it alone—are you with me?

3

Why Is It So Hard to Believe
I'm Amazing?

The scene is set. God has created the world in seven glorious days. Adam and Eve live in Paradise. And then the devil shows up with a single question: "Did God really say . . . ?" (Gen. 3:1). Insecurity makes its debut. Eve responds, then reconsiders. "The woman was convinced" (Gen. 3:6 NLT).

Everything changes forever.

I find it interesting that the enemy didn't blatantly tempt Eve. He didn't ask, "So, how about we head off to Las Vegas and run wild?" He was much more subtle. And his question is hauntingly familiar. I've heard other versions:

"Did God really say you have what it takes?"

"Did God really say you're loved?"

"Did God really say who you are is okay?"

And, like Eve, I often respond, reconsider, and become convinced. What if Eve had said, "Yep, God sure did say that, and I'm not listening to another word. Hit the road, buster"?

What if *we* said that?

"Yes, God really did say I can do all things through Christ" (see Phil. 4:13).

"Yes, God really did say he loves me with an everlasting love" (see Jer. 31:3).

"Yes, God really did say I am fearfully and wonderfully made" (see Ps. 139:14).

Everything could change forever.

I've never met a woman who found it easy to believe she's amazing. I'm not talking about the puffed-up pride we sometimes see from celebrities (that's really just another form of insecurity). I mean "I truly know who I am in Christ, embrace that fully, and live in it completely all the time." I used to think I had to find a silver bullet that would kill my insecurity and replace it with confidence. I now believe that because we're all Eve's daughters, this insecurity is something we'll face throughout our lives. Can we have victory? Yes, my sisters, we can. But it's not a one-time, easy fix. It's a battle. This chapter is all about equipping you to win again and again.

So first of all, let's drop that guilt that we struggle with this, okay? Even Jesus was tempted, and he was perfect. We're all going to wrestle with our identities, feel drawn to insecurity, and want to fill those holes within us in other ways. That's not a sin. What matters is what we do next. We have a choice between living in the truth or giving in to the flesh. And what we pick ultimately shapes us and the course of our lives.

Can we pause for a little confession here? I have been putting off this chapter. Yes, ma'am. I've had one of *those* weeks. You know, the kind that makes you want to polish off gallons of ice cream at a time, hide under the covers, and/or run off to a desert island (as long as it has plenty of ice cream too)?

Oh, yeah. I'm there. And I have felt anything *but* amazing. Yet God keeps tapping me on the shoulder and reminding me that what I write is just as much for my healing as it is for yours. I'm on

[handwritten margin note: ♡ I struggle w/ feeling like temptation is sinning... →]

[handwritten annotation at top: a lot of times i even feel like eating is a sin... like i know gluttony is, but where does that start?]

this journey with you. He put some things on my heart that helped me, and I believe they'll help your heart too. Let's walk this road of words together, friend, and see where he wants to take us. Feel free to bring a spoon and some hot fudge with you if it helps.

Beyond Eve: Uncovering the Other Lies in Our Lives

From the moment we take our first breath as a beautiful baby girl, the enemy wants to suffocate our souls with the question, "Did God really say . . . ?" As our lives unfold, all of us experience the lies that come from that question in many different ways.

When you're a child, you accept everything you hear as true. Santa Claus? Of course! Easter Bunny? Yes! A fairy that leaves money under your pillow when you lose a tooth? Let's stay awake and try to see her! Over time those beliefs change because someone, whether a kid on a playground or a loving parent, tells us the truth. But there are many other lies we believe as children that don't ever get replaced.

You're not good enough.

You'll never amount to anything.   *[handwritten: mhm... ☹]*

You don't fit in here . . . or anywhere.

Those lies are just as much a myth as Santa Claus and the Easter Bunny. But many of us never have anyone take us aside and say, "Hey, that's not true. This is what's real."

We all have lies we carry around inside us. Usually they're so familiar we don't even pay much attention to them. Pause for a moment and ask God to show you some of the lies you've believed about yourself. You can even write one below.

◦ A lie my heart sometimes still hears is:

[handwritten: I'm not good enough]

[handwritten: I have to be perfect]

[handwritten: It's all your fault]

Whoever said "sticks and stones may break my bones, but words will never hurt me" must not have experienced childhood. Sentences slung at our souls wound deeply. I imagine you felt a sting as you filled in the blank above. *Sure did...*

Some of my lies? *"You're so ugly." "No one likes you."* Ouch. As I revisited those lies recently, I pictured God, with his hand over my heart, touching the places where those syllables still sting. And a passage from the Gospels came to mind (see John 8:1–11). A woman accused is brought to Jesus. The leaders are ready to stone her. But Jesus "stooped down and wrote in the dust with his finger" (John 8:6 NLT). Jesus said whoever had never sinned should cast the first stone. *And they all walked away.*

What Christ wrote in the dust is a mystery. But whatever it was, *I know it was truth.* And now we stand as women accused. The enemy is ready to throw stones at us. In the dust of our hearts, I picture Jesus writing truth that covers those accusing words:

- Loved
- Accepted
- Chosen
- Mine

My eyes are overflowing a bit now (as I imagine those of the woman accused did too) with happy tears of freedom and grace. Others may speak into our lives. But Jesus has the final say. He covers the lies with love. May he heal us and help us to believe.

The accusations and lies in our lives come in different ways. Some are completely undeserved. For example, insensitive parents or insecure peers may tear us down to build themselves up. Other lies slip in through poor choices of our own and remain long after we've been forgiven.

Whatever the source, God's intent remains the same: to replace those lies with truth. While we can't cover every lie in this chapter, let's take a look at a few that women commonly struggle with and replace them with truth instead.

Lie #1: "I Have to Be Perfect"

I know Perfectionism. Let's call her "Ms. P" for short. She showed up in my life somewhere in the middle of elementary school and decided to stick around. Do you know her too? Oh, on the outside she's prim and proper. But beneath all that she's a bossy, inconsiderate, joy-stealing, lie-telling, impossible-to-please taskmaster who's never satisfied. She doesn't play well with others. I don't know why I kept her around for so long. I tried to get her to leave a few times, but she always came back—until I found some truth that finally sent her packing.

You see, Ms. P liked to quote a verse to me (no surprise there—the devil did it when he tried to tempt Jesus in the wilderness). Her favorite Scripture was, "Be perfect, therefore, as your heavenly Father is perfect" (Matt. 5:48). Every time I heard those words, I thought about how I was falling short and must try harder.

But I finally decided to look a little closer at what that verse might really mean. I looked for other verses that used the word *perfect*. Lo and behold, look what was hiding in Hebrews: "By one sacrifice he has made perfect forever those who are being made holy" (10:14). What? I've already been made perfect? I thought at first my Bible might have a typo. But it turns out it's true. I've already been made perfect. And so have you.

Here's how it works: There's only One who is perfect. To be perfect, I'd have to be him. But wait—"I no longer live, but Christ lives in me" (Gal. 2:20). When I gave my life to Jesus, he gave his to me too. In God's eyes, I'm as perfect as Christ. All that sin? It's settled once and for all. Whew. Jesus shows Ms. P to the door and says, "I'll take it from here."

Also, the Hebrew word for "perfect" is different than our typical Western definition. It actually speaks more to the concept of being "complete" and how we are all we need to be in Christ.

Does that mean we're off the hook and can do whatever we want? Nope, that's where the second part of the verse from Hebrews comes in. We've been made perfect—check—but we're still in the process of being made holy. God's goal in our lives is *growth*.

So what's the difference between growth and our typical idea of "perfection"?

- *Perfectionism is all or nothing.*
- Growth is little by little.
- *Perfectionism is all about the goal.*
- Growth is more about the journey.
- *Perfectionism is about outward appearances.*
- Growth is about what happens on the inside.
- *Perfectionism is about what we do.*
- Growth is about who we're becoming.

I love the verse in Proverbs that says, "The path of the righteous is like the morning sun, shining ever brighter till the full light of day" (4:18).

Growth in our lives often looks like this chart:

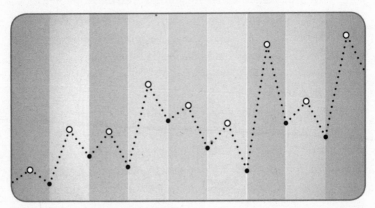

We go through peaks and valleys. We make some progress and then slip up. When that happens, *it feels like we're all the way back at the bottom.* But we're not—we're further along than we were before. We've gained new wisdom, developed our strengths a bit more, and leaned a little harder into God.

I know God looks @ us and doesn't see sin.... but How can he want it "just as [we] are"?

If Ms. P could draw on the previous chart, she'd make a red line across the top, and anything below it would be failure to her. But God sees our lives in a much different way. The red he places over our lives is the blood of his Son, and it covers us completely. Then he takes our hands, calls to our hearts, and says, "Let's go! I want to share life with you—just as you are, every step of the way."

Why You Don't Have to Be Perfect

I know Perfectionism.
She calls my name and says,
   "*You will never be good enough.*"
And sometimes I listen.
I cower in a corner.
Or I endlessly run.
But it's always about fear.
Then these words stop me in my tracks,
grab me by the heart,
and invite grace to speak instead:
   Perfect love casts out fear (1 John 4:18)
I don't have to be perfect.
I only need to be perfectly loved.
And I am.
   So are you

Lie #2: "I Need to Be More Like Her"

Let's pretend we're sitting at a middle school lunch table, eaves-dropping on giggly girls.

"My boyfriend is captain of the football team."

"I found the coolest jeans last weekend!"

"I got an A on the science test."

Is anyone else's heart racing just thinking about being back there? Good grief! Okay, I've regained my composure. The point is that as women we compare. A lot.

We tend to berate ourselves for this tendency. But really, I just think it's part of how we're wired.

Women were created by God to be inherently relational. This means we're always checking in, asking ourselves, "How's she doing? How's she doing? How's she doing?"

This is a reflection of our tender hearts and compassionate natures. It's a beautiful thing that makes us excellent mamas, wives, and friends. Where we get tripped up is when we follow that first question with, "How am I doing compared with her?"

Hold up. That's not helpful.

If we fall short, then we're insecure.

If we're doing better, then we're prideful.

If her life seems harder, then we don't feel entitled to our pain.

God's answer? Focus on him and his plan for your life.

There's a little scene at the end of the Gospel of John that I find a bit funny (it's okay to think that, right?). Jesus and Peter are having a heart-to-heart. Another disciple walks up, and in his typical style, Peter asks, "What about him, Lord?" Jesus has an even better question: "What is that to you?" And then, "As for you, follow me" (John 21:21–22 NLT).

Your story and strengths belong to you. God doesn't compare them (or you) to anyone else, and you don't have to either. Big sigh of relief. So as we explore our strengths together (and live them out with others), let's go for these three steps: share, care, prayer. And skip the compare. (Unless you get the coolest jeans on sale. Comparing prices totally doesn't count. You'd better reveal the deal, sister. I'm just saying.)

Lie #3: "I Don't Have Anything to Offer"

Y'all, I am terrible at holidays. Decorating makes me hyperventilate. My gift-selection skills are challenged. I can't sing worth a hoot. My one redeeming quality is that I can make some serious treats. Yes, ma'am. So a few years ago I got a truffle recipe from a friend. It involves a package of Oreos, cream cheese, and melted chocolate. Easy-peasy, I thought.

So I slaved away in the kitchen making my confections, imagining that I would soon get a phone call that went something like this: "What, Martha? Did you say you'd like to have me in the studio tomorrow? Well, I already booked with Rachael. Maybe next year." Needless to say, the phone did not ring, and it's a good thing, because when I got done . . . those were the ugliest truffles ever!

Horrified, I determined in my heart that I would sneak them onto the "free food" table at work and no one would be any wiser. Alone in my shame at my desk the next day, I heard an excited group of ladies talking outside of my area.

"I don't know who made them! We've been trying to find out all day!"

"Yes, they're amazing. I've just got to get the recipe for those truffles."

Say what?

It turns out my ugly truffles were a hit. I decided to out myself to the shock and delight of my co-workers. As I sat back down at my desk, it seemed God whispered, "This isn't just about the truffles."

I thought about how I do the same thing with other areas of my life. When parts of my heart or life don't measure up to my expectations, I tend to hide them. But what if someone would be blessed by what I have to share and they miss out because I hide it?

I'm thinking most of you are Holiday Queens who are far superior to me in making all the seasons of the year bright. But maybe, just maybe, you've got a little bit of the "ugly truffle complex" going on somewhere in your life too. By that I mean there's some part of you that God has said is "fearfully and wonderfully made" (Ps. 139:14), but you're just not quite sure about that yet. Women seem to be pretty good at agreeing with God unless he's talking nice about us. Can I get an "Amen"? Amen.

Let's put all we've got on the table for him and share it with our whole hearts. I may never be hot stuff when it comes to holidays, but with God's help I hope I can get a little better at living in the truth.

One of the biggest lies the enemy tries to tell us is that we don't have anything worthwhile to offer. Girls, we do. And God says it's good.

(I know you just kept reading in the hopes of getting that recipe. So let's all say thank you to my friend Jennifer Moore for giving it to me. Her truffles turn out lovely—but we won't hold that against her.)

Sweet & Simple Truffles

- 1 16-ounce package of Oreo cookies
- 1 8-ounce package cream cheese, softened
- 16 ounces semisweet baking chocolate, melted

Yummy! ♡

Directions:
Completely crush Oreos and place in a bowl. Add cream cheese. Mix until blended. Roll cookie mixture into 1-inch balls. Dip in chocolate and place on wax paper to cool. Decorate truffles as desired.

Refrigerate until firm, about one hour. Eat them all, or keep refrigerated.

Lie #4: "Being Confident Will Make Me Prideful and Selfish"

It's the Last Supper. Jesus is headed to the cross. But first he washes his disciples' feet:

> Jesus knew that the Father had put all things under his power, and that he had come from God and was returning to God; so he got up from the meal, took off his outer clothing, and wrapped a towel around his waist. After that, he poured water into a basin and began to wash his disciples' feet. (John 13:3–5)

love love love

Did you catch that first line? Jesus was secure in who he was and whose he was, and that enabled him to freely serve. There's a myth that goes something like this: "Confidence will make you selfish." We fear becoming prideful, forgetting others, pursuing our own agendas. But here's the secret Jesus shows us: true confidence leads to service.

Insecurity does just what it sounds like—turns us inward. We focus on ourselves, our appearance, our house, our talents ... you get the picture. I imagine you really want to do all you can to help, serve, and be humble. Me too. If so, then we need to be secure, confident, and assured that we're loved. Easy? Not at all. Life changing? Yes, ma'am. And you won't become prideful, I promise. I know, I've worried about that too.

Pride is really just another form of insecurity. It's an effort to puff ourselves up so we seem bigger (and therefore feel safer). *If we want to become more unselfish, we've got to believe what God says about us.* Because when we do, we'll be able to stop looking inward and instead focus upward and outward on him as well as others.

Is this scary to you? Good grief, I feel like I'm going to hyperventilate. But we'll be okay. We're just scared because we've never thought about things this way before; it's unfamiliar territory. And what's unknown is always scary. But as we practice this, lean into God's love, and ask him to show us a new way of living, that fear will go away. I promise. And what's even better, *God promises.* "For God did not give us a spirit of timidity, but a spirit of power, of love and of self-discipline" (2 Tim. 1:7 NIV 1984). That sounds a lot like true confidence to me.

I'm ready to take the risk of thinking about all of this differently. Will you try it with me?

Lie #5: "I Am Who Others Say I Am"

We tend to accept what others say about us as the truth about who we are. And it may be—as long as it aligns with what God says about us too.

Lord, help me to be confident in your love.

Brandy prayed this over me when she came over to talk/pray w/ me a while ago... I love it.

Think back to those lies you thought about at the beginning of this chapter, the ones that still sting your soul when you think of them. Now picture Jesus saying them to you. "He would never say that!" you're probably thinking. And you're right. There is no condemnation in Christ, so if someone else has spoken condemning words over you, then they are not true—no matter how real they may feel.

We talked about how as children we believed whatever we were told. The apostle Paul describes it this way:

> When I was a child, I talked like a child, I thought like a child, I reasoned like a child. When I became a man, I put the ways of childhood behind me. For now we see only a reflection as in a mirror; then we shall see face to face. Now I know in part; then I shall know fully, even as I am fully known. (1 Cor. 13:11–12)

At some point, we have to deliberately choose to put those lies behind us. As Paul also says, until we're in heaven we won't see the complete picture—even about who we are. But we can begin to look into God's truth and ask him to show us what we need to know. This process takes time. It's not simple. It will feel awkward, uncomfortable, and as if what you're telling yourself isn't real at all. Your emotions will be the last to get on board.

God created our brains in amazing ways. When you think in certain ways, your mind makes literal, physical pathways. Think of it as building a road. As you grow up and new situations present themselves, your brain naturally goes the way of least resistance. It returns to those well-worn patterns. When you decide to replace lies with the truth, you're really creating new pathways in your brain. Think of it as constructing another road and letting grass grow over the original one. It takes time and perseverance. But it is possible. The hard work that it requires means holding on to the truth no matter what your emotions may try to tell you instead.

Jesus tells her to FLEE from her sin...

· · · · · · · · · **Replace the Lie: 5 Minutes** · · · · · · · ·

○ A lie I've believed:

I'm not good enough...

○ The truth God wants me to remember instead:

with Him, I am complete. He wants me as I am.

○ Scripture that shares this truth:

John 8:1-11

○ God has the ultimate word on who you are—not your spouse, friends, parents, co-workers, or spiritual leaders or even you. And he declares you're loved, valuable, accepted, and irreplaceable.

Did God really say . . . ?
Oh, yes, he did!

wow... ♡ Thank you LORD!

┌─────────────────────────────┐
│ In Case You Ever Wonder │
└─────────────────────────────┘

You question . . .
Is who I am okay?

> *You're more than okay—you're His.* (Ps. 139:14)

You ask . . .
Do I have what it takes?

> *You've got all you need.* (2 Pet. 1:3)

You wonder . . .
Can I do this?

> *You can do all things.* (Phil. 4:13)

So go for it, girl.
Dare to make that difference,
take that step, follow that dream.
God will go with you—

> *and love will see you through.*

June 14th ♡

(Jessica Vaughn's Louyie's song)

♫ ♪

God, here is my whole heart
i. here are my open hands
I am a child, and my life
is lived for you. God,
here is my future i. here's
my dream. These words
are eternal + so here's
is life with you...
... Life is good
with you...

SORRY
4 tha
doodling
lol
-STD

4

Why Do I Feel This Way?

A woman walks into my counseling office. She talks of loss in her life. As tears slip down her cheeks, she grabs a tissue and says, "But I shouldn't feel this way."

Another woman arrives later in the day. She describes abuse and wrongs against her that have left deep scars on her heart. Her voice gets louder until she stops midsentence and says, "But I shouldn't feel this way."

A final client steps through the door and talks of a new opportunity. It's way out of her comfort zone. She starts to explore the unknown, then folds her shaking hands and says, "But I shouldn't feel this way."

I've responded like this too. Emotions knock on the door of my heart, and I turn them away. I hear old lines spoken by well-meaning people, like "If you're not smiling, you won't be a witness for Jesus" or "If you feel fear, you're not showing faith."

man tells me this...

But in each of the scenarios above, the emotion was just a message about what that woman was experiencing.

For the first woman, sadness was saying, "You've experienced a loss."

For the second, anger was declaring, "You've been wronged."

And for the third, fear was cautioning, "You've got an exciting opportunity—but there are risks involved too."

Those emotions hopefully prompt the first woman to seek comfort, the second to tend to her wounds so she can eventually forgive, and the third to pray and plan as she moves ahead.

Of course, we also have positive emotions—joy at a wedding, contentment around the dinner table with those we love, enthusiasm as we begin a new job. Those uplifting feelings tell us important things too. *All* of our emotions are gifts from God to help us process *everything* we experience.

Emotions are also a big part of what makes you amazing. They allow you to respond to life in deeply personal ways. They connect you with others. They reflect your awesome Maker.

Research has shown that there are six universal emotions: anger, fear, disgust, amusement, sadness, and surprise.[1] How we display those emotions shows up in facial expressions that are recognizable in even the most remote parts of the world. The women I described above could walk through any door in any country and their feelings would be clear to those around them. Isn't that incredible? Our emotions display our hearts—our beautiful, broken, blessed, glorious hearts.

Your Approach to Emotions

Beyond the common emotional ground shared by all humanity, how we experience and express our feelings varies widely. Think of each basic emotion like a color. Give a box of crayons to a class of kindergarteners, and they'll all recognize red but use it in very different ways.

We approach emotions in a similar fashion. Some of us grab all the colors every chance we get, while others are more careful and methodical. Again, picture that kindergarten class. One little girl may be wildly scribbling a rainbow while another daintily fills in the details. Doesn't that image make you smile? It made me grin as I wrote it. There's something about recognizing our quirks and differences that brings us joy. I believe it does the same for God. After all, he's the One who created them.

So let's take a closer look at your unique approach to emotions. While we can do so in a lot of different ways, let's start with the simplest: head or heart. Take a look below to see whether your head (those lines on the coloring page) or heart (all that color) tends to be the dominant force in your life.

· · · · · · · · · · *Head or Heart: 5 Minutes* · · · · · · · · · ·

While we all use both our heads and our hearts,
circle the option on each line that sounds like you *more often:*

○ I prefer facts.	○ I prefer feelings.
○ People are more likely to describe me as logical.	○ People are more likely to describe me as emotional.
○ When someone expresses a strong emotion, I often want to withdraw.	○ When someone expresses a strong emotion, I often try to find a way to engage with them.
○ In conversation, I most often say, "I think. . . ."	○ In conversation, I most often say, "I feel. . . ."
○ I agree more with this statement: "Use your head."	○ I agree more with this statement: "Follow your heart."
○ I grow in my relationship with God most by learning a new truth about him and applying it practically.	○ I grow in my relationship with God most by experiencing him in an intimate way through a personal situation.
○ I find it fairly simple to compartmentalize my life. I can think about one thing at a time.	○ I find it difficult to compartmentalize my life. How I feel affects every area.
○ This is one of my favorite verses: "Do not conform to the pattern of this world, but be transformed by the renewing of your mind" (Rom. 12:2).	○ This is one of my favorite verses: "Trust in the LORD with all your heart and lean not on your own understanding" (Prov. 3:5).

LOL

If you circled more items on the left, then your head leads the way for you most of the time. If you circled more on the right, you're a live-from-the-heart kind of girl.

If you're dominated by your head, then you're more vulnerable to avoiding emotions. They may make you uncomfortable and appear to cloud your otherwise clear thinking. You probably don't like being emotional yourself, and you may withdraw when others display emotions as well. You like the facts, just the facts, when you make a decision. After all, what more do you need? This can keep you from being easily swayed. It can also sometimes lead you to miss divine opportunities that don't make sense from a human standpoint. Some of your strengths are likely to be steadfastness, a practical and efficient approach to life, and the ability to stay calm (and bring calm to others) in a variety of situations.

If you're dominated by your heart, then you're more vulnerable to being controlled by emotions. You may jump to conclusions or make decisions without getting the facts you need. You're highly sensitive to others, which helps you be a caring friend and co-worker. It also puts you in danger of "catching" the emotions of others much like someone else might catch a cold. Your emotions can be so strong that when they're in line with God, they can serve as a helpful guide. They may also lead you to assume an opportunity is from him without using wisdom to evaluate it. Some of your strengths are likely to be empathy, a passionate approach to life, and the ability to perceive and respond to the needs of those around you.

Of course, we're all on a continuum. None of us use just our heads or just our hearts. And that's the way God designed it—we're to love him with our hearts *and* minds. The purpose of the exercise above is simply to help you understand which way you naturally tend to lean because it impacts your life, makes you vulnerable in certain ways, and can also be the source of many of your strengths. As we move forward, we'll talk more about who you are emotionally and how you can use that to serve God and others.

How Does God Want Us to Respond to Our Emotions?

Let's talk about that kindergarten class one more time. Imagine a little girl with a coloring book in front of her. Someone taps her on the shoulder and says, "Use this yellow crayon to draw a sun." Then someone else pipes in and says, "No, use this red one to make a fire." A third declares, "You have to make the water blue now!" She may have been coloring contentedly, but now she's unsure. That's often what it feels like when many different emotions try to get our attention. How do we make sure our hearts really reflect what God wants to see?

Fortunately, there's another voice asking for our obedience and attention. It's the voice of the One who loves us. He made the crayons. He created the coloring page. He alone holds the vision for what we're creating with and for him. So what are we supposed to do with all of the other messages we receive? Listen to them, but ultimately obey him.

Emotions make great messengers but bad bosses. If we listen to what the messenger has to share with us, then turn to our heavenly Father and ask, "What do you want me to do?" all is well. If we turn to the messenger with our back to the Maker, then our emotions can lead us astray. While they can share important information with us about our experiences, God always gets the final say.

Peggy, a reader on my blog Heart to Heart with Holley, shared how she replaces the messages emotions give her with the truth from her heavenly Father she really needs:

- Emotion says, "Nobody cares."
- Truth says, "Jesus cares for me."

- Emotion says, "I'm angry and will show her!"
- Truth says, "Be angry and sin not."

- ○ Emotion says, "I'm afraid to hear the doctor's report."
- ○ Truth says, "Fear not, for I am with you."

- ○ Emotion says, "I can't do this anymore."
- ○ Truth says, "My grace is sufficient."[2]

What's Your Emotional Style?

Who we are emotionally grows and changes over time. The little girl in kindergarten is content to express who she is in simple ways. But it won't be long before she trades that box of crayons for boxes of shoes and endless accessories. Instead of creating an image on a page, she creates one for herself. In much the same way, we all develop a unique emotional style—a one-of-a-kind, complex way of showing our hearts to the world as women.

Imagine I pick up you and a friend and take you to your favorite store. As you walk through the door I say, "Surprise! I'm sending you on a shopping spree. You both get to pick an outfit. There's only one rule—it has to reflect *you*." While you and your friend might have a lot in common, you're most likely going to get something entirely different. Maybe you're a "jeans and T-shirt" kind of girl while she heads right over to the pearls and pumps. Even if you choose something similar, you'll probably pick out a different size or color.

What if I took you to another store, but this time it was filled with emotional expressions instead of clothes? The same thing would probably happen. Your friend might feel totally comfortable in bold yellow joy while you feel more at home in the laid-back blue of peace. There would be all kinds of reasons why you made your choices—ranging from where you grew up and what you were taught in church to how your brain is wired.

God, the ultimate designer, has custom created an emotional wardrobe for you. And it's *beautiful*. It's also essential to accomplishing his purpose for your life. So let's explore it together.

The next few sections may feel a little like going into a dressing room. I'm going to ask you some questions, have you try a few things, and give you time to get feedback from your heavenly Father too. We'll find what fits you just right and helps you express the amazing woman he's made you.

The Start of Your Emotional Style

When we look at the trends that come out in fashion each year, they're always new and old at the same time. Designers don't start from scratch. They look back to the past to put a fresh take on the familiar, and usually it works well. When it comes to family fashion, we all know sometimes it's best not to let history repeat itself. Think about that infamous photo where everyone is wearing matching pink plaid outfits for Easter. Enough said.

Since our families are important influencers in our lives, let's start by exploring what emotional hand-me-downs they passed on to us. They might be quality vintage, or it could be time for a new look. This isn't about right and wrong or blaming anyone—it's simply about understanding.

· · · · · · · · · **Families and Emotions: 5 Minutes** · · · · · · · ·

Read the descriptions below and then circle the title (Stuffers, Screamers, Surfers) of the one that reminds you most of your family.

(Stuffers:) *but we celebrate accomplishments*

These families like to keep emotions where they seem safest—on the inside. Have a bad day? Keep it to yourself. Have a really big accomplishment? Settle down. Home is a safe, peaceful place. Please don't rock the boat.

Wardrobe item: A sturdy, all-season raincoat

Screamers:

The neighbors already know if you're in a family of screamers. Emotion? Bring it on. Or better yet—bring it out. Emotions are made to be expressed, not suppressed. Conflict is present and passionate. So is making up. When it comes to emotion, these families are loud and proud.

Wardrobe item: A bright, bold purse that holds a lot

Surfers:

If you're in a family of surfers, everyone just rides the waves. Low tide, feeling a little sad? That's okay—we'll hang out down there with you. High tide, everything fantastic? We can get up to that place and share the joy too. Conflict ebbs and flows naturally. Emotions are just part of life.

Wardrobe item: A pair of shoes that can handle it all— wet or dry

Of course, these descriptions are intended to be lighthearted. They're also stereotypes, so no family fits neatly into one or the other. What's important is recognizing that every family does approach emotion in certain ways that teach us about how we "should" engage with emotion too. Sometimes that's really helpful. Other times it leads us astray. What matters most is recognizing those patterns, testing them against what God says is true, and proactively choosing what to do about them in our lives. Otherwise we just naturally repeat what's familiar.

So let's follow that up with a few more questions about emotion in your family:

In my family, it was okay to feel . . .

(circle three positive and three negative)

◦ Afraid	◦ Ecstatic	◦ Jealous
◦ Amused	◦ Embarrassed	◦ Joyful
◦ Angry	◦ Empty	◦ Lazy
◦ Annoyed	◦ Encouraged	◦ Lonely
◦ Anxious	◦ Enraged	◦ Loved
◦ Ashamed	◦ Enthusiastic	◦ Mad
◦ Blessed	◦ Envious	◦ Overwhelmed
◦ Bold	◦ Excited	◦ Peaceful
◦ Bored	◦ Exhausted	◦ Pressured
◦ Brave	◦ Fearful	◦ Protected
◦ Broken	◦ Foolish	◦ Quiet
◦ Calm	◦ Forgiven	◦ Sad
◦ Cautious	◦ Free	◦ Satisfied
◦ Certain	◦ Frightened	◦ Scared
◦ Cheerful	◦ Frustrated	◦ Shocked
◦ Comfortable	◦ Fulfilled	◦ Shy
◦ Compassionate	◦ Furious	◦ Silly
◦ Competent	◦ Giddy	◦ Strong
◦ Confident	◦ Glad	◦ Supported
◦ Confused	◦ Grateful	◦ Surprised
◦ Content	◦ Grieved	◦ Suspicious
◦ Courageous	◦ Guilty	◦ Sympathetic
◦ Defensive	◦ Happy	◦ Timid
◦ Delighted	◦ Hopeful	◦ Understood
◦ Depressed	◦ Humble	◦ Valued
◦ Determined	◦ Hurt	◦ Weary
◦ Disgusted	◦ Hysterical	

In my family, it was not okay to feel . . .

(circle three positive and three negative)

Afraid	Ecstatic	Jealous
Amused	Embarrassed	Joyful
Angry	Empty	Lazy
Annoyed	Encouraged	Lonely
Anxious	Enraged	Loved
Ashamed	Enthusiastic	Mad
Blessed	Envious	Overwhelmed
Bold	Excited	Peaceful
Bored	Exhausted	Pressured
Brave	Fearful	Protected
Broken	Foolish	Quiet
Calm	Forgiven	Sad
Cautious	Free	Satisfied
Certain	Frightened	Scared
Cheerful	Frustrated	Shocked
Comfortable	Fulfilled	Shy
Compassionate	Furious	Silly
Competent	Giddy	Strong
Confident	Glad	Supported
Confused	Grateful	Surprised
Content	Grieved	Suspicious
Courageous	Guilty	Sympathetic
Defensive	Happy	Timid
Delighted	Hopeful	Understood
Depressed	Humble	Valued
Determined	Hurt	Weary
Disgusted	Hysterical	

Imagine we're back in that dressing room, and you're trying on your mama's dress from many years ago. It might fit just right. Or it might need a few changes. And, of course, the most important part is making sure it's in line with what your heavenly Father wants you wearing too. The same is true with our emotions: Much of what we inherited from our families can be good and helpful. But other parts, well, need some altering. And occasionally a piece may need to be tossed out completely.

Every one of us thinks our normal is *the* normal. Our way of life, responses, and, yes, emotions make sense to us. But ultimately, our reality has to be tested against God's ways of doing things. He says, "My thoughts are not your thoughts; neither are your ways my ways" (Isa. 55:8).

- What's one emotional pattern you learned from your family that you want to keep?

  fun / lighthearted　(?)

- What's one you've outgrown and need to replace with God's way of doing things instead?

  annoyed

Experiences and Our Emotions

We're born into our families, and they influence our hearts from the second we come into this world. As we grow up, experiences also impact our emotional style. The good, the bad, and the ugly all play a role in shaping how we learn to respond to life.

Dr. Ryan Rana, a Christian counselor and friend of mine, says we all have an emotional range. In other words, if emotions are on a continuum, then we've each got a comfort zone. My translation of that range looks a lot like this:

negative emotions	neutral	positive emotions
(anger, sadness, fear)		*(joy, anticipation, affection)*

<u>God's intent is for us to appropriately experience the full range of emotions.</u> Even fear plays a helpful role when we encounter a dangerous situation. But often life comes along and we learn that some of those emotions aren't allowed or don't feel safe. In particular, abuse can cause us to narrow our emotional range.

So, Dr. Rana explains, instead of being open to the full continuum of emotions, we may stop ourselves from feeling certain ones. For example, a woman who had a difficult childhood might decide to protect herself by limiting the negative emotions she allows herself to feel. Her range would look like this:

negative emotions	neutral	positive emotions
(anger, sadness, fear)		*(joy, anticipation, affection)*

X

The X represents how far she'll go with those negative emotions. She might let herself experience a little bit of sadness, but not much. Most of the time she keeps it tightly controlled. She thinks, "If I don't let myself have negative emotions, that will keep me safe." But here's what happens:

negative emotions	neutral	positive emotions
(anger, sadness, fear)		*(joy, anticipation, affection)*

X   X

Without realizing it, she's placing an X on the other side as well. When we limit our negative emotions, we limit our capacity to experience positive ones too.

Have you ever tried on a coat that felt too tight—as if you couldn't even lift your arms? That's what we do to ourselves emotionally sometimes.

Now, before you start being hard on yourself if you identified with this example, remember this: at some point in your life, that emotional restriction served a purpose. You probably began it as a child (remember those lists above?). God created in us the ability to adapt and survive our circumstances. Those responses got you through whatever you had to face to where you are now.

It just may be that what once made sense no longer works now. It's time for a new emotional fitting! You may have responses in your emotional closet you "outgrew" years ago. But they're like that teeny tiny T-shirt you've still got from high school—you just can't bring yourself to throw them out.

So, girl, maybe it's time! You are God's beautiful, loved, cherished daughter, and he wants you to live fully. Let's take a look and find some things that fit you just right.

LORD, I want to "live fully" in You. Show me what this means.

I allow myself to feel . . .

(circle three to five)

Afraid	Ecstatic	Jealous
Amused	Embarrassed	Joyful
Angry	Empty	Lazy
Annoyed	Encouraged	Lonely
Anxious	Enraged	Loved
Ashamed	Enthusiastic	Mad
Blessed	Envious	Overwhelmed
Bold	Excited	Peaceful
Bored	Exhausted	Pressured
Brave	Fearful	Protected
Broken	Foolish	Quiet
Calm	Forgiven	Sad
Cautious	Free	Satisfied
Certain	Frightened	Scared
Cheerful	Frustrated	Shocked
Comfortable	Fulfilled	Shy
Compassionate	Furious	Silly
Competent	Giddy	Strong
Confident	Glad	Supported
Confused	Grateful	Surprised
Content	Grieved	Suspicious
Courageous	Guilty	Sympathetic
Defensive	Happy	Timid
Delighted	Hopeful	Understood
Depressed	Humble	Valued
Determined	Hurt	Weary
Disgusted	Hysterical	

I don't allow myself to feel . . .

(circle three to five)

○ Afraid	○ Ecstatic	○ Jealous
○ Amused	○ Embarrassed	○ Joyful
○ Angry	○ Empty	○ Lazy
○ Annoyed	○ Encouraged	○ Lonely
○ Anxious	○ Enraged	○ Loved
○ Ashamed	○ Enthusiastic	○ Mad
○ Blessed	○ Envious	○ Overwhelmed
○ Bold	○ Excited	○ Peaceful
○ Bored	○ Exhausted	○ Pressured
○ Brave	○ Fearful	○ Protected
○ Broken	○ Foolish	○ Quiet
○ Calm	○ Forgiven	○ Sad
○ Cautious	○ Free	○ Satisfied
○ Certain	○ Frightened	○ Scared
○ Cheerful	○ Frustrated	○ Shocked
○ Comfortable	○ Fulfilled	○ Shy
○ Compassionate	○ Furious	○ Silly
○ Competent	○ Giddy	○ Strong
○ Confident	○ Glad	○ Supported
○ Confused	○ Grateful	○ Surprised
○ Content	○ Grieved	○ Suspicious
○ Courageous	○ Guilty	○ Sympathetic
○ Defensive	○ Happy	○ Timid
○ Delighted	○ Hopeful	○ Understood
○ Depressed	○ Humble	○ Valued
○ Determined	○ Hurt	○ Weary
○ Disgusted	○ Hysterical	

how?

I sin when im angry

When we look in the Bible, we see the full range of emotions—especially in the Psalms. David expresses everything from wild joy to deep sorrow. *And all of those honored God.* Remember what we talked about earlier? It's what we do with our emotions that matters. For example, "In your anger do not sin" (Eph. 4:26).

So give yourself permission to feel and to find the right "emotional fit" for your heart.

It's okay to be sad.

It's okay to be happy.

It's okay to be mad.

I'm not talking about "venting" the way the world often tells us we need to do. God clearly wants us to use self-control through his Spirit and show love to those around us when we're expressing our emotions. If we're emotionally restricted or numb because of our wounds *or* if our emotions are wildly out of control, it's a sign that something is broken within us.

I'm def broken (Lol)

If that sounds like you, especially if you've experienced abuse, I recommend seeking help from someone you trust like a counselor or mentor. It can take time and a listening ear for our emotions to heal and for us to be comfortable with them again.

Then when you're ready, step out of the dressing room and give those emotions a twirl.

Emotional Evidence

It's one of the great mysteries of womanhood that we all have moments when we stand in our closet, look at our clothes, and still think, "I've got nothing to wear." And I've got a confession: it's been one of those weeks for me emotionally. Of course that would happen when I'm writing this chapter! I'm not dressed up but I've got someplace to go—a big ol' pity party. You know the kind where the theme song is, "Nobody likes me, everybody hates me, I'll just go eat worms"? Yep, that's been me the last few days.

Tonight as I sat on the couch moping, this thought crossed my mind: *Your emotions have nothing to do with reality right now.*

It caught me off guard (in case you haven't figured it out, I'm a live-from-the-heart kind of girl, and I tend to take what I feel at face value). But the more I considered it, the more I realized it was true. Now, there have been weeks when my emotional state would have been appropriate because it would have been a response to something that had happened. That wasn't the case this time. My circumstances and emotions were vastly different. When that happens, it's time for an emotional style reality check.

Imagine you're back in that dressing room and I'm one door over. I slide on that neon pink self-pity dress that caught my eye on the rack. I tell you as I step into the hall, "Oh, I have a feeling this is going to look *good.*" Then we both turn to the mirror, and it looks like I've been hosed down with Pepto-Bismol. You know what I'm talking about, don't you? Our emotions are like that sometimes too. We think what we feel is right and real. But then we take a closer look and find we couldn't be further from the truth.

The higher you scored on "Heart" in the first section, the more likely this is to happen to you. But we're all susceptible to being caught up in emotions that are nothing more than a mirage at times.

As I thought more about my pity party, the Israelites came to mind—especially the story of Joshua and Caleb (see Num. 13–14). You remember that one, don't you? Let's all have a quick review together. The Israelites have been trekking across the desert to the Promised Land. They've seen miracles galore, and God has provided for them. He's also said, "This land is your land—go get it! And by the way, it's *good.*" So they send up some spies to check it out. Sure enough, it's a wonderful land beyond their wildest imaginations. But there are also giants in the land. The spies (except Joshua and Caleb) come back and say, "Sure, it's great. But there's no way we can defeat those folks. We should just give up." Joshua and Caleb step up and say, "No way! God gave this land to us. And he'll give us the victory we need too!" You know the rest of the story. The naysayers win out, and the Israelites wander in the wilderness for forty years.

We all have a point at which we have to choose which evidence to believe. Do we rely on our emotions alone? Or do we look into God's truth and let him tell us what's real? Fear won that day in the desert—and an entire generation paid the consequence. Only Joshua and Caleb lived to actually see the Promised Land.

Faith is more important than emotion. Again, I'm not talking about the "fake it until you make it" or "grin and bear it" approach to emotions. The Israelites having those emotions in the desert wasn't the issue. It was that they chose to obey their fear rather than God's command. At the end of the day, we've got to listen to and follow God's Spirit more than our own hearts. He's the ultimate reality check. We also need sisters of faith who will speak truth to us when we can't see it or simply don't have the strength to believe it in that moment. Seek out "Joshuas and Calebs" who will do more than just go shopping with you—they'll make sure you get to the Promised Land too.

The Most Important Accessory for Your Emotional Style

In those moments when we look in the mirror of truth and realize our emotions aren't lining up with reality (that little pink self-pity dress is a disaster waiting to happen), what can we reach for instead?

Thankfully, God promises to give us something better to wear. And it's just right for our calling in life. We're not going to prom, ladies. We're going to a battlefield. That's why he tells us to guard our hearts, and he's given us the perfect outfit to do so. We each have a unique emotional style. But no matter what that may be, God still wants to give us just the right accessories. And they complete it, *complete us*, in a way that's powerful and beautiful.

Finally, be strong in the Lord and in his mighty power. Put on the full armor of God so that you can take your stand against the devil's schemes. For our struggle is not against flesh and blood, but against the rulers, against the authorities, against the powers of this dark world and against the spiritual forces of evil in the heavenly realms. Therefore put on the full armor of God, so that when the day of evil comes, you may be able to stand your ground, and after you have done everything, to stand. Stand firm then, with the belt of truth buckled around your waist, with the breastplate of righteousness in place, and with your feet fitted with the readiness that comes from the gospel of peace. In addition to all this, take up the shield of faith, with which you can extinguish all the flaming arrows of the evil one. Take the helmet of salvation and the sword of the Spirit, which is the word of God. (Eph. 6:10–17)

LORD help me to do this...

While all of these armor accessories are important, one stands out above the rest: the breastplate of righteousness. That's because it's the one that covers the heart. And that's really what we've been talking about all along. "Above all else, guard your heart, for everything you do flows from it" (Prov. 4:23). All of this talk about emotions matters because our hearts affect *every other part of who we are and what we do.*

At first I didn't understand why righteousness would be what covers our hearts. But then it became clear: *choosing to do what is right in spite of our emotions protects us.* Think of times in your life when you've let your emotions get the best of you. I'm recalling some now, and the first word that comes to mind is "ouch." Exactly. When we let our emotions get out of control, we get hurt. And often others do too. When God says, "Obey me rather than your emotions," he's really looking out for our best interests.

But it seems like a tall order, doesn't it? Choosing what's right regardless of how we feel is no easy task (at least for me—maybe

I'm the only one). So I dug a little deeper into this idea of guarding our hearts, and that brought me to this Scripture: "Do not be anxious about anything, but in every situation, by prayer and petition, with thanksgiving, present your requests to God. And the peace of God, which transcends all understanding, *will guard your hearts* and your minds in Christ Jesus" (Phil. 4:6–7, emphasis added).

Worry is a sign that we're letting our emotions get the best of us. (And believe me, I know. When it comes to worrying, I'm a pro.) So when we start sensing those feelings taking over, God invites us to come to him instead. When we say thanks along with our requests, we're reminding ourselves of what's true regardless of the circumstances at the moment (remember Joshua and Caleb?). God says that then his peace, which is beyond all understanding, will guard our hearts. It's like a bulletproof vest that looks gorgeous too. Simply stunning.

Stepping onto the Red Carpet of All God Has for You

On the show *What Not to Wear*, Stacy London and Clinton Kelly surprise women with wardrobe makeovers. At the end of each episode, the woman gets to say a few words about her experience. Almost all of them express something like this: "I feel freer to be who I am and pursue my dreams." Many also add that they feel beautiful for the first time.

I'm sure none of you need a wardrobe makeover (although if you'd like to nominate me, please go for it!). But I do hope our little journey leaves you feeling much the same way. God made you an emotional being. That's a beautiful, powerful, glorious thing. After all, the reason we have emotions is because God has them too. We read in the Bible about him feeling everything from anger to sadness to joy. We have the capacity to reflect him through our emotions because we're created in his image—every part of us. Those tears you cry. That smile you give. The anger you express at injustice.

God has given you a wardrobe of emotions fit for a princess because that's what you are in his eyes. Wear them royally, with your heart held high, and show the world what it means to be a passionate woman who has the courage to truly experience life and express herself (and the One who knows her heart best) with love and grace through it all.

I'm imagining a car pulling up to the curb.

You step out of it, confidently placing your feet on the red carpet of God's plans for you.

I wave wildly, snap a picture, and smile from deep inside.

Oh, girl, your heart is looking fabulous today.

5

Where Am I Going?

My car came with a GPS (global positioning system). Despite its best efforts to get me from one place to another, the phrase I most often seem to hear is, "Make a U-turn if possible." My husband somehow set it to the British version, so it sounds a bit like I'm being reprimanded by Mary Poppins all the time—quite distressing. I'm still hoping they'll come out with a Southern version that says, "Now, honey, it sure seems like you've had a rough day. Why don't you pull on over and get yourself a nice, big mocha?"

But for now it's Ms. Poppins and I zipping down the road together. Whenever she starts giving me directions, the first thing I do is look for the little red dot on the screen that represents my car. It essentially tells me, "You are here." After all, before we know where we're going, we need to understand where we are at the moment, right?

We've just spent time in the last chapter getting all dressed up in our emotional style. And as every girl knows, the next step when you're all dressed up is to find somewhere to go—and then get there quick. But it seems when I don't pause first to be certain I know where I am, that's when I get myself into the most trouble. I turn too soon or pass up an intersection, which leads to frustration and even discouragement. Thinking we're one place in life when we're actually somewhere entirely different can derail us from being the amazing women we are and doing what we're called to do. So let's pause and look for that dot.

When I think about the journey of our lives, of course the first thing that comes to mind is when God took the Israelites from Egypt to the Promised Land. You remember that, don't you? The Israelites had been in slavery for hundreds of years. God sent Moses to tell Pharaoh to let the people go. Through a series of miracles, the Israelites were finally free and began their journey through the desert to the wonderful land God had for them. And all along the way, God himself was their divine GPS!

Although I'm sure God did a much better job than my "Mary Poppins," the Israelites still ended up doing more than their share of wandering around too. Like for me, a lot of that happened because they just couldn't grasp where God had them at the moment and hang on to that truth in the middle of their circumstances. As they say, if you can't be an example, be a warning. So take it from the Israelites and from me that things work out better when you know where you are and where God wants you to go.

As I looked at the story of the Israelites again, I wondered how they knew when to stay put and when to move along. It turns out the answer is right there in the middle of the story:

> Whenever the cloud lifted from above the tent, the Israelites set out; wherever the cloud settled, the Israelites encamped. At the LORD's command the Israelites set out, and at his command they encamped. (Num. 9:17–18)

The cloud above the temple was God's presence. So to sum all that up, *wherever God went, the Israelites went too.* He asks us to do the same in our lives. Our role is not to rush ahead but instead to stay right by his side.

That means we're going to have different phases of our lives. Sometimes we'll encamp and sometimes we'll set out. We'll take a closer look at what that means soon. But first, let's have a little heart-to-heart about why this is so hard for us as women.

The Road Less Traveled Is Always the One You're on Right Now

Remember how we talked about our tendency to compare? That doesn't just apply to our strengths—it often extends to where God has us in life. We think, "I need to volunteer for every committee at church because Susie does and she's so godly." Or we might tell ourselves, "I need to quit every committee at church because Anna did and she's so peaceful." We feel like we need to do more, less, or something entirely different than everyone else. We end up zigzagging from spot to spot on the map and wear ourselves out in the process. All the while God is saying, "Dear daughter, I'm here, right here. Won't you join me?"

Here's the good news: God has a journey for *your* life. It looks different than anyone else's. The road he's carved out for you is yours alone. It's always the road less traveled because you're the only one who is ever going to walk it. Oh, sure, he'll give you wonderful traveling companions to go with you. But don't let that fool you: that doesn't mean their paths are the same as yours—just that they're parallel for a time.

So if you've been feeling guilty that your path doesn't look like Spiritual Samantha's then breathe a deep sigh of relief. Your GPS (God Positioning System) is going to get *you* exactly where you need to go. And he promises to be with you every step of the way.

With that said, there are some common stops along the way in our journeys. The Israelites experienced them too. Taking a closer look at those can help us accurately place our "You are here" dots and give us a better understanding of those places.

Keep in mind that where you are in different areas of your life may vary. For example, professionally you might be in the Promised Land while personally you're feeling like you're in the desert, or vice versa. If you relate to several of the spots below, that's totally normal, and I'll give you a tool to help you map them all at the end.

When You're in Egypt

We all begin our journeys in the same spot the Israelites did—Egypt. Most biblical scholars believe that Egypt, a place of slavery, represents how we're all born into sin. We're controlled by it. Then God comes along and promises to set us free.

If you're a Christian, you don't live in Egypt anymore. If you haven't started a relationship with God yet, you can do so right now by giving your life to him. Just tell him something like this:

> God, I believe that you exist, that you love me, and that
> you sent your Son to die on the cross for my sins. I ask
> your forgiveness for those sins, and I receive your gift of
> a right relationship with you and eternal life in heaven.
> All I am and all I have is now yours. Amen.

Once we make that commitment, our address is no longer in Egypt because God has set us free. But we can sometimes find ourselves in that old place again. Let me be clear: I'm not talking about your salvation. Once we belong to Jesus, "our citizenship is in heaven" (Phil. 3:20). But we may end up back in Egypt for a visit. That happens when we let sin take over our lives again.

You know that feeling, don't you? Instead of moving toward what God has for you, it seems you're going backward. Your life feels out of control. It might be because of an addiction, a destructive relationship, or a pattern you just can't break. Whatever it is, you don't have to stay in Egypt! If you've given your life to God, you're his always. Sometimes we just need to stop and realign with his direction for our lives again. You can start that by praying something like this:

> Lord, thank you that I am yours and that you have a plan for my life. I've gotten off track and ended up in Egypt again. Please forgive me. I want to make a U-turn right now. I want to be where you are and live in your presence. Help me change. Amen.

Egypt is a powerful place, and we often need the help of others to get free. Have you ever gotten your car stuck in the mud or seen someone else do so? The wheels endlessly spin, but there's no forward motion. Usually the only way to get the car out is to have someone else pull it onto solid ground again. If you're feeling "stuck," then find someone you can trust—a friend, spiritual mentor, or counselor—who can help you get back on the road. There's no shame in that, girl. We've all been there and will most likely go there again. His grace is your highway out of Egypt and on to better things. As Karen, a reader on my blog *Heart to Heart with Holley*, powerfully declared, "The same God who delivered me from the sins of my past will deliver me from the sins of my present!"[1]

· · · · · · · · · · · · · *Am I in Egypt? 5 Minutes* · · · · · · · · · · ·

Is there an area in my life where I feel like I'm in Egypt?

- ○ In bondage
- ○ Out of control
- ○ Oppressed
- ○ Separated from God's presence

If so, what area is it?

  ○ God, I want out of Egypt. Please help me to

_____

  ○ Someone I trust and can confide in about this is

_____

> *And I have promised to bring you up out of your misery in Egypt*
> *into . . . a land flowing with milk and honey. (Exod. 3:17)*

When You're Encamped

I always wondered how the Israelites could have taken so long to complete a journey that turned out to be about eleven miles. What were they doing all that time? It turns out much of it was spent encamped. In other words, God just told them to stay put for a while. As long as the cloud stayed over the tabernacle, they remained in camp:

> When the cloud remained over the tabernacle a long time, the Israelites obeyed the LORD's order and did not set out. Sometimes the cloud was over the tabernacle only a few days; at the LORD's command they would encamp, and then at his command they would set out. (Num. 9:19–20)

Okay, ladies, it's time for a little confession. I don't do well with being encamped. I'm a "let's get on the road" kind of girl. Yes, ma'am. Pack up those tents, put them in the car, and let's go! And yet there have been multiple times in my life when God's direction to me has clearly been the worst four-letter word of all in my vocabulary: *wait.*

As I look back over those times, I can see that waiting was indeed part of the overall plan and served a purpose. There are many reasons why God may tell us to encamp for a period of time. For the

Israelites, it was an extended "time-out" because they'd blatantly rebelled against God. But that's not always the case. And trust me, if that's why you're waiting, you'll clearly know it. So let's take a closer look at some of the other reasons why God may have us "encamp" for a while.

∼ We're Weary ∼

Making progress in life is hard work. When we insist on moving forward as quickly as possible, we can wear ourselves out in a hurry. Sometimes when God makes us wait, it's one of the most merciful things he can do. It doesn't inherently mean we've done something wrong. In fact, it can indicate just the opposite—that we're right between some really big things God has for our lives, and we need to rest up.

Let's talk about another biblical story we probably all know, from 1 Kings 18. It's one of my favorites because I'm a Texas girl and this is the original showdown. I'll set the scene: Elijah is a prophet of the Lord who challenges the prophets of Baal to prove who's the real God. Everyone shows up. The prophets of Baal make an altar and ask their god to bring down fire on it. Nothing happens. Elijah does the same, and fire comes down in an astounding way. It's an unmistakable victory.

So what does Elijah do next? He hightails it out of town, sits under a tree, and says, "I have had enough, LORD. . . . Take my life" (1 Kings 19:4). Then he falls asleep. So God strikes him with a bolt of lightning. The end.

You'd think that would make sense, right? Nope, that's not what happened. Instead God sends an angel to take care of Elijah, to feed him and make sure he gets even more rest. Then the angel says, "Get up and eat, for the journey is too much for you" (1 Kings 19:7). After that meal, Elijah has the strength to travel for forty days. At the end of that time, God shows up in Elijah's life in another powerful way.

God knows we're human. He knows we get worn out. Sometimes he simply says, "Take a break, child." I have friends with young kids, and naptime doesn't ever seem to be very welcome. The kids almost always protest. But in the end, my friends make sure their little ones get the rest they need for their own good. We can be like those reluctant kids too. We're so set on getting where we want to go that the last thing we want to do is nap (or encamp). But our heavenly Father, in his infinite tenderness, knows that sometimes that's exactly what we need most.

~ We're Healing ~

As I began to write this section, I glanced up at the wall. A plaque just above me reads, "As for God, his way is perfect" (Ps. 18:30). It shows a peaceful path between tall trees. I leaned back in my chair and sighed a bit, relieved at the reminder that God's ways are perfect—but mine don't have to be. And they never are. One of my favorite songs talks about how God blesses the broken roads of our lives.

Life's hard. We get hurt. That means sometimes what we need most is for God to stop us right in the middle of our road as we limp along and say, "Daughter, sit down. Rest. Heal. Let me tend to your wounds."

After a particularly painful season in my life, I walked into the bathroom at an office and burst into tears. My emotions caught me off guard. I had been telling everyone I was just fine! As I found a quiet corner to process things for a moment, Jesus seemed to show up right beside me. Later that day, I wrote this about it on *Heart to Heart with Holley*:

> Hot tears slam my cheeks, slide down, rivers of unbidden emotion.
>
> I'm shocked at their appearance—hot lava exploding from a mountain that had just been covered in daisies.

I slip into a bathroom stall, place my head in my hands, sniffle into a square of paper. That year ... *so good, so hard.*

I felt more like a warrior than a writer.

My heart has the scars to prove it.

But then, softly, a whisper comes, "Put down your sword."

And I notice, for the first time, how my heart has stood in ready-to-fight position for so long, stiff, waiting to dodge the next blow.

I relent. And something inside clatters to the ground. I see the wounds, still fresh, not noticed in the heat of the battle. I touch them tentatively. Cover protectively.

Then again, softly within ...

"If I will wash your feet, will I not wash your wounds?"

I have a choice. *Drop my guard or guard my hurts.*

I choose the first.

And His hand touches all that aches, His voice whispers truth, His love wipes *around, over, down.* It stings a little. I flinch with old fear. But slowly I relax, lean into Him, remember the time before the war, and I know it is finished.

No longer a warrior.

I'm a child, small, safe, with Daddy's hands making it all better.

Victory.

Surrender.

I leave the bathroom stall, finally, look into clear eyes in the mirror.

And I am never the same again.

....

We want to move forward in our lives. We want to keep saying "I'm fine" and pressing ahead as if that's really true. But Jesus, in his infinite love for us, sometimes slows us down for a season so that he can heal our hearts.

~ We're Being Prepared ~

I have a new obsession: the Food Network. I know, I know—it's not the deepest thing out there. But in a time when things feel a little chaotic in life, it's wonderful to know that sugar, flour, and eggs in the oven at 350 degrees predictably do what you intend.

But before that can happen, there's a lot of preparation. Whole shows are built around it. Rachael Ray, Paula Deen, and others talk to the audience while slicing, dicing, mixing, and stirring. Imagine an episode where they skipped all of those steps.

It might sound like this: "Hey, y'all, today we're baking Make-You-Gain-a-Dress-Size Mango Muffins. I'm in a little bit of a hurry, so instead of mixing and measuring, we're just going to put the whole bag of flour and sugar right in the oven and see what happens."

I imagine the results might not help the ratings! Yet I often approach God's purpose to my life the same way: "Hey, God, today I'm really ready to get to the next phase of my life. You know, the one where everything is wonderful? So I think I'll just mix some unfulfilled desires with quick fixes, throw in some steps taken in my own strength, and see what happens."

Whoopsie. It doesn't usually turn out quite like I had in mind.

God's plans for our lives take preparation. That's not my favorite part—I just want to get to the end result. But sometimes God asks us to "encamp" so that he can do the necessary work in our lives for his purposes. Then when the time is right, we get to dig in and enjoy!

~ It's Just Not Time Yet ~

Ladies, I know none of us like this, but it's just got to be said: sometimes *it's just not time yet*. There's no logical explanation for the delay. God is simply doing his thing. "'For my thoughts are not your thoughts, neither are your ways my ways,' declares the LORD" (Isa. 55:8).

When this happens in our lives, the enemy tries to slip in and tell us all sorts of nonsense. For example, "If you were a better person, then this would have worked out by now."

My friend Julie Sawyer Philips has walked this path. For years, she prayed to be a wife and mom. Finally, the first request was answered. Although she and her new husband applied to adopt a child, nothing seemed to be happening. During that time, they had the opportunity to have dinner with the daughter and son-in-law of the couple who ran the orphanage where they had applied. With all of them having busy schedules, only one particular day and time would work.

When they finally got together, the couples took time to pray and asked God to bless the child he had for John and Julie. Four days later, the phone rang and a voice on the other end said, "We have a baby boy for you!" When Julie considered the time difference, she realized her new son had been born the very same day those prayers were offered. During the years Julie had been "encamped," God had been working out every detail. She said with a broad smile on her face, "Isn't that amazing? I can tell my son there was never a moment of his life when he didn't have a family."

You may be "encamped" in a way you don't understand either. God offers this hope: "He who began a good work in you will carry it on to completion until the day of Christ Jesus" (Phil. 1:6). In other words, whatever journey God begins in your life and heart, he promises to finish—in his perfect timing.

~ *Whatever the Reason . . .* ~

Ecclesiastes 3:11 says, God "has made everything beautiful in its time. He has also set eternity in the human heart; yet no one can fathom what God has done from beginning to end." That verse speaks to what it's like to be in the mysterious middle—of circumstances, of unmet expectations, of the journey from Egypt to Home. When we're in the "middle" of life, we can take comfort in knowing we're right in the center of God's hands too.

If you feel "encamped" in your life right now, it may be for any of the purposes we talked about above. Whatever the reason, use this time to rest and receive the truth your heart needs for the journey. You are loved. God has a purpose for you. He is working out his plans for your life.

And just when you least expect it, you'll be on your way so he can take you all the way to the Promised Land.

· · · · · · · · · · · · *Am I Encamped? 5 Minutes* · · · · · · · · · · ·

Is there an area in my life where I feel like God is asking me to "encamp"?

- ° Waiting
- ° God may seem silent
- ° Doors aren't opening for me to move forward
- ° I feel the need to rest or heal

If so, what area is it?

- ° God, sometimes simply staying where we are is difficult. Please help me to

_____

- ° Someone I trust and can confide in about this is

_____

> The LORD replied, "My Presence will go with you, and I will give you rest." (Exod. 33:14)

Setting Out

Encamping doesn't last forever, and when the cloud of God's presence lifted, the Israelites knew it was time to move. When God does the same in our lives, we may have several responses. Which one sounds most like you?

○ **The Settler**

"What? Set out? I'm quite content right here. I just got things the way I want them. You go ahead and maybe I'll join you later. Change is pretty scary, after all."

- Strengths: Good at maintaining security and peace. Willing to stay with something as long as it takes. Faithful and trustworthy.
- Areas for growth: Tends to view change, even when it's from God, as negative. May get stuck in a rut and refuse to move forward.

○ **The Explorer**

"Bring on the change! I'll race you to the Promised Land. I may not be sure where I'm going, but I'm making good time. Life's an adventure and new is fun."

- Strengths: Willing to take risks and go in a different direction. Moves forward and often helps others do so as well. Embraces and encourages change.
- Areas for growth: Sometimes takes risks or tries new things for the experience rather than being led by God. May put tasks ahead of relationships for the sake of progress.

○ **The Traveler**

"I'm packed and ready to go. I feel a little uneasy, but I'm still willing to take the next step. We'll see what happens. Life is just as much about the journey along the way as it is the destination."

- Strengths: Takes life in stride and tries to move at the pace of God and others. Flexible and adaptive. Interested in what is ahead but doesn't rush to get there.

- Areas for growth: Sometimes can end up wandering longer than necessary. May be indecisive or too easily sidetracked by others.

We each play these roles at some point in our lives, but one is probably your natural tendency. And this is never more apparent than when God says, "It's time to set out!" By understanding how we normally respond to change, we can pause and be sure we're really doing what God wants and not just what's most comfortable for us.

We can also ask ourselves the following questions when it's time to take a step or make a change.

~ *Am I Being Led or Driven?* ~

Sonic is a popular fast-food restaurant in the South. Home of the infamous cherry limeade, it's also reminiscent of the days when carhops brought food to you. One afternoon I pulled in, and as I waited for my order to come, I glanced at the car next to me. A toddler about two years old was perched in the driver's seat with his little hands wrapped around the wheel and a look of determination on his face. I laughed out loud since the car was safely in park and he was right in the middle of his mama's lap.

As I thought more about that scene and how it seemed oddly familiar, I slowly realized I was a lot like that toddler. I wanted to grab the steering wheel of my life and zip down the road. It seemed God gently whispered to my heart, *"If you're driven, you can't be led."* I knew in that moment that me being in charge of my life wasn't any wiser than that little boy driving down the highway. God in his mercy was letting me know that I could take a seat on the passenger side and he'd gladly get me where I needed to go.

We can be driven by all kinds of things—fear, insecurities, ambition, pride, comparison, or lies from our childhood. But we can only be led by one Person. Jesus promised the Holy Spirit would lead us into all truth (see John 16:13). Instead of God's presence being a cloud above the temple, we have God's presence within us. "Your body is a temple of the Holy Spirit" (1 Cor. 6:19 NIV 1984).

The next question naturally seems to be, "But how can we know if it's the Holy Spirit leading us?"

First, simply begin to make a habit of asking God to speak to you and then listening for his voice in your life. As you do, make sure what you hear lines up with God's Word—anything that's from him always will. Also ask for guidance from others you trust. "Surely you need guidance to wage war, and victory is won through many advisers" (Prov. 24:6).

Then take a step. Sometimes the step you take won't be exactly right, and that's okay. "Many are the plans in a person's heart, but it's the LORD's purpose that prevails" (Prov. 19:21). Ask God to redirect you as needed. Learning what God wants for our lives is a process. As the book of Romans says, we're to "test and approve" God's will (12:2). In other words, if God is asking you to set out, then sometimes the only way to know is to go!

~ Is My Pace Matching God's? ~

Like we talked about earlier, we all approach change differently. If you're a Settler, you may tend to go a bit slower than God might want at times. If you're an Explorer, you may race ahead. God wants us right by his side. And when we are, the journey doesn't wear us out, and we even find joy along the way.

One morning my husband and I set out for a bike ride. A brilliant blue sky hung above us, and the first kiss of fall found its way onto our cheeks as we began to zigzag down the trail. Biking hasn't always been easy for me (okay, it never has). I do enjoy it—especially on flat pavement. But we live in a hilly part of the country, and every ride is full of ups and downs (anyone else feel a spiritual analogy coming on?).

My husband is a great biker, and my big breakthrough came when he taught me how to use my gears. You see, I had been doing everything in the hardest gear. I was showing off, really. I thought if I could tackle the biggest, baddest hill in that gear, then I must be good.

But that's just silly. And I understood why when I learned you can make it easier to pedal just by a little flick of your fingers. Now my gear fits the terrain. I can adapt, shift, and make the most of where I am at the moment.

When I find just the right gear, it almost feels like flying.

God has been giving me some "gear lessons" in the rest of my life the last few months too. Just like I am on my mountain bike, I tend to be a bit intense in my spiritual life. I think, "I'll just do it all in the hardest gear. That will prove what a good little Christian I am." Can anyone say "craziness"? But now, instead, the One who loves me is gently showing me how to shift, adapt, and allow seasons of rest between seasons of pushing hard. It's changing everything for me.

What pace do you tend to go? What gear do you tend to use? When we take time to align ourselves with God's pace and purposes, our journey suddenly feels different. As Isaiah 40:31 says, "But those who wait on the LORD shall renew their strength; they shall mount up with wings like eagles, they shall run and not be weary, they shall walk and not faint" (NKJV). It's clear from those words that this kind of waiting isn't passive—it's more about keeping pace with God.

And when we do? Well, it almost feels like flying too.

∽ *Am I Making God My Ultimate Destination?* ∽

Think of a trip you took with someone you love. Maybe it was a family vacation, a honeymoon, or a way to celebrate a milestone. While you may have gone to a beautiful place, the best part of all was probably the relationship.

When God asks us to set out, we can get so focused on moving forward, on getting to the Promised Land, that we forget that the real point of the journey is our relationship. Yes, God moves us forward, but most of all he simply wants *us*.

It can seem hard to believe at times, but it's true—the God of the universe wants to share life with you. Every step. Every day. All the way to your forever home with him.

• • • • • • • • • • *Am I Setting Out? 5 Minutes* • • • • • • • • • •

Is there an area in my life where I feel like God is asking me to "set out"?

- ○ An urge to take the next step
- ○ God seems to be speaking and guiding
- ○ Doors may be opening for me to move forward
- ○ I'm sensing the need for change—even if it's hard or uncomfortable

If so, what area is it?

- ○ God, it seems you're asking me to "set out" with you. Please help me to

- ○ Someone I trust to walk with me through this is

> *Have I not commanded you? Be strong and courageous. Do not be afraid; do not be discouraged, for the LORD your God will be with you wherever you go. (Josh. 1:9)*

The Promised Land

After we escape from Egypt, do some camping, and move forward when God says to, then we finally make it to the Promised Land.

For believers, heaven is the ultimate Promised Land. But God gave the Israelites a Promised Land in this life as well. I believe he often does the same for us too. Let's define a Promised Land as this: *a desire of your heart that God guides you into through an intimate journey with him.* Maybe you were single for years and God brought along your husband. You might have been trying to have a baby and suddenly you saw the bright pink "yes" of that line on a pregnancy test. Perhaps you got the position at work you'd waited so long to get. Or your health returned after a struggle with illness.

All of our Promised Lands look different. And because we live this side of heaven, none of them are perfect. We'll still disagree with that husband God gave us, grow a little weary of changing diapers for the baby we wanted so badly, or realize this job has more responsibilities than we bargained for when we asked for it. But even in the middle of all that, we know this is where our hearts belong.

Also, we won't make it to all of the Promised Lands our hearts long for this side of heaven. We live in a fallen, broken world, and some of the desires of our hearts will only be met when we cross from here to eternity.

Sometimes we become so sure that we won't make it to our Promised Land in this life that we're taken by surprise when we do. Or perhaps we've been so intent on getting there that we're not quite sure what's next when we actually arrive. After my husband and I reach a destination and set down our suitcases, the first question out of one of our mouths is usually, "What should we do now?" We pull out a guide to the area and make a plan.

After all the praying, waiting, and moving forward, it's time for us to explore what God has given us too. Fortunately, he gives us a guide to use as well. So what does he say we're to do when we get to our Promised Land?

～ Possess It ～

When the Israelites arrive at the edge of the Promised Land, God tells them to go in and make it fully theirs. He asks us to do the same too. That can take a lot of hard work and fighting some battles. Possessing the Promised Land isn't a one-time event but instead a process.

> *God's Guide:* "The LORD your God will drive out those nations before you, little by little. You will not be allowed to eliminate them all at once, or the wild animals will multiply around you" (Deut. 7:22).

Like Joshua and Caleb, we're to believe that the Promised Land will ultimately belong to us, but the way that actually happens usually takes time and courage on our part.

～ Defend It ～

As the years went by, the Israelites drifted away from their faith in God and eventually were exiled from the Promised Land for many years. When we get to where God is taking us, it doesn't mean we can get so comfortable that we let our guard down or neglect our relationship with him.

> *God's Guide:* "Be careful that you do not forget the LORD your God, failing to observe his commands, his laws and his decrees that I am giving you this day. Otherwise, when you eat and are satisfied, when you build fine houses and settle down, when your herds and flocks grow large and your silver and gold increase and all you have is multiplied, then your heart will become proud and you will forget the LORD your God, who brought you out of Egypt, out of the land of slavery" (Deut. 8:11–14).

While the Israelites did have to fight the nations around them, the biggest threat ended up being from within. Gratitude and obedience are the best defenses for our Promised Land.

∼ *Enjoy It* ∼

Once we're in our Promised Land, God wants us to enjoy it! After wandering in the wilderness so long, our joy muscles can get a little weak. Give yourself permission to celebrate where God has brought you and what he has entrusted to you.

> *God's Guide:* "The LORD your God is bringing you into a good land—a land with brooks, streams, and deep springs gushing out into the valleys and hills; a land with wheat and barley, vines and fig trees, pomegranates, olive oil and honey; a land where bread will not be scarce and you will lack nothing; a land where the rocks are iron and you can dig copper out of the hills. When you have eaten and are satisfied, praise the LORD your God for the good land he has given you" (Deut. 8:7–10).

· · · · · · · **Am I in the Promised Land? 5 Minutes** · · · · · · ·

Is there an area in my life where I feel like God has brought me to the Promised Land?

- A desire or prayer answered
- A sense of being where I belong
- Renewed joy and anticipation
- Passion to possess and defend what's been given to me

If so, what area is it?

- God, thank you for bringing me to the Promised Land. Please help me to

- Someone I can celebrate this with is

> *When you have eaten and are satisfied, praise the LORD your God for the good land he has given you. (Deut. 8:10)*

Your Life Map

The Israelites' divine GPS guided them every step of the way and eventually got them to the Promised Land. God promises that if we follow him, he'll do the same for us too.

Let's think back to my little GPS—the one in my car that we talked about in the very beginning. I mentioned how I "zoom in" to the little red dot representing my car because it helps me know where I am and where I'm going. We've been doing the same for your life.

One more way I use my GPS to stay on track is to "zoom out" so I can get the full view. Then I see that little red dot in the full context of where I am and where I'm going next. Because our lives are complex, we actually have more than one dot. As I said before, you might be in one place personally and someplace totally different professionally. That's even more reason for us to step back and see the big picture.

To tie everything together, let's build a map of where you are in different areas of your life. Take a look back over your answers in each section of this chapter and use them to fill this in:

· · · · · · · · · · · · · **My Life Map: 5 Minutes** · · · · · · · · · · · ·

Under each section draw a dot and write the areas of your life that fit in each one.

Egypt

Promised Land

Encamped

Setting Out

Where do you have the most dots? They might all be clustered in one area right now, or you may literally be "all over the map"!

By knowing where you are in life, you can ask God for what you need in each area. You can also let others in your life know how they can come alongside you. Perhaps most important, you can give yourself grace by understanding that these are stops along the way. You won't be where you are forever. God promises that when you trust him, he'll take care of you wherever you are and get you where he wants you to go.

In the meantime, I'm going to step in and pretend to be your personal GPS for the day. Here's what I'm saying to your heart: "Way to go, girl! You've made a lot of progress in this chapter. Now pull over and celebrate because God has you headed somewhere good. He's given you all you need and made you exactly who you need to be for your journey. He'll get you where he wants you to go in his perfect timing."

6

Who's **with** Me?

The women gather, laugh, hug, and reconnect. I stand at the back of the room. I ask the silent questions we rarely dare to speak aloud.

Will I fit in?

Will anyone like me?

I'm at a conference. I know many of these women. I've met some in person and connected with others online. We call each other friends, support each other through hard times, cheer each other on . . .

And yet.

Insecurity pushes me into the corner. I become a wallflower, not growing but wilting in the feeling of being alone right in the middle of a crowd.

Eventually the feeling passes.

But I know it will come again.

I think we all experience this as women. We're part of families. We join churches. We do bunco in our neighborhood or join the school board. We are on Facebook, send emails, write cards to one another.

We know what it's like to be connected and yet feel alone.

Throughout the journey we talked about in the last chapter, we look to our left and right, our hearts asking the question, "Who's with me?"

Of course, the Sunday school answer is "God."

And that's true—God promises to always be with us.

Yet it seems he also created within us a deep desire to share life with each other—flesh and blood. In the Garden of Eden he declared, "It is not good for the man to be alone" (Gen. 2:18). It's not good for women either. We need others to speak truth to us, remind us we're amazing, walk alongside us, and encourage us in all God has called us to do.

We may tell ourselves, "If only I were closer to God, I wouldn't feel like I needed other people so much." But Adam lived in a perfect place. There was no sin. He had an intimacy with God we can only imagine. Yet God still said that Adam being alone wasn't good.

So that ache you feel, that longing you can't name? You don't need to feel guilty about it. It's the magnet God places within you that draws you to other people. It's part of his plan. *It's good.*

When God says being alone is "not good," the contrast is stark. Remember the seven days of creation? After sky, water, birds, animals, light, and dark, God says, "It is good." And yet now he is announcing the opposite. A life without relationships with other human beings isn't good—isn't what he planned.

In today's world of going-it-alone, pull-yourself-up-by-your-bootstraps thinking, it often seems we disagree. Oh, perhaps it's not stated directly. But even in churches it sometimes feels as if needing other people is a sign of weakness.

If only my relationship with God were stronger, then I wouldn't be lonely.

If only I could get my act together, then I wouldn't care at all what other people thought.

But wanting other people in your life isn't weakness. Instead it's a reflection that you are created by a God who is inherently relational. Look at the lengths he's gone to just to have a relationship with you.

Why was Adam being alone not good? *Because it's not like God.*

Father.

Son.

Holy Spirit.

The kingdom we serve in is one of love, relationship, and intimacy. We're not made *for* each other, but we're certainly made to share life *with* each other.

What You Have to Offer as a Woman

As the daughters of Eve, being made to share life with others is especially true of us—it's central to what makes each of us amazing. God created Eve with relationships in mind. When we think of Eve being created as a "helper" for Adam (Gen. 2:18), we tend to assume that word describes her role. But what if it's much deeper than that? What if it describes her heart?

Think of the women in your life. Encouraging, comforting, cooking, painting, working . . . it's almost all for someone else. They labor on behalf of love. This "helping" varies in its intensity. Sometimes it's a soft hand brushed across the hot brow of a sick child. But often it's fierce, strong, wild, bold.

The word for "helper" is the same word often used when God helps us. David uses it in the Psalms: "We wait in hope for the LORD; he is our help and our shield" (33:20). Here the help that comes from God is the kind one needs in war—it stands side by side with a shield.

We, as women, often do go to battle. We fight cancer. We fight for our marriages. We fight for our children. And in doing so, *we help*.

Perhaps we have defined this word too narrowly because a part of us grasps what it truly means. Deep inside we have sensed our full calling . . . and it frightens us. So we define, and let it be defined for us, that "helping" is quiet and safe.

And sometimes it is. It has been said that humility is "strength under control." So at times we do help in the ways servants do—not because we must but because our hearts love deeply enough to put the needs of others before our own. This is a beautiful part of being a woman.

But other times, perhaps, we hold back our help because it would mean stepping out of our comfort zones and getting messy, dirty, and involved. We know it would take all of our strength, we might get wounded in the process, and people could misunderstand.

Yet it remains that we are "helpers" created and called by the One who is our help. So we must look to him for the complete picture of what that word means. God's heart is the place where "woman" began, and though we may look elsewhere, it is still the place where we (as women) find who we are in the end.

The world needs you as a woman to do what only you can do, to love the way only you can love, to offer what you have to share.

Believe me, sister, it's beautiful and worth much more than you can even imagine. :) ♥ *encouraging*

Why We Hold Back

If we have so much to offer, why is it so hard to open ourselves up? What keeps us from fully giving ourselves in relationships? After connecting with thousands of women, I've discovered several common reasons—all of which I can personally relate to as well.

We're Afraid We Won't Be Loved

I pull jeans from my closet and hold them up to the light. I'm about to fold them neatly into my suitcase when I notice the rough cuffs.

I grab scissors and snip at loose ends. They only fray more. I tug and pull. (Did I mention these are my *good* jeans?) I sigh and lean back against the wall. And as I do, I realize my jeans aren't the only thing with frayed edges.

My heart has them too.

I shouldn't be afraid of this trip. I'm looking forward to seeing old friends and making new ones, to learning and time with Jesus.

And yet (confession coming) a part of me still feels insecure.

Fear pulls at the edges of my heart.

My jeans are frayed.

And I am afraid.

Neither of us seems quite good enough at the moment.

And as I stand there, jeans still in hand, a change begins to happen. It seems Jesus lays his hands on those frayed edges, those places I wish were different, and he stitches them up with grace. He tells me again,

- Love all. Please One.
- Be who I've created you to be.
- You are enough because I am enough in you.

Each line is like a thread that mends something inside me. I run my thoughts along those frayed edges of my heart, amazed—they suddenly feel smoother and more whole.

And my jeans?

I put them in my suitcase.

I decide I'll just wear them anyway.

I'm slowly learning it's not about being perfect but about being perfectly loved.

"There is no fear in love. But perfect love drives out fear" (1 John 4:18). This verse has come to mind over and over as I've thought

I'm slowly grasping God's love for me + others to be true.

about relationships and why they're so hard for women. We strive for perfection, after all. It seems like the ideal insurance policy against rejection, doesn't it? If our house, habits, and heart are just right, who wouldn't love us? And yet all the time we know that we aren't perfect, that we won't ever be this side of heaven. Round and round it goes until God stops us as he did me that day with my jeans and tells us again, "Beautiful daughter of mine, you don't need to be perfect. You are already perfectly loved."

The hard part is translating that into our relationships. Perhaps we can grasp that God loves us, but it seems more uncertain that our friends or family are likely to follow suit. I recently pondered that, and it seemed God whispered to my heart, "There is no fear in love—if you are acting out of insecurity, then you are not living in love." That hit home.

I protested, "But God, I want people to like me. I want people to be happy with me. Isn't that what it means to be loving?" And as I dug deeper into his Word it became clear that, no, being loving doesn't mean pleasing people. *We are to love people, but we're only asked to please God.* "Am I now trying to win the approval of human beings, or of God? Or am I trying to please people? If I were still trying to please people, I would not be a servant of Christ" (Gal. 1:10).

We're called to care about others, to be kind and considerate, to try our best to bless them. But, ladies, we don't have to make everyone happy. *And if we don't have to make everyone happy, then we don't have to be perfect.* God has already declared us good enough, worthy in his sight, valuable, and with much to offer the world.

Please listen to this: if you are loving toward others and following God's will as best you can and someone else talks negatively about you or rejects you, then they are responsible to God for that sin. Yes, it's sin for someone else to gossip about you, criticize you to others, or cut off their relationship with you in an unloving way. *And you are not responsible for the ungodly responses of others.*

If others have wounded you in this way, I'm so sorry. I'm asking God right now to heal those hurts, to release you from the burden of feeling it must have been your fault and from the endless striving of trying to make things right—or to be just right.

I used to walk on eggshells around other people, say yes when I wanted to say no, and worry endlessly about what someone might whisper behind my back if I didn't please them. Then I realized that they're accountable to God for their words and actions. If I'm doing my best to be loving, God says, then others are to come to me and tell me if I've offended them. (The same works in reverse—others are not responsible for pleasing us either.) And we're to guard our lips against criticizing them or gossiping about them as well. We're not here to please each other. We're here to please the One who put us on this earth.

So if you've felt afraid to put yourself out there because you feel less than perfect, because you're afraid what others might say, then reach out your hands and open your heart, sweet sister. You are already perfectly loved, and you only have to please the One who has already declared you are a delight to his heart.

We Only Feel Safe When We're Hiding

Adam and Eve forget their purpose is to please God. They fall, then hide. But God doesn't let them stay there. He finds them again.

Hide-and-seek. Our hearts have been playing that game ever since.

Every kid has their favorite hiding places. Mine were under my brother's bunk bed, behind an old chair in the garage, and in the laundry basket (how I fit in there, I'll never know). What were yours? At first hiding was fun. But at some point, I just wanted someone to come get me.

how is it always the same? sometimes God is wrathful

As a child, I hid physically. As an adult, I'm more like Adam and Eve. My insecurity makes me hide emotionally. God asks my heart, "Why are you hiding?" On any given day, the answer varies:

- Insecurity.
- Perfectionism.
- Hurt.

But his response is always the same—to call me back to confidence in him, remind me of who I am, and bring me back into the light of his love.

God seems to prefer *seek-and-find.* "You will seek me and find me when you seek me with all your heart" (Jer. 29:13).

Here's how it works: we come out of hiding, and then we're free to pursue God's heart, chase his will, freely follow his path for our lives. I remember how as a child playing hide-and-seek, one person would eventually yell, "Olly olly oxen free!" I still have no idea what that means, but it seems God makes the same declaration to our hearts: it's safe to come out of hiding. In the game of life, we're free, loved, found forever.

We don't have to hide in our relationships with others either. As we talked about earlier, we're called to love those in our lives, but we don't have to please them. The hardest part is having the courage to live that way—to stand in the open rather than hiding.

While God does want us to be open with others, he also encourages us to put boundaries in place as we do so. He talks repeatedly about guarding our hearts. So what's the difference? *Hiding is a response out of fear, while guarding is a proactive choice to protect what matters most.* In other words, we're not to deliberately put something of worth where it won't be valued. Some people in our lives can't or won't treasure our hearts. In those cases, it's okay to limit how we share ourselves with them. What God wants us to avoid is making a habit of hiding that leaves us feeling alone and as if no one really knows us.

· · · · · · · · · · · · **Safe Person Checklist** · · · · · · · · · · ·

How do you know if someone in your life is safe? The short answer: if they love you the way God does. First Corinthians 13 gives us a checklist. No one does this perfectly, including us! What we're looking for is someone who tries to love this way, even if they mess up at times.

A safe person . . .

- Practices patience
- Treats you with kindness
- Finds joy in your blessings and success
- Stays humble
- Considers your needs
- Gives unselfishly
- Is slow to become angry
- Doesn't hold grudges
- Defends you
- Trusts you
- Hopes for the best
- Sticks with you no matter what

Let's look at the opposite of that list too.

An unsafe person . . .

- Frequently gets impatient
- Treats you unkindly
- Envies you
- Is prideful
- Doesn't take you into consideration
- Takes whatever they can get
- Quickly becomes angry
- Holds grudges
- Wounds you
- Is suspicious and untrusting
- Believes the worst
- Abandons you when you need them most

I have to let friendships go sometimes? is that bad?

They need me/don't want me/ Idek...

The first list is how God intends for you to be loved—and how he wants you to love others too. If you've experienced or expressed anything else, it's not from him. Find the people in your life who will love you like this, and forgive the ones who can't or won't. Broken people have sharp edges, and you may have been deeply wounded. If that's what's driven you into hiding, then God wants to set you free to feel safe and to love again.

It may seem scary to think of being in relationships with others, of coming out of hiding. Jesus knows what it's like to live in this world. He knows what it's like to have someone you love betray you, to be abused, to be crucified when you're innocent. *He knows.* And he still says, "Love is worth it."

Coming out of hiding doesn't mean that we won't ever get hurt. We will. It doesn't mean people won't disappoint us. They will. But it does mean that we'll be able to love and be loved, to experience life the way God intends—with each other.

And God will help us guard our hearts. "He is my loving God and my fortress, my stronghold and my deliverer, my shield, in whom I take refuge" (Ps. 144:2). God wants to be your protection.

Oh, sweet sister, it's been hard hiding, hasn't it? It's exhausting, lonely, scary. God wants to whisper to all of our hearts, "Come to me. Stand with me. I will be with you. I will go before you. I will be your shield. You don't have to carry the burden of protecting yourself anymore. I'm here. I love you—and I want you to experience the love of others too."

Drop that mask. Tear down that wall. Step out from behind that barrier. *Dare to love.*

We've Got to Have Control

Sometimes it seems the best way to protect our hearts is to have control. Relationships are messy, after all. Unpredictable. We know if we put cookies in the oven and bake at 350 degrees for a certain amount of time, the results will be what we want. But if we put love into our lives and circumstances turn up the heat, we're not sure what may happen.

We've talked a lot about Eve and how as women we're still impacted by that one important choice she made in the Garden. Ultimately, that choice was about control. Eve wanted to "be like God, knowing good and evil" (Gen. 3:4) While it may hurt to admit, many of us want the same—especially in relationships.

Control can usually be traced back to one emotion: fear. We want to feel safe. And the only way to feel safe is to know what will happen. The only way we can know what will happen is to be sure we're in charge of it, right? + we aren't in charge!)

As a counselor, I see many of my clients struggling with issues of safety and control. It often leads to anxiety and depression in their lives. Naïvely, I assumed I didn't struggle with control because I had little desire to tell others what to do. But in his loving-kindness, God slowly began to peel back the layers of my heart and reveal that, yes, I did struggle with control too. My attempts to control just looked different. Instead of controlling others, *I controlled myself.* I set unrealistic expectations for my behavior. I put standards in place that were impossible to meet. I wanted to be perfect—which would be the ultimate display of control.

I began to realize there are two primary ways we tend to approach control as women. Both impact our lives and relationships.

~ *If you're drawn to external control . . .* ~

- You want to determine the behavior of others
- You are often tempted to be critical
- You may be seen as "bossy"
- You have high expectations for those in your life
- You feel unsafe in situations in which you can't determine the outcome
- You're drawn to positions of power

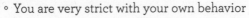

~ *If you're drawn to internal control . . .* ~

- You are very strict with your own behavior
- You are quite hard on yourself
- You tend to be anxious and find it difficult to relax
- You have high expectations of yourself
- You feel unsafe in situations in which you don't know what others expect
- You are continually pushing yourself to do and be more

All of us struggle with control in both of these ways at times, but there's usually one tendency we're drawn to more than others. (I also want to be sure to clarify that this kind of self-control is different than what the Bible talks about. Self-control as a fruit of the Spirit is a natural outflow of God leading our lives. It's ultimately God-control. The kind of control we're talking about here is self-imposed so that we feel safe.)

It's easy to read what's above and be hard on ourselves about it. But picture for a moment yourself as a little girl. You fear monsters under the bed, so you keep a little light on every night. You're not sure what's in that closet, so you never open the door. You hear a noise in the dark and insist your mom stays with you until you're asleep. We're not little girls anymore, but we still know that life can be full of darkness, "monsters," noises we don't understand, things that make us feel afraid. So we cope. *We control.*

Give that little girl inside of you some grown-up grace. Tell her you know she's scared and you're sorry she doesn't feel safe. Then tell her about the heavenly Father. The One who is the forever light, who loves her, who promises to keep her secure no matter what happens.

Notice I said "secure" and not "safe." Because the reality is that life and relationships *aren't* completely safe. Jesus said, "In this world you will have trouble" (John 16:33). We will get hurt. We will face loss. We will be disappointed. It seems as if control

LORD help me believe this. believe this.

is a cure for this—but it's only an illusion. It traps us tight within our fears. Freedom only comes when we find security in Jesus, when we realize that life is hard but he is good and *no matter what happens* he'll get us through it. Life is risk. Love is risk. As C. S. Lewis said:

> To love at all is to be vulnerable. Love anything, and your heart will certainly be wrung and possibly broken. If you want to make sure of keeping it intact, you must give your heart to no one, not even to an animal. Wrap it carefully round with hobbies and little luxuries; avoid all entanglements; lock it up safe in the casket or coffin of your selfishness. But in that casket—safe, dark, motionless, airless—it will change. It will not be broken; it will become unbreakable, impenetrable, irredeemable.[1]

Control keeps us alone. God invites us instead to love—to that wild, unknown, heart-pounding reality of relationships. We're to give him the reins of our hearts, and then he loves others through us. Are you ready to let go of a little control and let more love into your life? *Yes.*

Learning to Love

Once we've faced all the reasons we might be holding back our hearts, then the question becomes "How do I build relationships?" The answer to that question is as unique as you are. Just as God has given you specific strengths and skills, he's also created you to connect with others in particular ways.

As women, we can struggle with feeling we have to be "all things to all people." We look at Chatty Cathy and wonder why we're not more outgoing. We listen to Deep Debbie and feel like we should be more insightful in talking about our faith. We squirm in crowds and feel safe one-on-one. Or just the opposite. Usually we simply sigh and ask, "Why do I act this way?" The beautiful answer to that question just may be, "Because that's exactly how God made you, sweet girl."

When we think about the biblical command to "love one another," it seems like the way we go about doing so should be one size fits all. But the way God expresses his love through you will look entirely different than the way he does it through someone else. *And that's good.*

So let's explore how he wired you, *amazing you,* to be a reflection of his love.

7

How Do I Connect?

Imagine we're on a playground. One feisty little girl leads her peers in a spontaneous game. Another talks quietly with a friend in the sandbox. Both seem utterly content in the way they connect with others.

Then we grow up and learn words like *outgoing* and *shy*, and the labels make us squirm. When certain social situations make us feel uncomfortable, we tell ourselves we shouldn't feel that way. We pile on the guilt for not being "loving" and try harder. But the truth still remains—particular ways of connecting with others feel as natural now as they did back when we were those kids on the playground.

What if God made us that way? What if he wired our social tendencies just like he did our other strengths and skills? Perhaps the way you connect with those around you is just as needed as the other gifts in your life. Maybe it's even at the heart of what makes you amazing.

but is it? (just being a deep *with this* A.)

Your Social Strengths

As we talked about in the last chapter, God is relational. And I believe he formed each of us with certain ways of reaching out to others. So let's take a closer look at what that means for you in the following sections. (And yes, they all start with *S* because I'm an alliteration addict and just can't help myself.)

These are general categories. They're intended not to box you in but instead to help you do a little exploring. We're all complex, unique individuals, and there's no way to fully capture who we are in a few sentences. So use these tools in whatever way is helpful to you. Follow them completely as they are, make up your own, or somewhere in between. They aren't absolutes—just ways of thinking about who we are and how we connect. God knows you better than anyone, so also ask him to be your partner in this process and show you what you need to know about who he's made you.

Also, even within the category that fits you there will be variations between you and someone else who chose the same one. We're all on a continuum and have our own spot. Just treat these as starting places and adapt them to wonderful, one-of-a-kind you.

Setting

Amanda slips into the party. Her palms feel sweaty and her knees knock a little. There are so many people! She glances over at her friend Molly who's loudly telling a story and has an entire group laughing. "Why can't I be more like her?" Amanda wonders. She drifts across the room and spots her friend Sarah in a quieter corner. She quickly grabs the chair next to her and settles in for a long chat. It turns out Sarah has had quite the week and really needed an empathetic ear in the middle of all the chaos. Amanda has always been a great listener. As she tunes out the crowd, her racing heart slows and she feels comfortable again.

You have a dominant social setting preference. One way to recognize it is by asking yourself what you usually choose if you have an evening free to do anything you'd like with others. Do you plan a party? Have dinner with a few friends? Make time for a long chat over coffee with just one person?

Your answer gives you a glimpse of who you are and how you relate to others. Which of the descriptions below sounds most like you?

One-to-One:

You prefer situations in which you can focus intently on an individual. You listen carefully and seek to offer your full attention. Your conversations are likely to have depth, and you want to hear what's really going on in the other person's life and heart as well as share the same. While you enjoy people, you probably don't have the desire for an extensive inner circle. That would require spreading yourself too thin. After all, a relationship is a significant, serious investment that requires the best of you.

In a group of people, you may feel overwhelmed or frustrated that you can't give each person the attention you'd truly like. You also may have little patience for small talk and chatter, seeing them as a distraction from what matters most. You have a strong capacity to make people feel truly valued and heard.

One-to-Few:

You are drawn to situations in which you can be in a close circle of people. Most often, those in that circle are people you already know. You feel safe and comfortable because you have history and an understanding of who is around you. You don't necessarily need to have deep conversations because you know so much about each other, although you can do so at times. You enjoy hearing how each person approaches life and learning from them. You also like seeing how each individual engages with the others in different ways. You are a peacemaker and relationship maintainer.

You don't necessarily mind meeting new people but don't naturally go out of your way to do so and may avoid situations completely if people you know aren't going to be there. You know how to talk as well as listen and can do so with one person or the whole group as the conversation flows. You make people feel comfortable and as if they belong.

One-to-Many:

socially . .

You thrive on groups of people. You have a seemingly endless capacity for connection. While others might be intimidated by having lots of people around, you are excited by the opportunity. You could be called a "social butterfly," and you often act much like one—flitting from person to person with ease.

Most of your conversations are more casual because you need to spread your emotional energy around, although you can go deeper if someone really needs you. If someone takes too much of your time, you may start feeling trapped. You're able to lead, speak in front of a group, or coordinate many people if needed. You love seeing how different people are, and there's no such thing as a stranger to you—just another friend waiting to be made. You make people feel included and help them engage in life and with each other.

Of course, we're all going to experience each of the settings above at different times. Understanding our preference doesn't mean we avoid the others. But it's important to know because the one that fits closest with you is where you'll have the most to give to others. If you're more of a one-on-one girl, then you might want to consider being a life coach. If you're one-to-many, then that leadership position in women's ministry might be a really great opportunity for you.

You can also get rid of the guilt you feel for not feeling equally comfortable in all of these situations. It doesn't mean anything is wrong with you—it's simply how you're wired. For the sake of others, we choose to be in situations out of our comfort zones. But that doesn't mean we have to feel ecstatic about it. God made you to love others in your own wonderful way.

Which one sounds most like you?

○ My strongest social setting is:

*One—to-one
(but I'm super comfortable in social situations)*

Structure

Pam stands in front of a microphone and smiles at the women in front of her. This conference has taken months of careful direction and planning. Now the day has finally come and everything is in place. Well, almost. She notices someone has forgotten to put coffee in the back. Pam makes a quick mental note to ask for that to be taken care of before the first break. Then she takes a deep breath and welcomes the women for the day. She knows it's up to her to set the tone, and she's up for the challenge.

Now that we've looked at which settings you're drawn to with others, let's talk about the structure of those relationships. There are three primary relationship structures: leading, partnering, and following/serving. Depending on where you are (work, home, etc.) these may vary for you. But there's usually one that you naturally gravitate to more of the time.

If you made graphs of each of these they would look like this:

Leading	Partnering	Serving
You		Others
↓	You ⇄ Others	↓
Others		You

Leading:

If you prefer the leading structure of relationship, then you're confident being in charge. You enjoy setting direction and inspiring others to join you on the journey. Those in your life likely listen to you and look to you for advice. When you're not depending on God as your ultimate leader, you may come across as controlling. But when you're being directed by him, you have the ability to take many people to places God wants them to go and to guide them well along the way.

Partnering:

If you're drawn to the partnering structure of relationship, then you view everyone in life as your equal. You want to be side by side or face-to-face. You see connecting with others as an endless process of give-and-take. You care little for power but don't want to be taken advantage of either. You may become agitated by issues of balance and fairness. You have a strong capacity for coming alongside others and encouraging them, sometimes simply by your presence through whatever they face. You believe we're all better together.

Serving:

If you fit closest with the serving structure of relationship, then you see humbling yourself as the best way to lift others up. You're willing to do whatever is needed and offer support without resentment or envy. You likely feel uncomfortable with the spotlight and avoid attention. You may sometimes use service as a way to make yourself feel needed or earn love rather than giving freely and confidently. If you find a worthy leader, you are quite content being a follower. You're a strong, steady support and gain joy from helping others in the journey of life.

Which one sounds most like you?

○ My strongest social structure is:

leading (I guess)

Sight

Alison and Meg have been best friends for years. Although their lives are busy, they try to make time for lunch every few weeks. When they get together, it usually goes the same way. Meg stops to talk to at least three people she knows before she makes it to the table. She sits down commenting about the changes in the décor or the weather outside. She asks Alison, "How's it going? What have you been up to?"

Alison looks a bit startled when Meg suddenly bursts onto the scene, interrupting her thoughts. She smiles and tells Meg a little bit about the new idea she has for a project at work. She thinks Meg seems a little more tired than usual. She mentally runs through the reasons why that might be the case. Then she asks, "Meg, how have you been? How are you feeling?"

When it comes to life, we all have vision that's stronger in particular areas. Just as our eyes can be nearsighted or farsighted, we see more clearly in certain social situations. In this case, it doesn't need to be corrected—it simply needs to be recognized and maximized. When you do so, your way of seeing the world can become a strength.

There are two primary types of sight when it comes to relationships: external and internal.

External:

If your social sight is externally focused, then you're highly tuned in to your environment and the people in it. You notice details about the ones you love. You remember events in their lives like birthdays. You are aware of what's going on with them and take the time to show it. When you're in a conversation, you have the ability to watch facial expressions and body language while staying aware of your surroundings too. You're likely to ask "How's it going?" and really want to know what's happening in the lives of others. You show love in tangible, often practical ways.

Internal:

If your social sight is internally focused, then you are highly tuned in to the unseen world that exists around you and within those you love. You seem to intuitively understand what others are feeling or thinking, often without them telling you so. You are more likely to live in the realm of the heart. When you talk intently with someone, the rest of the room frequently fades away. You want to know the passions, desires, and dreams of those you love. You express that you care in ways that are invisible but still deeply meaningful—listening, speaking encouraging words, and silently providing support.

Of course, all of us can pick up on the external and internal cues around us. What this really describes is your primary focus in relationships.

Which one sounds most like you?

∘ My stronger social sight is:

_____

Sphere of Needs

Jill, Tina, Kris, and Valerie all sign up to go on a mission trip at church. A few months before they are to leave, they get together to do some planning.

Jill starts out by saying, "The most important thing is for people to know about the need. So many people don't even realize what's happening in that country! I'll put together a newsletter we can send to our friends and family."

"That sounds great," replies Tina. "I've been reading some of the stories and it seems like so many of the women in that place are just really hurting. I just want to go so I can listen, cry with them, and make sure they know how much they're loved."

Kris chimes in, "I think what matters most is just being there to spend time with people so we can build relationships—and continuing that even when we're back home. Our presence is what's really going to make a difference."

"And I've got big plans while you're doing that," says Valerie with a smile. "I'm bringing an extra suitcase with all kinds of food that I've been collecting. You can find me in the kitchen! I think the best way to feed a hungry heart is to feed a hungry mouth first."

When you use your social sight to focus on others, needs begin to appear. And of course you want to meet them. The needs that stand out most to you and the ways you feel compelled to fill them for others are the final aspect of your social strengths.

We can think of needs this way:

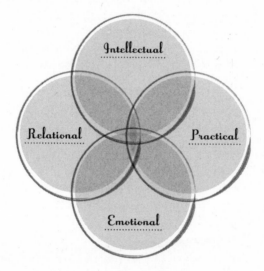

While we're called to help meet all of these needs in the lives of others at various times, and they often overlap, there's likely to be one or two we're especially called and equipped to fulfill.

Practical:

> If you're drawn to meet the practical needs of others, you're likely to see what needs to be done and then do it. You use your hands to meet needs—whether that is cooking, setting up, writing a check, or making something happen

in a tangible way. You feel satisfied when you see actual results from your giving.

Emotional:

If you're wired to meet the emotional needs of others, you offer your heart first. You know when someone is hurting or desires to have someone rejoice with them. You give through intangible ways most often—comforting, encouraging, bringing hope. You don't need to see actual physical results from the way you give other than a smile appearing or a tear being wiped away.

Relational:

If you desire to meet the relational needs of others, then you see your presence as the best gift you can offer. You show up whenever it matters most—in the hard times as well as the happy. You may not even talk about what the other person is feeling or be compelled to take a specific action. You simply want to be there for support, to share the experience, and to be a connector.

Intellectual:

If you focus on the intellectual needs of others, you're likely to try to connect them to truth first. You might offer to pray for them right away, share a helpful Scripture, or pass along a book that offers wisdom for their situation. You want others in your life to know what matters most because you believe it impacts every area of their lives.

You may wonder why there isn't a category labeled "spiritual." That's because I believe all of these are spiritual. Jesus said if we even give a cup of cold water to someone in his name, it matters and will be rewarded (see Matt. 10:42).

Also, as believers Jesus wants us to meet all kinds of needs in the lives of others. This is intended not to get us off the hook for serving in other areas but instead to help us see where we're probably called to give more of the time. If you could only do one of the categories above, which one would you pick? That's your primary sphere of needs, but stay open to serving in other ways as well.

Which one sounds most like you?

◦ My strongest sphere of needs is:

_____

_____

Why Does All of This Matter?

We often try to force ourselves to be like others or to simply do whatever we're asked. Then we wonder why we feel ineffective and exhausted. We are the body of Christ—and that means we not only have individual strengths to offer; we also have unique ways of loving others. Of course, sometimes we'll need to step outside of those for a special need or season. But knowing how we connect lets us serve in the center of the way God made us.

For example, if you're someone who circles one-to-one, partnering, internal, and emotional, then you would probably make a great counselor. But you'll likely feel frustrated as a youth worker taking forty teenagers on a mission trip to build a house. In contrast, if you circled one-to-many, leading, external, and practical, then that same trip is likely to thrill you.

So how do you make the most of who God has made you to be? Here are a few thoughts that apply to your social strengths as well as all the other strengths we've talked about along the way too.

Stay in Your Strengths When You Can

Sheila just started a new job. Through her previous work, she learned that she's very good at leading teams on projects. When she attends a meeting about an upcoming initiative, she wants to volunteer to be the team leader. It even seems a little voice inside whispers, "Fear not, for I am with you." But she's worried about not being good enough, so when it's time for assignments, she takes the task of working with one other person to record all the data collected during the project. Her co-worker

Debbie is made team leader by default. At that news, Debbie's face turns pale, and she mutters something about "feeling overwhelmed."

A few days later, Sheila stops by Debbie's office. It's clear her co-worker is upset, and Debbie confides again that she really wishes she didn't have to lead the team—she'd be much better at taking care of the practical task of collecting data with the other co-worker. Sheila breathes a sigh of relief and confesses that she too has been struggling with her part of the project. She whispers a prayer, "Thank you, Lord, for second chances." They meet with their manager later that day and make a plan to trade roles. Months later the project is successfully completed, and both women feel energized about taking on the next challenge.

I recently helped facilitate a study, and one section focused on using our gifts. At the end, a woman stood up and said something along the lines of, "If we try to meet the needs of others in ways God is not asking us to, then not only are we likely to burn out—we're also taking the place of whoever really is supposed to be meeting that need."

Yes, sometimes women use "that's not my strength" as an excuse to get out of a legitimate opportunity for service. But more often than I see them ducking out of what God is asking them to do, I see women taking on roles and responsibilities because they want to please people, they feel obligated, or they simply assume that's the "Christian" thing to do. If that's how you've been feeling, then give yourself permission to serve first in those areas that are in line with who God created you to be and how he designed you to love. *He'll rejoice, and we'll all benefit.*

> The body is not made up of one part but of many. Now if the foot should say, "Because I am not a hand, I do not belong to the body," it would not for that reason stop being part of the body. And if the ear should say, "Because I am not an eye, I do not belong to the body," it would not for that reason stop being part of the body. If the whole body were an eye, where would the sense of hearing be? If the whole body were an ear, where would the sense of smell

be? *But in fact God has placed the parts in the body, every one of them, just as he wanted them to be.* (1 Cor. 12:14–18)

No one can take your place. God doesn't have a "plan B" for you. You have gifts to offer the world, ways of connecting that only you can fulfill.

Here's the thing: God's not the only one with a plan for your life. The enemy has one too. And if he can't get you to rebel outright, then sidetracking you and getting you outside of your strengths is a pretty good alternative. Convincing an ear it needs to act like a hand is sure to limit its effectiveness, right? Your strengths are worth protecting. You are of incredible worth to the kingdom. Dare to be who you are—who God created you to be.

When You Need to Step Away from Your Strengths, Have a Strategy

"Hey, Candace, it's Molly. I'm checking with all of the moms in the classroom to see if they can help with the bake sale in March. Are you free that day?"

"Sure, I can make some cookies."

"Actually, we have all the baked goods taken care of already. We really need someone to work at the booth and talk to the other parents."

Candace takes a deep breath. She's much more comfortable in her kitchen than being the meet-and-greet mama. She senses a hesitation inside.

"Listen, Molly, I really do want to help. Can you just give me until tomorrow and I'll let you know for sure?"

"Sure," replies Molly. "That would be great. Thanks for considering it—talk to you later."

Candace hangs up the phone and whispers a prayer. "Lord, do you really want me to do this, or is it just a distraction?" She's learned that before stepping outside of her strengths, it's important to take time to pray. By the next day, she feels like she's got her answer.

She picks up the phone again—but she's not calling Molly yet.

"Amy? This is Candace. I know how good you are at talking with all the moms at school and the way you love a crowd. Will you be my bake sale buddy?"

Candace tells Molly the good news that she has two volunteers for the day. During the bake sale, Amy and Candace make a great team with Amy doing most of the talking and Candace ringing people up. Candace also loves the moments in between the busy times when she can spend some one-on-one time catching up with her friend.

It's often when we step outside our strengths for a season that we learn and grow. That's a necessary part of becoming all God wants us to be. But it's still important to have a plan. My husband and I like watching the travel channel. As soon as the guide on the show announces she's going into unknown territory, all kinds of preparation starts taking place. Clothing gets changed to adapt to warmer or cooler weather. Gear gets packed. Maps are pulled out. Because of that work, the trip usually turns out to be enjoyable. But imagine the guide said, "I live in Hawaii and today we're going to Alaska in the middle of winter. I'm sure what works here will be just fine there too." Then we'd fully expect to see chattering teeth and a very unhappy camper by the end of the episode.

In much the same way, we can find joy in any circumstance. But it always takes prayer and usually some strategic planning to make sure that happens when we're crossing the borders of our strengths into other territory.

Even if we do have a strategy, we're not intended to stay outside of our strengths for the majority of the time. Our strategy can act like a sunscreen for a little while, but we can't live out on the beach twenty-four hours a day—even if it seems wonderful at first—and not get burned. Like that travel guide, don't be afraid to step outside your strengths for a visit when God asks you to do so. But be sure to get yourself back home in the end.

Always Be Led by the Spirit

Karen strides into the room, thinking, "Oh, I've totally got this. They're going to be eating out of my hand in no time."

Wendy follows behind her, thinking, "There's no way I can do this. I'm just going to keep quiet and leave as fast as I can."

Whether we're talking about strengths or weaknesses, the biggest temptation is to rely on ourselves. When that happens with our strengths, it shows up as arrogance and pride. When it's our weaknesses, it leads to insecurity and shame.

Jesus invites us to a better way. He says we don't have to go through life in our own power anymore. Instead he promises that when we belong to him, the Holy Spirit comes to live within us. The Spirit is many things to us—a guide, a comforter, a counselor, and the One who leads us into all truth. He's the every day, every moment companion of our hearts.

The Spirit enables us to live the way God wants and to be all he's created us to be. "For God did not give us a spirit of timidity, but a spirit of power, of love and of self-discipline" (2 Tim. 1:7 NIV 1984).

- *Power*—We don't have to live in our strengths on our own. The Spirit is the One who enables us to do what we're called to do.
- *Self-discipline*—Even in the times when we don't feel like obeying, the Spirit will help us do God's will.
- *Love*—Whatever God wants us to do is ultimately about love, and the only way we can love like he does is through the Spirit within us.

"Being led by the Holy Spirit" can sound vague or super-spiritual. But it's really just moment-by-moment, day-by-day dependence. It's acknowledging that even in our strengths, we need a lot of help. And even in our weaknesses, God can enable us to do more than we imagined. We're amazing not because of who we are but because of who lives within us.

What Matters Most Is Love

Even when we live in our strengths, love still requires sacrifice. Jesus said that if we're going to follow him, we need to take up our cross and deny ourselves. The point is that it's *our* cross—not someone else's. Jesus didn't say, "Take up your cross and deny who God made you." The part of ourselves that we're called to deny is the sin nature within us that wants its own way. We're never to use our strengths (or weaknesses) as an excuse for being selfish. Instead we're to see all of who we are as an invitation to serve. "You, my brothers and sisters, were called to be free. But do not use your freedom to indulge the flesh; rather, serve one another humbly in love" (Gal. 5:13).

I'm thinking of you as I write these words. I imagine you with your head bent over this book, maybe with a highlighter in your hand, on your couch, in the passenger seat of a car, or on a plane. I'm wishing more than ever that we could have coffee today. I'd tell you, "You are loved. You matter. You have so much to give the world and the hearts in it."

Let's dare to love, to share life with each other, to offer ourselves in the way God has created us to do.

I need you.

You need me.

The kingdom needs *us*.

8

What Does God Want Me to Do with My Life?

I curl up on a chair in the corner of my bedroom. I hold a cup of coffee in one hand and my journal in the other. I've come with questions for Jesus.

I run my fingers along the fabric of the chair. It's almost fifty years old—an heirloom from my grandparents. I think of them and how they lived with intention, the ways they made a difference. I wonder if I'm doing the same.

My busy schedule flashes before my eyes. Go here. Do that. Commit to this. Say yes to that. My to-do list is never done. My expectations for myself are never met.

I sigh and begin writing on the blank pages in front of me. I explore, tentatively, how I feel God is calling me to a new season—of living entirely differently than before. I squirm in my seat. I question, "God, don't you want me to be busy all the time? Don't you want me to push myself to the limit for you and others? You've been teaching me about relationships. And isn't that what it really means to love?"

It seems my heart hears a whisper in response, "Daughter, I did not come to give you a full life. I came to give you life to the full."

And suddenly everything changes.

I know what it feels like to have a full life that leaves you empty. I don't want to live that way anymore. I imagine you don't either.

When I asked women on *Heart to Heart with Holley* to share their thoughts about this, it quickly became clear that this is a struggle we face in every stage throughout our lives:

> I'm afraid everyone (especially women) in the "modern" world knows this feeling. The problem is I want it all. My boyfriend, my house, my friends, my family, my job . . . and then I feel like I need to do more. . . . Why is it so hard to do the right thing—the best thing? (Marion[1])

> I am a mother of five that works full time as well as having all my children involved in school and sports activities. I feel like I have been running on empty for too long. I pray every day for God's strength to make it through one more day and for him to stay the center of the whirlwind. I know it is only because of him that I can go forward! (Jennifer[2])

> At 76 I still keep on being "busy" and "living life to the full." I need to be reminded sometimes to pause and give thanks for gifts God gives me daily through his grace! (Bernice[3])

God whispers to my heart, *to our hearts*, "I've come to give you better. I've promised you more."

It's a promise. Another dare. And most of all, an invitation.

God's Ultimate Goal

What does God really want for our lives? As we talked about earlier in the book, for many years I would have answered that question this way: "He wants me to be perfect." That belief sent me scrambling after impossible standards, trying to please people, and wearing myself out in the process.

Then Psalm 18 stopped me in my tracks one day. It says, "God's way is perfect . . . and he makes my way perfect" (vv. 30, 32 NLT). Did you catch that? *You are not responsible for making yourself perfect.* God will do so—and his idea of perfect is entirely different than ours. In the New Testament, the Greek word for "perfect" is *teleios,* and it's actually more accurately described as maturing growth or completion. For example, an oak tree is the *teleios* of an acorn.[4]

It's also a process that will only be complete in heaven. For now, God will bring our ways into alignment with his. And what are his ways? Love, love, love.

God is love, and *everything* he does is loving. "God is love, and all who live in love live in God, and God lives in them. And as we live in God, our love grows more perfect" (1 John 4:16 NLT). So, again, what does God really want us to do with our lives? Not make them perfect. *Grow in love.*

Love in a biblical sense isn't a touchy-feely, vague experience. It's a verb. It's a series of choices and actions in our lives. So the next step in our process is to look again at your life through the lens of love. How is God asking you to live in love—first with him and then with family, friends, and others he's called you to serve?

Your LIFE

Over the last several chapters we've looked at how God has created you—the strengths he's placed within you, the skills he's developed in you, the way you're wired to connect with others. When we put all of that together, we can capture what he's really calling you to do with your life.

In our culture, that's often called a mission statement. And while I think those can be helpful, it feels like the title can be a bit misleading. As believers, we all ultimately have the same mission. God gave it to us in Galatians 5:6: "The only thing that counts is faith expressing itself through love." We're here to express faith through love—for God, others, and ourselves.

But how that happens does vary with each one of us. By understanding how we're created and called to express love, we find focus and direction. We can say yes to what matters most and no to what isn't necessary without guilt. We can make sure our days are spent wisely and we live well.

So instead of a mission statement, let's talk about your LIFE statement—Love Is Faith Expressed. (Okay, okay, maybe it's a teensy bit cheesy. But it's easy to remember, right? And I am an unashamed acronym fan. So let's just go with it, okay?) I think *express* is such a wonderful word because it implies creativity, individuality, and you doing what you do in a way no one else can. Your LIFE is one-of-a-kind. It's a combination of all we've talked about in the previous chapters. *Drum roll, please* . . . We're now ready to summarize all of that in one sentence.

As I said before, we all start with a common foundation from Galatians 5:6:

I am created and called to express my faith through love . . .

Now you'll finish that statement with your unique way of doing so in the world. That part will have this structure:

. . . especially by (verb ending in "ing") + (what) + (who) + (how)

Here's my LIFE statement:

I am created and called to express my faith through love,

especially by bringing hope and encouragement
(what)

to the hearts of women through words.
(who) *(how)*

Another one might be:

I am created and called to express my faith through love,

especially by <u>meeting the practical needs</u> of
(what)

<u>my family, friends, and community</u> <u>through service.</u>
(who)   *(how)*

Try yours here (this is just a start—you can think and pray about it more later):

I am created and called to express my faith through love, especially by

_____

_____

(verb ending in "ing") + (what) + (who) + (how)

The sentence structure above is just a suggestion. You can write your LIFE any way that you'd like. It can be shorter, longer, or in an entirely different format. *There is no wrong way to do this.* Here are some phrases *Heart to Heart with Holley* readers used as part of their statements (when we did this we all used the word "bringing" as the verb).

I am created and called to express my faith through love, especially by bringing . . .

- the love and hope of Christ to hurting friends and strangers through spontaneous, God-inspired acts of service. (Valerie)

- leadership and creativity to my sphere of influence by caring for those God places in my care. (Amy)

- connection and covenant friendship to women through the spoken and written word. (Cari)

- comfort to those in any trouble with the comfort I have received from God. (Melissa)
- faithful service to my family by caring for their needs the way Christ wants. (Tammy)

It will take time for you to create a statement that really feels right. Think of this exercise as a rough draft, a beginning point. There's no pressure to get it done right away—or even to do it at all (I can't believe I just said that). This is just a tool. What matters most is thinking and praying more intentionally about how God wants you to express love through your life.

Circumstances and Seasons

I have a pitcher that I love. I've used it to pour lemonade, water, and tea. I've used it at parties, for dinner with my husband, and when family comes to visit at the holidays.

If that pitcher said, "I'm just made to pour iced tea on Saturdays," then it would only partially understand its purpose. That pitcher might feel like a failure if I wanted to use it to serve orange juice on Sunday mornings instead. But I would be happy about it.

God calls us his "vessel." That means we'll display our LIFE in various situations, amounts, and times. The words we write down are meant not to confine us but rather to bring focus and then set us free to be used by God however he chooses.

For example, speaking encouragement to a tired cashier is just as much living out my statement as writing a book that will be read by thousands. What God wants most in our stories is our hearts. After all, it's not about the size of the word but the meaning behind it. Big or small, he can use it all.

You may have seasons in your life when it seems everything you do flows with your LIFE. Other times you may feel your highest goal is just managing to take a shower. God loves you just the same in both of those. He can use you wherever you are and in whatever you're doing.

Yes, it's important to understand who he's made you to be and what he's called you to do, but living in that is a process that will unfold for a lifetime.

Expressions vs. Expectations

Josie writes down her LIFE statement and posts it on the refrigerator. She smiles as she makes the coffee and thinks, "This is going to be so much better!" Then the phone rings and a neighbor who's chronically in crisis needs her attention. She has to get off the call quickly to get the kids to school, which makes her sigh, "Oh, I'm not a good friend!" The phone call makes her late dropping the kids off, and she realizes the cookies for her son's class party are still on the kitchen counter. She mutters, "There goes being a good mom too."

The rest of the day passes in a blur—the meeting doesn't go as hoped, dinner doesn't taste the way everyone would like, the dishes are still in the sink, and she falls asleep next to her husband thinking, "Sorry, sweetheart, I haven't been much of a wife to you today either." The next morning she looks at the LIFE statement on her refrigerator again and shakes her head. How can one simple statement be so complicated to carry out?

We've all felt like Josie at times. We know what God wants us to do, and we even have his power to do it, but it's still hard to consistently say yes to his calling on our lives. That's often because so many other voices (real or imagined) are demanding our attention as well—telling us what "should" be done.

All those voices we hear have one name: *expectations.*

We have expectations *for* ourselves.

We have expectations *from* others.

As I prayed about this section and what God wanted me to share, I asked him to give me his perspective on expectations. The surprising discovery:

○ Expectations are laws we place on ourselves and each other.

Yep, laws.

An expectation equals "You must do X or you will be punished in some way."

Oh, the punishment might be subtle—rejection, guilt we lay on our shoulders, a look across the room that lets us know we didn't measure up. No one is going to throw us in jail. But consequences of the heart can seem even more frightening.

Let's take a look at the expectations in our lives. Try listing one in your life here. For example, "I must say yes every time someone at church asks for help or people will think I'm selfish."

I must _____ or this will

happen: _____ .

What's God's answer to those expectations, to those laws we create for ourselves or let others lay down for us? *Grace.*

LIFE is all about that too.

"You are not under the law, but under grace" (Rom. 6:14). We usually think of that verse in the context of Old Testament law. But it applies to the expectations in our lives as well. We are not to be under anything but grace, the love of Christ, and the leading of the Holy Spirit.

Girls, this is *really* good news. We can kick those expectations to the curb.

Your house doesn't have to be spotless.

Your work doesn't have to be flawless.

You don't have to please that finicky member of your family.

You don't have to look like a page out of a magazine.

You're already enough because Jesus is enough in you. You're loved, accepted, set free to live your LIFE to the fullest.

What Does "Much Required" Really Mean?

As I thought about being free from expectations, a bit of panic started to kick in for me. I thought of a comment recently made by someone in my life: "To whom much is given, much will be required. A lot has been given to you, so a lot is expected of you." I remember how I wilted at those words. And yet I knew that phrase came from the Bible. Why did Jesus say that, and what did he really mean?

I turned to Luke 12 and read that phrase in context. It appears in a story about servants and their master. Yes, it did say to whom much is given much would be required . . . *by the master.* A lot of the expectations in my life aren't from my Master. I make them up or take them on from someone else. In that case, I'm not required to meet them. *And neither are you.* As servants, we're not in control of our own lives, and we don't have to take orders from other servants either. Only God has the authority to tell us our duties, what's required of us.

That made me want to dig deeper. What did God require of me? I pulled out my journal again, ready for a long list. But a quick look at my concordance and a trip over to Micah 6:8 stunned me with its simplicity: "The LORD has told you what is good, and this is what he requires of you: to do what is right, to love mercy, and to walk humbly with your God" (NLT).

Period. End of story. No long list of rules. No endless expectations. It's all there in one verse. And it's all about relationships.

Let's take a closer look at those phrases from Micah 6:8:

- *To do what is right*—This is about practicing self-control, which leads to loving ourselves as well as others the way God intended.

- *To love mercy*—This is about our relationships with others. We are to love them as ourselves.
- *To walk humbly with your God*—This is about our relationship with God. We are to love him above all.

Amazing, isn't it? Yet it's so difficult to really live this way. The challenge is nothing new. The Galatians, those in one of the early churches, struggled with putting themselves back under the law too. The apostle Paul asks them this question: "After starting your Christian lives in the Spirit, why are you now trying to become perfect by your own human effort?" (Gal. 3:3 NLT). It's a question we're called to consider too.

What expectations in our lives are from God—and what have we added as laws he never intended for us to be under?

We did a little practice listing an expectation above. Write that expectation again below. Then next to it write the real source: yourself, others, or God.

Expectation: I feel like I have to...	Source: *(myself, others, God)*

Ask God to continue uncovering the hidden expectations in your heart as well as their sources. Also ask him to set you free from any that aren't truly from him.

You may fear, "But I won't be loving if I don't have those expectations!" But God is love—whatever he directs you to do will be loving to others too. What you may let go of (and this can be hard!) is what you're doing simply to please people. You are not required to please people. You don't have to meet their expectations. You are a servant with *one* master.

Fear vs. Love

One morning as Josie sticks her to-do list for the day next to her LIFE statement on the refrigerator, she notices a committee meeting that doesn't really seem to fit. She wonders, "Could I say no to that and yes to something better instead?" Her stomach begins to twist, and worries run through her mind. "What if everyone gets mad at me? What if quitting means I'm being selfish?" She pauses, sighs, then calls out to her husband, "I'll be home late tonight!"

One of the hardest parts of embracing our LIFE is letting go of some things we do out of fear. Doing so is always difficult because the lies that have been compelling us to do whatever it is will come rushing back in full force. You're likely to hear, "You won't be loved," "You won't be accepted," "You will fail." Hold on to the truth—you are loved, accepted, enough in Christ. Nothing and no one can take that away from you.

Being led by love is the cure to being driven by fear. "Perfect love drives out fear" (1 John 4:18).

If you're not sure whether you're motivated by fear or love in a certain activity, you can try writing it out this way:

○ I feel compelled to

_____

(Example: Have a completely clean house)

○ This is motivated by . . .

Fear	Love
(what people will think of me)	*(desiring to make a haven for my family)*

As you grow in love, you'll move further away from fear and toward love in different areas of your life. You don't have to make that happen right now. Instead, just be aware of it and begin asking

God to help you change. "He who began a good work in you will carry it on to completion" (Phil. 1:6).

When you think of what you might want to say no to in your life, the things that are all the way on the fear side would be the first to consider. Fear can creep in at times even when we're doing exactly what God wants us to do in love. But if the only reason we're doing something is out of fear, then it's not from God. As we talked about before, "God gave us a spirit not of fear but of power and love and self-control" (2 Tim. 1:7 ESV).

Pause for a moment and consider: If you knew you would be completely loved and accepted no matter what, then which items would be crossed off your to-do list for good? Consider letting go of those things in your life. If it's something that you really need to do, then begin asking God to heal your heart so that you can do so more out of love and less out of fear.

At one point in my life, it seemed God kept emptying my hands of so much. I asked, "Why are you doing that?" And I slowly came to realize God has to empty us of ourselves before he can fill us with him. Does that mean we have to let go of all he's given? No, but we hold it loosely. We surrender. We say, "Not my will but yours be done."

And we look at our lives closely, like one mining for gold. We are of great worth, amazing women of God, and that means what we allow into our lives should be of value too. We can sift through our schedules and ask, "Does that really belong there? Is this a glimmer of false security? Is fear compelling me to do this?" We filter, sort, pay close attention. We toss away what is not of him and deeply treasure all that remains. Then we hold it up to the light and polish it until it shines even more brightly—and we do too.

As you let go of some things you're doing out of fear, it may seem as if a void opens up in your life. Our expectations are often also our *motivations*. If the expectations are gone, then why do you do what you do? It's not about being free to do whatever you want (which you may fear might happen if you don't have those requirements). The goal is to replace those expectations (the law) with the same thing Jesus did and what we've talked about all along—love.

Just Say No to Guilt

The closer you get to what God has truly called you to do in your LIFE journey, the more the enemy will resist you. You'll likely have thoughts like, "Oh, I've totally messed this up," or "I don't do this enough," or "How can I live this out when I am a stay-at-home mom/have to work/am battling chronic illness right now?"

Listen, girl, if it's important enough for you to put in your LIFE statement, then I can almost guarantee you are already living it out in some way. For example, maybe creativity is part of your statement and you long to be an artist with paintings in a gallery, but right now you're raising toddlers. Then I bet you're finger painting with them, or teaching them colors, or helping them find beauty in the world.

Whatever you are wired by God to do, you'll find a way to do where you are—and *all* of that is equally important to him. We tend to think there's a pinnacle to our purpose, a high point we have to reach. But God cares more about the journey and our partnership with him in the process. Remember what we talked about earlier? Perfection is simply about growth, a little at a time.

When You Worry, You've Wasted Your Life

We sit and talk. Eventually she clears her throat and quietly asks, "What do you do if you feel like you've wasted your life?" The silence hangs thick in the air between us.

It's a heavy question of the heart.

And I think of the One who had the most meaningful existence ever. For so many years, he was simply a carpenter.

I say this out loud, pondering.

"He didn't need more practice," I say, "and it sure seems like he could have started his ministry earlier and gotten more done. But for some inexplicable reason, he spent years working with wood. Years we would have called wasted."

She looks up, smiles. We part ways. Next time I see her, she holds a sheet of paper in her hand. It has these words on it. I ask her if I can share them with you. She says yes.

> Why did he need to be a carpenter? Maybe, just maybe, he was a carpenter for me. . . . Each hurt is a board, each disappointment a piece of wood, and each trial a plank.
>
> Jesus, the carpenter, is taking each piece of wood and nailing it together. He is nailing together a future that is unclear to me, but I have peace because he is my carpenter. I take great comfort in Ephesians 2:10: "For we are God's workmanship, created in Christ Jesus to do good works, which God prepared in advance for us to do" [NIV 1984].
>
> I understand that my past was not wasted. He is using it all to "build" me so I can do the good works God has prepared for me to do. I don't know what he has in store for me in the next phase of my life; however, it doesn't matter because he is building me into his masterpiece.

Those "wasted" years? In the carpenter's hands they can be transformed into a beautiful part of your purpose.

We might think that Jesus could have gotten a lot more accomplished if God had just let him get started sooner. But God isn't interested in how much we can do. If he can create the world in seven days with a few words, then getting it done isn't an issue for him! Instead God is interested in us doing only what he's asked us to do, when he wants us to do it, and most of all simply living in love along the way.

Keep Growing, Girl

You are *free*. Free to love. Free to live in joy. Free to be who you are. If you're loving God, others, and yourself, then *you're already doing enough*. That's right. And you're already amazing because you are God's creation, his child, and he lives in you. Sounds scandalous, doesn't it? But it's true.

What God wants most of all is you. Just as you are. Then he'll show you how he wants to use your life to partner with him in fulfilling his purposes. It won't be a burden but instead a glorious adventure—with plenty of room for mistakes, growth, and joy along the way. Bonnie Gray from the blog *Faith Barista* beautifully says it this way:

> It encourages me to know that Jesus knows how unnatural it is for me to come to Him as I am. I know that the Holy Spirit prays for me during these moments because out of nowhere, I'll be struck with how much God loves me, and how much I need Him.
>
> And I go to Him. Not because I'm so great in any sense. But because God is great in His love for me.[5]

I'm looking at the trees in my backyard as I write these words. I can't see them growing. But I know it's happening because day after day, year after year, they simply keep reaching a little higher toward heaven. I imagine for a moment that each leaf is a little bit of love. And I think of you—how you're out there growing too. Day after day, year after year, simply reaching a little higher toward heaven, drawing closer to God's heart.

That's all he wants, sweet friend. Not your striving. Not your standards. Just you.

The trees stretch out their arms, and we stretch out our hearts. I close my eyes and imagine the arms of the One who loves us reaching back, always finding us, always willing to carry us, always reminding us that life is about love—giving it, receiving it, gloriously growing until our hearts are home.

9

What Are **My Next Steps?**

Here's how my morning went. I got up early (which is a minor miracle), ate breakfast with my husband, rode the exercise bike for twenty minutes while reading my Bible, took a shower, and sat down to pray and write in my journal about this chapter.

Then I checked my email.

One hour, fifty-four messages, six websites, and two Facebook stops later, I felt like the world was falling apart. I had more items on my task list than time in my day, unanswered requests, and a morning that seemed like it had quickly gotten derailed.

So what did I do? Exactly what every deeply spiritual woman does in these cases.

I ate a chocolate brownie with peanut butter frosting.

At 9:00 a.m.

Then I laughed long and hard at myself because this chapter is supposed to be about implementing your Life Is Faith Expressed statement effectively. And a big part of that is being organized, right? Ha ha ha. Pass the brownies, honey.

I will be the first to admit that I don't have this part figured out when it comes to schedules, detailed lists, and a fully organized world.

And I'm starting to believe (warning: scandalous statement coming) that it doesn't matter much to God. Did I just say that? It must be the peanut butter frosting talking.

What I mean is that we put a lot of pressure on ourselves to do things a certain way and/or to do it all. But God doesn't put those standards on us. Remember how we talked in the last chapter about expectations being like living under the law? Well, the woman-made standards in our lives are the same way.

Are we to be responsible stewards of our lives, time, emotions, energy, and resources? Yes, of course. But how that looks in our daily lives is going to be as unique as we are. You have a purpose no one else has, and how that unfolds will look different for you than for any other woman in your life.

Run YOUR Race

LIFE gives us direction, but we still need to know specifically what steps to take next. These verses show us the starting line: "Let us throw off everything that hinders and the sin that so easily entangles. And let us run with perseverance the race marked out for us, fixing our eyes on Jesus, the pioneer and perfecter of faith" (Heb. 12:1–2).

What Hinders You?

First we're to look in our lives for *what hinders*. That's anything in your life that is getting in the way of you living God's purpose.

Rebecca likes to do things herself. It feels like helping others (after all, they're busy too), and it also ensures that things turn out the way she wants. But Rebecca's plate just keeps getting fuller. She knows God wants her to spend more time with the college girls at her church. Unlike many of the other responsibilities in her life, that one brings her joy and fills her up. She also sees a real difference in the lives of the girls. But right now it seems to land at the bottom of her list. Rebecca drifts off to sleep, exhausted, thinking, "Maybe someday when things slow down . . ."

Rebecca's long to-do list is something that hinders. To throw it off and run her race, she's probably going to need to learn to delegate some tasks and let go of others. As you can probably tell, something that "hinders" is anything that trips you up and slows you down. This can be hard to recognize because unlike "sin that entangles," what hinders us often seems good. And many times it is—it's just not what's best. My wise college mentor, Beth English, used to say, "Holley, the hardest choices in life aren't between good and bad. They're between good and best."

Wayne Cordeiro, author of *Leading on Empty*, says 85 percent of what we do, anyone can do. For example, watching television, checking email, and attending meetings. Another 10 percent could be done by someone if we trained them. That last 5 percent is what only we can do. After facing burnout, making new choices about that 5 percent became a life-changing revelation for Wayne:

> I had to rethink what was most important to me—what God had asked me to do—and how I would restructure my life. I had to think what my last 5 percent would in-clude. What were the things that only I could do and, if neglected, would affect the rest of my life? Here are the responsibilities I wrote down:
>
> 1. A vibrant, growing relationship with my Lord and Savior, Jesus Christ
> 2. A healthy and genuine relationship with my spouse
> 3. An authentic family that is close to God and close to one another
> 4. A God-pleasing ministry

5. A physically healthy body and a creative soul
6. Taking time to enjoy life with family and friends

Wayne goes on to say, "Your choice of what is most important will shape your soul. We won't be accountable for how much we have done, but for how much we have done of what *he asked us to do*."[1]

You have a gift to offer the world, a calling only you can fulfill, a race only you can run. Throw off everything that hinders and move forward in all God has for you.

What Entangles You?

Next we're looking for *sin that entangles*.

Rebecca sometimes turns to gossip or criticism to vent. "She's so lazy," Rebecca tells her husband. "If she had any motivation at all, I wouldn't have to do everything myself." She pours out more of her frustration but ends up feeling even worse. And nothing in the situation changes, so she repeats the same cycle the next day.

Like all of us, Rebecca sometimes spends time and emotional energy with little return. Sin can momentarily make us feel better, but in the end it's a high price to pay. It quickly empties our emotional bank accounts and separates us from God and others.

When we find ourselves entangled in sin, we can ask forgiveness, turn away from the sin, and get back on the path to keep going in our race. This battle with sin isn't a one-time fix. As the apostle Paul tells us, it's a step-by-step reliance on Christ:

> Now if I do what I do not want to do, it is no longer I who do it, but it is sin living in me that does it. So I find this law at work: When I want to do good, evil is right there with me. For in my inner being I delight in God's law; but I see another law at work in me, waging war against the law of my mind and making me a prisoner of the law of sin at work within me. What a wretched man I am! Who will rescue me from this body that is subject to death? Thanks

be to God, who delivers me through Jesus Christ our Lord! So then, I myself in my mind am a slave to God's law, but in my sinful nature a slave to the law of sin. (Rom. 7:20-25)

Dare to embrace who you are. Dare to do those weird things you do. Dare to trust God's whispers into your life more than the demands of the world around you about "the right way." You have the Holy Spirit within you, and he will show you what you need to change in a way that's gentle, life giving, and affirming.

Let's revisit the two areas we talked about above: what hinders and sin that entangles. Pause for a few moments here to pray and think through what those might be for you. Then jot them down below:

○ My LIFE statement (rewrite it here):

_____

_____

○ What hinders me (anything that holds me back):

_____

_____

○ Sin that entangles me (anything that trips me up):

_____

_____

Let's move forward. With sin, the process begins by acknowledging that we've hurt God. We ask forgiveness, receive it, and then request his help in starting to live differently. Sometimes the process of change is instant and complete. Other times, it takes place over a period of time as we learn new patterns of behavior to replace what we've been doing.

With what isn't sinful but simply hinders us, it's also a matter of growth over time. Remember the true biblical definition of perfection? It's about maturity and becoming complete. That takes time and many small steps in the right direction.

Move Forward in Faith

Everything that hinders.

Sin that so easily tangles.

Those are the obstacles God wants us to clear out of our paths. You can stop worrying about everything else.

Read that again, girl.

You can stop worrying about everything else.

Yes, that includes how clean your neighbor thinks your house should be, that "suggestion" the preacher gave so adamantly from the pulpit about what you have to do, the better way your friend seems to handle that part of her life. *All of it.*

We are running "the race marked out *for us*" (Heb. 12:1). That means we're only concerned about the obstacles *in our lane.* If someone feels she needs to do something, then let her do it—it's probably in her lane. But that doesn't mean it's in yours.

This isn't about self-improvement. It's about aligning our lives with love in the way God created us to do. To do that, we need a lot of grace and an approach that makes sense based on who God made us. Every runner has a rhythm that works best for her. You're the same way. When we set out to make changes, we need to be sure we're moving to be more of who God made us—not more like someone else.

I remember sitting with a group of artists during a brainstorming session one day. We looked through magazines to get ideas and inspiration. I found a feature that shared different rooms where creative people worked. One overflowed with supplies, swatches of fabric, and collected items. I remarked to the girl sitting next to me, "I could never write in a space like that. I need my house to be uncluttered before I can create." She replied, "That's because you need to shut out everything else and focus internally to write. As an artist, I need to be surrounded by things that I can see when I look up because that's what gives me new ideas as I go."

She was completely right. For years, I'd felt guilty about not having a home filled with more decorative items. I felt like a failure and as if I couldn't possibly be truly creative. My artist friend had probably carried around guilt about not having a home that was a bit tidier and more orderly. But we both had what we needed to do what we were called to do.

It's the same way with every area of our lives. Any changes we make need to support who we are and the way we're intended to love others. We need to pray for wisdom and then trust the part of us that says, "This works for you." Like me, we may not even be able to articulate why until someone else points it out to us. We can waste a lot of energy trying to fix what isn't broken.

What Are Your Next Steps?

When my husband and I vacation, we walk everywhere. There's a moment when I panic a little—usually when my husband pulls out the map and cheerfully says, "Let's go here, here, and here." And I reply, "That's a looonnnggg way. Can't we just go to Starbucks?"

But we set out ... and by the end of the day we've made it and I'm happy. I've learned the trick is not giving in to that moment when the journey seems like too much.

Just start with one step.

Now that the path is clear for you to run your race, you can start thinking about what God is actually asking you to do with your LIFE. That statement is intended to be general, but when it comes to our everyday lives, we need to get more specific.

When we start taking several steps in a particular direction, it becomes a destination (in other words, a goal). Where we're heading should always be led by Jesus and in line with our LIFE. The idea of doing more than just taking some small steps can be intimidating. But when it comes to making changes in our lives,

I'm starting to realize that the process doesn't have to be as complicated as we often make it.

I've got plenty of experience setting unrealistic goals. Around the new year I start imagining how I will exercise for an hour every morning, bond with my husband every night, and write the most brilliant book ever published.

However, three days into the plan, I realize my shiny new ambitions will never be realized. And while all of my good intentions are staring me in the face, I realize something is drastically wrong. Rather than providing much-needed motivation, the goals created to help me live a full, balanced life have instead become the seeds of future disappointment.

One day I was driving to work and telling myself once again, "When things slow down, I will go to the gym and work out all the time. I'll get in shape. It will be great." Then I thought, "I've been telling myself this for five years. Things are never going to slow down. I've got to do what I can." That was the beginning of a revolution.

The "Do What You Can Plan"

The "Do What You Can Plan" is exactly what it sounds like—you do what you can to take steps and move in the direction God has for your LIFE. It began as an article I wrote for an online magazine called *Zia*. The magazine is no longer in existence, but the principles I wrote about are still very much a part of my life.

For me, the "Do What You Can Plan" meant doing whatever little bit I could each day. For example, if I could only fit in ten sit-ups, then that's all I would do. A year later, I'd lost the weight I wanted to shed and dropped a clothing size. I was shocked that I'd actually reached my goal by doing so little. So I decided to start applying the "Do What You Can Plan" to other areas of my life and spent some time figuring out exactly what made it work. Here are a few things I discovered along the way.

∼ Small Can Be Really Big ∼

We often get caught up in thinking we have to do something really big to achieve our goals, but sometimes the little things really can make a difference. Someone once told me that coming to the point where change happens is like adding one drop of water to a bucket every day. One day the bucket just overflows, but it's all the little drops along the way that made it happen. So when you're setting goals and thinking about the steps to reach them, think small. Say tomorrow you make a personal goal to walk a mile every day. If you take your dog for a walk around the block and that's all you can do for the day—that's great. Over time, those steps will add up, and you'll go farther than you imagined.

Jesus said if we have faith as a mustard seed, then we can move mountains. Have you seen a mustard seed? I was shocked the first time I did! Those things are *tiny*. It seems the point isn't how much we have on our own but whose hands we place it in. God knows how to turn our little bit into a whole lot.

∼ Easy Is Not a Four-Letter Word ∼

We all lead busy lives. Figuring out how to reach our goals when so many other things are asking for our attention is tough. I confess that I love to make complicated goals that are hard to maintain. The perfectionist in me comes out in full force, and before I know it, my goals need three notebooks and four spreadsheets just to keep track of them.

But the easy way is often the best way. For example, if you are trying to get in shape, think about how you can do that as part of your everyday routine. I do squats when I dry my hair in the morning and while unloading laundry. My husband thinks this is hilarious, and the dog shoots me a look of confusion now and then, but it's a small price to pay. Asking yourself how a goal can fit your everyday life is more than easy; it's essential.

God does ask us to do really hard things sometimes. When that's the case, we need to obey. But it seems we often use our energy and emotion on things that don't matter as much. Then when he does give us a big assignment, we're already exhausted. This is about using what we've got in the most effective way so we can be ready for whatever is ahead in God's plans for us!

～ *The Meaning Matters* ～

If your goal is a good one, it will take more than killer willpower to see you through. For me, a goal needs to have deeper meaning. If all I want to do is fit into a smaller pair of jeans, that's not enough to motivate me. I want to be fit so that I can have the energy and motivation to love God and those around me. When I don't feel good physically, I'm not a very fun person to be around. I growl, eat way too much chocolate, and in general don't make the world a nicer place to be. Dr. Gary Oliver, executive director of the Center for Relationship Enrichment, says that focusing on growth rather than change can give goals more meaning. How does this goal fit with your LIFE? Change is outward while growth is inward. By figuring out how your goal fits with something deep inside you, you will be much more motivated to do what you can to accomplish it. "Seek first his kingdom and his righteousness, and all these things will be given to you as well" (Matt. 6:33).

～ *What to Do with Slipups and Setbacks* ～

The seemingly evil twins of slipups and setbacks always seem to get the best of me when setting goals. I have good intentions, but before I know it, I'm downing the last piece of cheesecake at a party. The "Do What You Can Plan" has two little words to say about slipups and setbacks: "Oh, well." If it's actually a sin (such as using food to satisfy a need that only God can), then we need three words: "Please forgive me."

Since this plan is about doing what you can, not achieving perfection, what matters most is just getting up and doing what you can tomorrow. Slipups and setbacks are also great opportunities for learning. Think about what you might do differently in the future. Even create a strategy if needed. For example, you could eat a healthy dinner before you go to the next party so you're not ravenously hungry.

God gave us grace for a reason—he knew we'd need it. And he promises an endless supply. What matters most to him isn't that you always get it right but instead that you stay right by his side.

∼ Sunny Side Up ∼

The "Do What You Can Plan" is all about keeping things positive. It's a lot friendlier than the "You Tried Again This Year but Failed as Usual Plan." Our brains are wired to respond better to being told what we can do than what we can't. If you've ever tried giving up chocolate for a week and found yourself shrieking like a banshee by Wednesday, you know what I mean. Rather than figuring out what you're not going to do, think about what you are going to do instead. For example, next time I throw chocolate to the wind, I'll splurge on strawberries and pineapple to take its place when I have a craving for something sweet.

Another part of staying sunny is celebrating. I'm trying to get better at savoring accomplishments. I tend to reach a goal and then instantly set out toward a new one. Celebrating can look different for everyone. Maybe you go out to eat at your favorite restaurant, buy some new shoes, take a nap—or all of the above. Celebrating is positive reinforcement, a concept we're all familiar with. It makes our brains more willing to cooperate next time we set a goal.

Gratitude is also at the heart of celebration. Sometimes we're so busy pushing forward that we forget to stop and thank God for how far he's taken us. God is there for us in hard times, and he loves rejoicing with us too. So let him share the joy.

Going the Distance

The "Do What You Can Plan" is essentially about making goals work for you rather than the other way around. It's about small changes that make a big difference. It's about knowing that life is a meaningful journey and every step takes us closer to where we want to go. And along the way, it's okay to eat chocolate sometimes, to mess up, and to make things a little easier if we can. We can all do a lot if we just do a little. And with God, there's nothing that's impossible for us. Here's even more good news:

- Yes, Jesus says we can do all things through him—
- but he never says we have to do it all!

Deidra Riggs, who blogs at *Jumping Tandem*, wrote a post on the website (in)courage about going to the gym and telling the trainer she wanted to run a half-marathon. The trainer inquired about Deidra's running history and gently suggested a 5k might be a great place to start. Then she helped Deidra make a plan to do it. The next day Deidra stepped on the treadmill feeling a bit disappointed, until wisdom from her trainer changed everything:

> "Distance first. Then speed," she said. And with those two short sentences, I think she just may have saved me from disaster.
>
> Because we big picture people want it all and we want it now, don't we? We don't always consider the many steps it takes to reach a goal. . . .
>
> I probably would have cranked up the speed on that treadmill to some ridiculous number, worn myself out in two minutes flat, and given up on the whole idea. But those two sentences rang in my head for the entire twenty minutes it took me to run my little 1.5 miles.
>
> I was pleased with myself. Motivated, even. And in that moment I realized that I wasn't ready for the "all"

that we big picture people crave. Not yet. I needed this
one little piece, first. This accomplishment. This is what I
could handle right then. This is what fit. This was something I could build on.[2]

Maybe, like Deidra, you're ready to run a marathon in life. Or
you might be sitting on the curb wondering if you even have what
it takes to make it to the end of the block. Either way, the best place
to start is with one small step. It's the only way to bigger things
with God. As Jesus said, "Whoever can be trusted with very little
can also be trusted with much" (Luke 16:10).

~ My "Do What You Can Plan" ~

Change God wants me to make:	Small next step:	How I'll celebrate:

Your Organizational Personality

As you set out to make changes, let's get a bit more clarity about
how you approach life. This is important because the thing
about change is that it takes time. And that requires structure
and discipline. That's what trips a lot of us up. We pick the
right change but the wrong way (for us) to go about getting it
accomplished.

So let's look at some typical ways women approach life. Then circle the one that sounds most like you.

The Princess of Planning

You love order and structure. It gives you great satisfaction to take your thoughts and put them in tangible form—whether that is in a planner, a digital calendar, or a list. You want to know what's coming and be prepared. You enjoy details and can relax most when you know everything is in order. You like to think ahead and usually make time to do so. Others value your responsibility, conscientiousness, and consistency.

- *Strengths:* You get things done. You don't overlook details because you have them all recorded. You plan effectively and usually accomplish your goals.
- *Next steps for your "Do What You Can Plan":* Set aside time to create a concrete strategy for change. Write out what you want to accomplish and the steps to making it happen. Purchase or create whatever supplies you need to do so—a calendar, new journal, or chart—and put time in your schedule to pray and review your progress.
- *Watch out for:* Your goals becoming more important than your relationships with God and other people, being too hard on yourself, and becoming impatient when you don't see measurable results quickly.

The Queen of Creativity

You like variety and thrive on what's new. You have good intentions when you begin but often get bored with your goals before they're completed. You don't necessarily like details or feel compelled to keep track of your life in a tangible way. You like your options open. Too much order or planning feels restrictive. You're inspired by ideas, the intangible, beauty, and learning. You tackle a challenge for the joy of it, and when it's not as much fun, it may be hard to continue. But if you're deeply passionate you can work long and hard and create in a way that's often amazing to others. You put your heart into your daily life and operate on intuition much of the time. You may not be able to articulate exactly how something will get done, but you're definitely clear on why it matters and who it will benefit.

- *Strengths:* Your creativity brings freshness and excitement to the world. Others enjoy you because you encourage and inspire them to see things in new ways.
- *Next steps for your "Do What You Can Plan":* Get rid of the idea that you will find the perfect system and stay with it forever. Embrace your creativity when it comes to pursuing your goals. Remove structure except where it's absolutely necessary. Buy an unlined journal, put a whiteboard on the refrigerator, start a notebook of ideas. Add variety to your plans so that your goal stays the same but how you achieve it can change multiple times throughout the process.
- *Watch out for:* Chasing after the new so much that you abandon worthy goals prematurely, giving in to boredom and quitting rather than finding a creative solution to push through it, and rebelling against all structure and order.

The Royal Highness of Relationships

You believe life is all about connecting with others. You focus on who is in front of you, who's on the phone, or that email you just got that needs a response. Your schedule revolves around people, not projects. The only purpose for planning or tasks would be so that you can build your relationships even more. Your warmth and friendliness ensure your social life is full. When someone needs you, you drop everything to make sure you can be there for them. The direction of your life is determined by those around you.

- *Strengths:* You make people feel valued, loved, and important. You are friendly, open, and there whenever anyone needs a hand or just a hug.

○ *Next steps for your "Do What You Can Plan"*: Because you're so responsive to the needs of others, you may overlook your own. Begin to look at goals you might see as selfish (e.g., exercising) as an extension of the way you care for others (e.g., it gives you energy to play with your kids). You're not going to be motivated to do something unless you find a way it helps someone else too. So intentionally list that out with your goals and remember it. Also, whenever possible include others in accomplishing your goals by either having them join you in what you're doing or keeping you accountable.

○ *Watch out for:* Abandoning your goals because they are different from the goals of others, listening to what people want you to do before you take time to ask God what he wants, and allowing others to put unrealistic demands on you that make it difficult to take care of yourself.

These are just intended to be a lighthearted look at how we can approach change. You may see yourself a little bit in each one—or you might make up your own! The point is just to acknowledge that even if we have the same changes in mind as someone else, how we make those happen will be different. Who God made you is good, so go with it, girl.

Trying to force yourself to live in a way that doesn't make sense for who you are will just lead to frustration and wasted energy. It's okay to figure out what works best for you, and who knows, it might even be *fun*. As long as it's in line with God's Word, feel free to move ahead. "I run in the path of your commands, for you have set my heart free" (Ps. 119:32 NIV 1984).

Keep Realigning Your Life with Love

As you begin to do what you can and live in grace, love will begin to grow even more in your life. With each choice you make, you become a little more of who God made you and draw a little closer to his purpose for your life. The LIFE that's yours to share with others becomes clearer. It's like the lines in the road keeping you on course.

Go out there and run the race he's got for you, girl. The world is watching and heaven is cheering you on (and I am too).

10

Is It Okay to Take Care of **Myself?**

Jamie leans into the wall and places her head in her hands. "I'm so tired of being tired," she whispers. She thinks about asking for help, taking time away, just doing things differently. But another voice seems to interrupt, "Just get a grip and do what you need to do. A lot of people are counting on you. What's the matter with you?" She's heard those thoughts before. Jamie looks up and sighs, then tells herself she's just got to make it through another day.

Women are a generous gender. We give to our spouses, kids, neighbors, co-workers, church members, friends, and even the grocery clerk who is having a bad day. We pour out until one day we wonder, "Why do I feel so empty?"

One reason is a myth that says, "It's selfish to take care of myself." Oh, most of us would check "false" on that one if we had a test in front of us. But when we look at how we live, the answer seems quite different. We just talked about running your own race, and every athlete knows that self-care is essential to crossing the finish line well. In much the same way, taking care of yourself is going to be important to accomplishing your "Do What You Can Plan," fulfilling God's purpose for your life, and loving the people in your life well.

Another way to think of it is like a bank account for your heart. Certain things are like deposits: coffee with a friend, a long bubble bath, time spent praying. Others are withdrawals: an overwhelming project at work, a child with the flu, an especially busy season of life. We live in a fallen world, and there's never going to be a time when our emotional bank account always stays full. We don't need to feel guilty about it getting low sometimes. But we do need to be intentional about replenishing it so that we have something to give next time we're needed.

These are three common ways people try to refill their emotional energy accounts:

- Trying to earn the approval of others—In this mindset, we treat life like a job and the approval of others like a paycheck.

- Taking what we want because we're entitled to it—In this scenario, we grab all we can get because we believe we deserve it.

- Receiving what our hearts need as a gift of grace—We remember Jesus said to love others *as ourselves* (see Matt. 22:39), so we invest in ourselves because he says we're of great value.

I've done all of the above. You too? Our goal is to move more toward the third option. So let's pause for a moment and take a look at your emotional energy account.

Withdrawals	Deposits
(things that take emotional energy in my life right now)	(things that increase/restore my emotional energy in my life right now)
Example: Conflict with my teenage daughter	Example: Coffee with a dear friend

Hint: If you're having trouble thinking of things, then fill in the blanks below:

○ I feel the most drained after I

_____

(withdrawals)

○ I feel the most energized after I

_____

(deposits)

Sometimes we overestimate the emotional balance in our account because the withdrawals may be *good* things. For example, a teacher who is an introvert may love the kids in her classroom and feel very called to the profession. But being with other people all day long is going to be a withdrawal. Does that mean she should stop teaching? Nope, not at all. It just means she's going to need some things in the "Deposit" column so she can be restored.

As women, we often sabotage ourselves with false guilt. We tell ourselves that being married is a privilege, having children is a joy, going to work each day is a blessing—so we just need to suck it up and stop being so tired all the time. We should put on a happy face, say thanks, and get on with it, right?

As we've talked about before, how you feel is legitimate. What takes away from your emotional energy as well as what adds to it isn't bad or good. It's neutral. It's just reality. It usually doesn't say anything about what kind of person you are, how much you love the people in your life, or how much faith you have. It's just part of the way you're made.

When you give to a charity or another organization, it's a good choice. But it's still a withdrawal from your bank account. If you endlessly gave without replacing those funds, you'd end up bankrupt. You wouldn't be able to give to the charity any longer or cover the needs in your life. That's a lot like how our hearts work too. Even Jesus took time away to be renewed. It's not selfish to make a deposit in your emotional bank account. It's an investment that you'll be able to use to bless someone later.

Some withdrawals in our lives do need to be stopped. Imagine if you gambled away your life savings. Addictions, affairs, and other issues make us a slave to sin and drain away everything we have. If you're stuck in a destructive pattern, find someone you trust who can help you get free before you're emotionally and spiritually spent.

You are the only one who knows what's in your emotional bank account. "Each heart knows its own bitterness, and no one else can share its joy" (Prov. 14:10). So it's your responsibility to understand how God has made you and what you need.

We've talked about this before and it's worth mentioning again: women tend to compare. My friend who's an uber-extrovert gets a huge deposit in her emotional account every time she goes to a conference. I, on the other hand, go home with few funds left even though I love being there. So I know that after I get home, I need time alone to refuel and be ready to go again.

I don't believe in balance—there's never a time in our lives when the withdrawals and deposits work out perfectly. Life is too messy and unpredictable. That's not the goal. Instead, it's simply to be aware of what we need and give ourselves permission to receive it.

No matter what renews us, the source is ultimately the same: "Come to me, all you who are weary and burdened, and I will give you rest" (Matt. 11:28). Jesus doesn't want us to be exhausted. He doesn't expect us to be all things to all people. So take a deep breath, lean back into his love, and ask him what your heart needs to be filled with today.

Why It's So Hard to Receive

We feel the exhaustion. We know when we're discouraged. We sense the loneliness. So why is it so hard to receive what we need?

Receiving Is Risky

Jamie desperately wants to ask for help on a project at work. But she's afraid if she does, it won't seem as if she adds as much value to the team. So she stays late again and finishes everything herself. "Surely they wouldn't ever doubt my worth now," she tells herself as she finally closes her eyes to sleep.

In order to receive, we have to open our hearts, hands, and lives. We put ourselves in a position that's vulnerable. When we give, we're usually more in control. We get to determine what, how, and when. It's a risk—but it's usually one we've calculated. Receiving feels messy, more unpredictable. But it's essential. Look at the world around you. Everything in nature is about give and take, offering and receiving, grasping and releasing. If you only feel safe when you're giving and consistently resist receiving, then you may have some fears holding you back from getting what you need.

Try: writing down or saying out loud to someone you trust what you're actually afraid will happen if you receive.

Receiving Feels Selfish

Jamie's husband stands beside her at the kitchen sink. "Hey, why don't you let me finish those dishes? You look exhausted." Jamie looks up at him quizzically. She knows he doesn't like doing dishes. She would love to take him up on the offer, but then she thinks, "It's not fair to make him do this just because I'm tired. I need to do my part." "Thanks," she responds, "but I can take care of it." Her husband sighs and walks away. A few minutes later she hears the TV turn on in the living room. Jamie dries the last plate and wonders why she's feeling resentful.

We touched on this before, and it's probably the most common reason women avoid receiving. We've got big, generous hearts and we want to bless those around us. We long to be good wives, mothers, and friends. When we receive, it feels like we're taking away from someone else. After all, "it is more blessed to give than to receive" (Acts 20:35), right? But in the upside-down kingdom of God, what looks like taking is actually giving. You bless others by letting them give to you—just like you feel blessed when you give to them. If you're always receiving and never willing to give, then you may have some entitlement to hand over to God. But I imagine very few of you are that way. For most women, we're more likely to be out of balance by giving far more than we allow ourselves to receive.

Try: saying yes when someone offers to help you.

Receiving Seems Unproductive

The kids are in bed. The house has been picked up. Jamie settles down on the couch and opens a novel. But before she's through the first chapter, a thousand thoughts seem to run through her mind. "I could be cleaning out that closet. I probably should get a jump start on that report for work. What was that last item on my to-do list?" She sets the book down and grabs her list from the counter. By midnight she has several more items checked off, but the next morning she wakes up feeling even more behind.

We like our to-do lists and all those check marks at the end of the day. It's hard to add something like "read a book" or "enjoy a walk with a friend" to our list of highly urgent tasks. Often when we spend time receiving we walk away feeling guilty and as if we're wasting our time. But receiving is actually an investment in our future productivity.

I hate stopping to put gas in my tank. I'm usually zipping from one place to another. Pulling over feels like a hassle. If I decide to skip that stop, I might make it a few more miles down the road faster, but eventually it's going to catch up with me. Filling your gas tank after you've made it all the way to empty is a lot more trouble than practicing a little prevention. Just like our cars, we've got warning lights. It might be exhaustion, irritability, anxiety, or depression. When one of those starts creeping in, just look at it as the little light on your internal dashboard telling you, "Stop for a refill soon!" Over a lifetime, you'll actually be a lot more productive if you learn to receive.

Try: treating receiving just like any other task on your list.

Receiving Feels Undeserved

Jamie's little girl runs up to her. "Mommy, you're so wonderful!" she declares. Startled by this sudden expression of affection, Jamie brushes her daughter's hands away before she even realizes what she's doing. After all, she hasn't been the mom she'd like to be this week. Her daughter looks confused. "I'm sorry, honey. Mommy didn't mean to do that. Come here and let me try again."

Sometimes we push others away or withhold what we need from ourselves because we don't believe we've earned it. When we're better, skinnier, wealthier, holier, or a better mom, wife, or friend, then we'll deserve to receive. We treat receiving as a reward. But God clearly tells us that receiving is always about grace. That's true for the spiritual aspect of our lives and every other area too. If we wait until we're perfect to receive, then it's never going to happen. You can receive now because you are God's child, dearly loved, redeemed, chosen, and cherished. You can receive not because of what you do but because of who you are in him.

Try: resisting the urge to deny compliments or push away affection from others. Simply say, "Thank you."

Receiving Simply Isn't Part of Our Plan

Jamie stands in front of the refrigerator and marks another event on the family calendar. Then she checks her email and accepts a meeting request for the following week. Her phone buzzes with a reminder about a birthday party starting in a few hours. Jamie laughs and sighs to herself as she thinks about her schedule. "It seems like everyone gets a place in my plans but me."

Receiving seems like it would just happen naturally, right? But life is often too busy or complicated for that to happen. Think back to your "Do What You Can Plan." Did you put anything about receiving in there? If not, then you're missing an important piece. Life is busy. Phones ring. Emails arrive. Guests show up. We think, "When things settle down, then I'll take better care of myself." But things never do settle down. There's no such thing as normal. There will always be more to do, ways to improve, and new items on your list to accomplish. Receiving requires making it a priority and part of your plan just like you would anything else that matters in life.

Try: including receiving along with the other plans you make.

Receive, Then Invest

Albert Lexie has been shining shoes for over forty years. In 1981, he created the goal of donating $100,000 in tips to help a children's hospital. Little by little, Albert made it happen. It wasn't all at once—instead it came through a series of small deposits which he intentionally made knowing that those would all add up to a lot.

Whenever we're talking about receiving, it helps to remember what we want to invest in with our LIFE. It's all about paying it forward.

Most of us are familiar with the parable of the talents Jesus tells in Matthew 25, but let's do a quick recap. A master goes on a journey and entrusts three servants with talents (a talent was a certain amount of money in those days). The first two servants invest what they've been given. The master praises them when he returns. The third servant buries his talent, and the response is a stern rebuke. The message is clear—our master wants us to be wise stewards of what he's given us. But the part we often miss is this: to create a return, we also have to be willing to receive. If the servants had responded to the master by saying, "I'm really doing fine. I can just use the talents I have," then they wouldn't have been able to give him a return on his investment and bring joy to his heart as well.

It's a paradox: receiving is about you and not about you all at the same time.

To keep this perspective, it's helpful to know how we want to invest the deposits we're intentionally making in our lives or the ways we're open to receiving from others and God. If we only think about the first part (ourselves) but not who will benefit in the end (the kingdom and others), then deposits in our emotional bank accounts will continue to make us feel guilty.

For example: "I will make a deposit in my emotional account by taking fifteen minutes alone each day (if you stop there then you're likely to feel guilty) *so that* I can be a more energetic wife, mom, and friend" (there's the return on the investment—for your family, the kingdom, and you).

Let's give it a try:

◦ I will make a deposit in my emotional account by

_____

_____

◦ so that

_____

_____

Ask yourself:

> Why am I doing this?
>
> Who will it benefit in the end?
>
> How will I make sure it happens?

When God looks at his daughters, he sees each of us the same. He wants us to love ourselves the way we love others in our lives. It grieves him when we treat ourselves poorly, just like it would if we treated one of our sisters in Christ that way. If someone were harsh or demanding with a close friend of yours, you would come to her defense. If she were exhausted or burned out, you would try to help her get some rest. Sometimes we need to do the same for ourselves. Telling women they're not allowed to receive is one of the subtlest and most dangerous tactics of the enemy. He might not be able to make us ineffective by getting us to fall into a major sin, but he can accomplish the same thing by driving us to become utterly empty and exhausted.

You are worth investing in, sweet sister. You are a daughter of the King, a holy princess, a woman with a purpose in this world and a calling on your life. You are of infinite value, and no one can take your place. You're our one shot at what you have to offer. God doesn't have a backup plan for you. So take care of yourself. You're blessing all of us when you do, and you bring joy to the heart of God too.

Your Personal Investment Plan

Everything we've talked about comes down to one thing: love. The end goal of taking care of ourselves isn't simply to be happy or personally satisfied. It's so that we can love God, others, and ourselves.

It's okay to take care of yourself because you are someone's beloved. You are the bride of Christ. You belong to the One who hung the stars in place, who knows every detail of your day, who is waiting for the moment when you're finally together forever. You matter to him. He wants the best for you.

If you haven't figured it out yet: *you're amazing because you're God's creation and he lives in you.* You're valuable because you belong to him. You're worth investing in because he paid the ultimate price for you.

Dare to take the risk. Love yourself because he loves you.

We live busy lives. Making deposits in our emotional bank account takes planning and being intentional. It may take our bank sending us an "overdrawn account notice" before we realize we've spent a bit too much. In much the same way, many of us wait until we're burned out before we realize how drained we are emotionally.

I've been there. In *Leading on Empty*, Wayne Cordeiro explains how God has wired our bodies. He's given our brains a supply of serotonin, a chemical that gives us a feeling of well-being. When we're in chronic stress, those levels get used up. So our bodies switch to the backup plan: adrenaline. Think of it like the little bit of money you set aside in case of emergencies. But we càn only live on that for so long. When that supply is depleted, we truly are "in the red"—physically, emotionally, and often spiritually.

At that point we need serious restoration. That happens through rest and also intentional deposits. If we get to the point of being totally overdrawn, it can take six months to a year to restore our serotonin levels. By proactively making deposits ahead of time, we can ensure we don't get to that point. We keep our emotional bank accounts full so that when there is an unexpected expense, we have enough to cover it.

· · · · · · · **Creating Your Personal Investment Plan** · · · · · ·

In each of the areas below, brainstorm ways to be renewed. *These are not goals.* They shouldn't make you feel pressure or as if they are something you must do. These are deposits in your bank account—not withdrawals. For example, social might be "coffee with a friend" and physical might be "taking a walk on a nice afternoon to enjoy God's creation." Use the deposit list you made earlier in this chapter as a starting place and then add anything else that comes to mind. Take a few moments to ask God to show you how he made you and what you really need.

Also, if you don't enjoy it, then don't do it. The reason? While we need to push through and do hard things out of discipline in our lives (and you probably have those on your "Do What You Can Plan"), those won't maintain or rebuild your serotonin levels. That only happens when you're doing something you enjoy. If you're feeling guilty right now, remember, this is about *receiving so that you can invest.*

Here's an example in each area to get you started:

- Emotional—Watching a movie that makes me laugh
- Mental—Reading a book I really enjoy
- Spiritual—Writing a page in my prayer journal
- Social—A "girls' night out" with friends
- Physical—Walking the dog

·········· **Ultimate Goal: Invest in LIFE** ·········

> *"Love the Lord your God with all your heart and with all your*
> *soul and with all your mind and with all your strength. . . .*
> *Love your neighbor as yourself." There is no commandment*
> *greater than these. (Mark 12:30–31)*

What's of Greatest Worth?

Think back to the parable of the talents we talked about earlier in this chapter. When the master returns and praises the servants, he says six words that are of the greatest worth in our lives: "Well done, good and faithful servant!" (Matt. 25:23).

That's what it's all about in the end: receiving and then investing so that one day we too can hear from the lips of the One our hearts love, "Well done."

You are valuable.

And you have so much of value to offer.

Take care of you.

And finish well.

11

What God Really Wants Your Heart to Remember

I call you. "Can we meet for coffee again? There are some things I want to remind you of just one more time."

We talk of what we've been through together in these chapters—of discovering more about who we are and who God made us to be.

We laugh, sip from our cups, and smile, maybe even shed a tear or two.

"It's been a good journey," I say, "and there are some things I want you to carry with you always. I think the One who loves you does too."

I pull a box from under the table. It has a big, fluffy bow on top and a ribbon around it.

You clap your hands. "Is that for me?"

"Of course!" I declare.

You slip off the ribbon and gently left the lid.

You pull out the piece of paper and run your hand along the edges. It looks like it belongs to you, with you—like it was made *just for you*.

You read the words at the top aloud, slowly: "What God Really Wants Your Heart to Remember."

Sip by sip, line by line, we talk through each phrase on the page together . . .

You Really Were Made for More Than This

I understand how it works when you read a book like this. You close the last page with good intentions. Then the phone rings, the kids throw spaghetti, the dog eats your new shoes, and you wonder what in the world just happened.

Your heart cries, "I thought I was made for more than this."

You quiet that voice quickly and tell yourself to stop feeling that way.

But the truth is, you *were* made for more than this.

You *are* made for more than this.

The trouble isn't feeling that way—it's expecting it all to happen here. That discontent within you is a homing beacon, reminding you of Eden and redirecting you toward heaven. The disappointment only comes when we expect all of the *more* we're promised in the then and there to happen in the here and now.

"He has made everything beautiful in its time. He has also set eternity in the human heart; yet no one can fathom what God has done from beginning to end" (Eccles. 3:11).

We hold eternity in our hearts—all we've been, all we will be—and we don't understand it. How can we? All we feel is that longing, that ache within us.

So we try to change our circumstances. We alter this or that. We want things to be different. But that longing never really goes away.

It won't completely.

Not this side of heaven.

What we've been talking about isn't making our lives perfect. Instead it's about learning to turn to Jesus when our hearts feel restless, to have the courage to be who he made us here and now no matter what, to cross the finish line into everything he has for us in eternity with a smile on our faces, knowing we ran well every step of the way.

When we tell ourselves, "I was made for more, so I'm going to... run off to Jamaica, start a new relationship, switch to another job for the hundredth time," we miss what that ache inside us means.

When we stifle that longing and say, "I wasn't made for more, so I'll just settle for this forever," we do the same. That leads us to be apathetic and miss out on the joy, adventure, and good plans God does have for us in this life.

The hard line we walk is this: "I was made for more—more of Jesus, more of who he created me to be, more of his purpose for my life, more of his love flowing through me—and I'm going to pursue that with all my heart. But I also realize that I won't have all he has for me until I step into eternity. I'm not going to let that get me off track. I'm going to keep going and remember that 'The path of the righteous is like the morning sun, shining ever brighter till the full light of day' (Prov. 4:18)."

If you feel that "I was made for more" feeling again even after all the hard work you've done in this book, don't let it make you think you're missing something or you've done it wrong. Just let it be a reminder that you're not home yet ... but you're on your way. And you're getting a little closer every day.

> *Oh, yes, you're made for more ...*
> *more than the worry, the weariness, the*
> *   what-has-to-get-done.*
> *You're made for more ...*
> *more of Jesus, more of His presence in your life, more of all He*
> *   has to offer.*
> *Joy, hope, peace, grace, goodness.*

And right there in the middle of it all is you,
beautiful you,
deeply loved, chosen, called,
and on your way Home
to the One who cherishes you
  so much more
than your heart can even know.

You Really Were Made for Right Here, Right Now Too

Our hearts pull us toward home as they whisper, "You were made for more than this," and yet we're also made for this moment. Out of all of history, God chose this time for you to be on earth. He knew the exact second you would enter this world with a cry and change it forever.

In between the laundry, the endless trips to the office, the mundane parts of being human, we can forget that we're part of a bigger story, a greater plan.

And here's the thing: we only get one you. There never has been, and never will be, another you in this world. God doesn't have a backup plan or replacement policy. That's why I feel so passionately about you being who you are and embracing it. We don't need a copy of someone else—we need the one and only, original you.

How do we live in this place, suspended between history and eternity? How do we find the courage to offer who we are in the middle of the mess? My dear friend and fellow writer Ann Voskamp leads the way in her book *One Thousand Gifts*:

> Time is a relentless river. It rages on, a respecter of no one. And this, this is the only way to slow time: When I fully enter time's swift current, enter into the current moment with the weight of all my attention. I slow the torrent with the weight of me all here. I can slow the torrent by being all here. I only live the full life when I live fully in the moment.[1]

Ann says this present moment is the only place we can fully experience God because he is *I Am*. We find him not in the future or in the past. Instead we find him right here with us, beside us, in us. When we take hold of that, take hold of him, then we become all we're called to be today.

We may think back with regret on who we wish we'd been. We may look forward with fear about who we might (or might not) become. But the only place where we can offer ourselves, where God can use us, is the moment we're in right now.

Living that way requires awareness and intention. I hope our journey together has helped you gain a bit more of both. What you have to give, what you have to share with the world, is far too important to be missed. We need you to be you—not tomorrow, next week, or next year but where you are at this very second.

The temptation will always be to say, "After I . . ." or "When this happens, then I'll . . . ," but life doesn't work that way. You, your circumstances, your life will never be everything you want them to be. Don't let that stop you.

Embrace this moment. Be who you are. You're the best gift you can give the world.

> *I'm thinking of you today . . .*
> *the past pulling at your sleeves,*
> *the future tugging at your hands.*
> *Take a deep breath.*
> *Just for a moment.*
> *Just in this moment.*
> *Ah, yes, look at you—*
> *beautiful you.*
> *The sunlight of now*
> *is on your face,*
> *the glow within you is spilling out too.*

That's the thing about light—
we can't save it up
or carry it back.
It's always for now,
always for where we are today,
because it flows from the One
who is *I Am.*
We can only reflect Him in the here and now
because that's where He is.
Yes?
So keep shining, girl . . .
and know the world is better, brighter for it.

All You Are Really Can Be Used for Good

If we really were sitting at a table in a coffee shop, I imagine a straw would be somewhere nearby. At this point, I'd reach for it and hold it up in the air between us, my fingers grasping the middle. Then I'd say, "As the saying goes, 'Every stick has two ends.' The core characteristics about us are like that too."

By this point you might tease me, "You and all of your analogies!" I'd grin and point to one end of the straw.

"See this end? That represents our characteristics acted out as strengths. For example, when I'm living in tune with God, my sensitivity looks like compassion."

Then I'd touch the other end of the stick. "But on my own, it drifts the other way and becomes anxiety."

I don't believe God wants us to throw out the "sticks" in our lives. He just wants us to move toward the end that is more like him. The same Paul who ended up writing to the early churches started out being belligerent, overzealous, and an oppressive leader. After Jesus appeared to him, Paul was determined, enthusiastic, and an encouraging leader. Same characteristics—different ends of the stick.

I've watched women (including myself) work hard to remove parts of themselves that God deliberately placed within them. It's a painful process that usually doesn't get us very far. Instead of eliminating, it seems God's goal is more that we simply surrender and obey as we are.

In the times when we can't seem to transform our weaknesses to strengths, God can still make up for (and even use!) our imperfections. Judy, a reader on my blog *Heart to Heart with Holley*, shared this story:

> God used a speaker, an ordinary, everyday woman (translated: just like me) whose voice quivered as she spoke to help me. Normally when I pick up on nervousness in a public speaker it makes me nervous for them. But this time God used it to speak to my heart. The thought He brought to mind was if the message the speaker shared about Christ meant so much to her that she was willing to endure nervousness, I could brave the fear of what He was asking me to do, too, because the message is worth it.
>
> When I had a chance to meet with the speaker a few days later, she mentioned that her nervousness hindered the message. I gratefully told her that her nervousness was the very thing God used to help me be at peace with myself and say yes to what He was asking me to do.[2]

God really can use all of you—strengths, weaknesses, imperfections, and challenges. The only time that can't happen is when we refuse to give an area of our lives to him. But whatever we place in his hands, he can lovingly make into something useful and even beautiful. Like that straw, we can experience his love flowing through *every* part of our lives if we'll just open ourselves to him.

All you are,
everything God created you to be,
becomes a gift when placed in His hands.
There's nothing He can't mold, shape, redeem,
form into something beautiful.
You don't have to be afraid or hold back—
just hold out your heart to the One who promises
to complete the good work He's already started in you.

All Things Really Are Possible for You

I'm sure you remember the story of Peter walking on water with Jesus. Peter starts off well, takes a few steps, and begins to sink.

Jesus asks, "Why did you doubt?" (Matt. 14:31).

I pause and ponder, "Who did Peter doubt? Jesus or himself?" And it seems there's a whisper in response . . .

Same thing.

What I mean is this: "I no longer live, but Christ lives in me" (Gal. 2:20).

I'm still quick to protest, "But I have so many weaknesses!" And then I remember that every promise given and every truth declared was for us, all of us, and none of us have it together. Our humanity isn't too much for God. "Many are the plans in a person's heart, but it is the LORD's purpose that prevails" (Prov. 19:21). There is nothing God can't do through a heart fully surrendered to him.

Nothing.

Lead an entire nation through a desert.

Knock down a giant with a single stone.

Fulfill his purpose for your life.

Let's believe that in us, through us, in spite of us, "With God all things are possible" (Matt. 19:26).

What does this sound like in our everyday lives? "This seems impossible for me. But nothing is impossible for the God who lives in me. That means all things really are possible for me too. I can do this with him."

Good news:
Nothing is impossible for you
because all things are possible for the God who lives in you.
There's no obstacle too great, no wall too high, no valley too low.
You can get through it, over it, beyond it together.
With Him, you have more than enough . . .
you have everything you need
and you're everything you need to be
for His purposes to prevail in your life.

What You Have to Offer Really Is Enough

One morning I thought of all I had to do, all the hearts I felt called to love, all the words I want to share with the world.

I felt very small and the need felt so very big.

Then it seemed God whispered, "Just offer what you have. I will make up the difference."

Yes, of course!

The loaves and fish.

You know that story. It's the one where Jesus is teaching a huge, hungry crowd, and there's nothing to feed them. All anyone has to offer is five loaves and two fish. But put those in the hands of Jesus, and "They all ate and were satisfied, and the disciples picked up twelve basketfuls of broken pieces of bread and fish" (Mark 6:42–43).

Yes, in the hands of Jesus a little is a lot, *even more than we need.*

I don't always approach it that way.

Instead I try to change the bread. I think, "Well, her bread is golden and gorgeous. If I can just make my loaves like hers, then what I have will be enough."

Or I tell myself, "I just need to decorate the bread! I'll draw the Mona Lisa on top with frosting. If I can just make my loaves perfect, then what I have will be enough."

Maybe you, my fellow traveler on this journey, might do this too?

But Jesus steps in, takes us by the hands, looks into our hearts, and says, "Daughter, you don't have to be enough or have a lot. Only offer all you are, all you have, to me. I will turn that into abundance beyond all you can imagine. All things are possible with me."

Not only is Jesus the supplier—he is the multiplier too.

It's not about what we have to offer. It's about whose hands we place it in.

And those hands? We can place our hearts safely there too.

Hey, you, the one with those "loaves and fish,"
wondering if what you have to offer can even make a difference.
Oh, yes, it can.
We need you, just you, to open your hands and your heart
to dare to give what you've been given,
to place it in the hands of the One who made you
and who can make what you have to offer
more than enough too.

You Really Can Live Differently

Our journey together has been all about believing we're amazing just as we are and pressing on toward all God has for us too.

The hardest part of moving forward for me isn't taking the next step, finding courage, overcoming obstacles. No, the biggest challenge has been the voice inside my mind. It's the one that says, "You can never do this. This is in the way. That won't ever change."

You've struggled with that too? We're not the only ones.

As Priscilla Shirer says in her book *One in a Million: Journey to Your Promised Land,* the Israelites also battled fear and insecurities:

> If there's a single word that doomed this generation of God's people from experiencing Promised Land living in their lifetime, it's this one: "nevertheless."
>
> They had heard with their own ears the assurances of God. They had seen and certainly tasted the cluster of fruit that more than verified, beyond their wildest imaginations, just how accurate God had been when He had described the land to them....
>
> Nevertheless.[3]

She goes on to say that we're all tempted to do the same. I discover her words as I sit on my back porch one evening. As I finish, I lean back and stare into the deep summer sky.

I ask God, "What do I say instead?"

And like shooting stars, two words blaze across my mind.

Even so.

Yes, the situation is difficult and the obstacles seem insurmountable. Even so, God will deliver me.

Yes, I left my comfort zone about a hundred miles ago, and all I want to do is eat a vat of chocolate. Even so, God can use me.

Yes, it feels like the valley is dark, the mountains are high, and the enemy is strong. Even so, God is able to get me to the Promised Land.

Even so.

Those two little words don't deny the difficulties or paste on a smile that says, "Everything is fine." They acknowledge life is hard. They recognize the obstacles. But in the end, they shift our gaze from what we see to who we know. And that changes everything—especially us.

You've begun to move forward, to make changes, to recognize the incredible woman you are and become more of who God created you to be. And the enemy would love nothing more than to convince you it's too much, you can't do it, there's not enough time . . . the list is endless. But it's not true, dear friend. You can change. You can grow. You already have—don't let anything stand in your way.

Yours is not a life of "nevertheless."

It's one of "even so."

> *Are you ready to take that next step?*
> *You can do this, sweet girl.*
> *With Him.*
> *In His power.*
> *That power created the world,*
> *spoke the stars into place,*
> *spread the sea from one shore to another.*
> *That's the power that lives in YOU.*
> *Move forward in faith,*
> *into all you are and all He has for you.*
> *You're already on your way.*

You Really Are Loved More Than You Know

I grew up in Houston, close to NASA. The evening news often contained talk about the latest mission or plans for venturing even deeper into the universe. Over the years it seemed this became clear: the more we discover about space, the more we realize how little we know. I paused to look up from my computer at the sky just now. The blue stretches far beyond my ability to see. It reminds me of this verse: "For as high as the heavens are above the earth, so great is his love for those who fear him" (Ps. 103:11).

As high as the heavens are above the earth. How high is that? Endless. That's the way God's love for us is too.

In *The Truman Show*, Jim Carrey plays a man whose entire life is a reality show. From the day he was born, everything in his life has been a performance without him even realizing it. Everything around him responds based on what he does. Our lives can feel that way too—when we mess up, it can feel as if the sky is going to crash down around us. But as much as it may seem like it, our lives aren't about us. They're about our Maker. And his love never changes. Yes, we can separate ourselves from fellowship with God because of the choices we make. But we can't stop him from loving us.

The apostle Paul says, "I pray that you, being rooted and established in love, may have power, together with all the Lord's holy people, to grasp how wide and long and high and deep is the love of Christ, and to know this love that surpasses knowledge—that you may be filled to the measure of all the fullness of God" (Eph. 3:17–19).

It seems Paul is praying for us to know how high the sky is, and that's impossible. But wait—one phrase stands out to me in this verse: "to know this love that surpasses knowledge" (v. 19). When the word "know" is used in a biblical context, it is often associated with intimacy. For example, "Adam knew Eve" is a polite description of their physical relationship. We can't ever comprehend the love of God, but Paul's prayer, and mine too, is for us to experience it in our daily lives in a powerful way.

Embracing God's love is done not with our heads but with our hearts.

It's not about understanding but instead about simply receiving.

We spend a lot of time trying to figure out how God can love us and what that means. But all we really need to know is that he does.

Really.

Truly.

Just as you are.
As high as the sky.
More than you can even imagine.

You're loved.
More than you know.
More than you see.
Deeper than you've even dared to dream.
All that you fear holds you back
has been wiped away, forgiven,
covered up by grace.
And the One who created you,
knows you, calls you His own
looks at you with love
and says, "You're mine forever."
Your heart has a home—
and it's not a place
but a Person who will never let you go.

There Really Is a Good Plan for Your Life

A few years ago, my husband and I set out on a hike with a few friends. I expected it to be easy. But as the miles wore on, the hill grew steeper, and more obstacles appeared, I began to wonder what I'd gotten myself into by agreeing to go.

At one point, my athletic husband disappeared around a curve ahead in the trail. He'd told us he would go ahead of us and scout out the trail. But as the minutes ticked by, I began to worry. Where was he? Why hadn't he come back for us? What was really in front of us?

Just then we broke through some trees and found ourselves standing on a beautiful overlook. The entire valley stretched below us. My grinning husband pointed out landmarks below that we'd passed. "See," he said, "that's the stream we crossed. There's the place we stopped for water. Those are the rocks we had to climb over."

And as I looked back on where we'd come from, it all made sense. That winding trail through the woods was a clear, wide ribbon. Those places I'd wondered about were just stops along the trail. Having arrived at our destination, I could look back and say, "Oh, yes, that was so worth it."

Our lives can be like that too. We go through each day and make a little more progress. We face obstacles, grow weary, and wonder when things will really get better. It may even seem as if God is nowhere to be found. Where are we headed? Why is it worth it to keep going?

But God promises us that in the end it will all be worth it and we'll understand everything we went through along the way. Jeremiah 29:11 says God has good plans for us, a hope and a future. Does that mean it will always be easy or what we want? Nope, not at all. What it does mean is that we can trust him—no matter what.

I imagine one day we'll stand before Jesus in heaven and we'll look back over our lives with a different perspective. The moments you lived in your strengths, the challenges you pushed through, the ways you made a difference—they'll all be something beautiful that you can give the One who gave everything for you.

Hello, you . . .
wondering what's next,
where you're headed,
what might happen now.
There's One who knows the way.
Every step.
Every day.
Every moment.

He never promised it would be easy
but He did promise you'll never be alone.
He has a plan for your life, your heart,
and it's good.
Better than you hoped.
Better than you dreamed.
More than you can even imagine.

. . . And You Really Are Amazing

My imagination is shifting back to that coffee shop. By now the sun has slipped lower in the sky, and our cups have long been empty.

I look at you and smile. "Thanks for spending this time with me."

A waitress comes and clears our table. She pauses for a moment and asks, "Can I get you anything else?"

I smile and answer, "I think we've got all we need."

And it's true: "His divine power has given us everything we need for life and godliness" (2 Pet. 1:3 NIV 1984).

You had all you need before you ever read the first page of this book. You're already amazing because God made you, formed you, and lives within you. You're amazing because you belong to him, because he has a plan for your life, because with him there's nothing you can't do.

I hope our time together has given you some new tools, let God whisper some truths to your heart, and offered you some courage to take the next steps into all he has for you. But before we ever crossed paths, you had everything you need. You still do. You always will.

I don't know what you'll do after you close this book. Maybe you'll walk over to a crib and pick up a baby newly awakened from a nap. Maybe you'll finish a lunch break and step into a meeting. Maybe you'll uncurl from the couch, grab your keys, and head into your day.

Whatever it is, I know that you have what it takes to accomplish God's purpose for your life.

I know that the people whose paths you cross are going to be blessed because of you.

I know that your life is a story being written by an Author who has more in store for you than either of us can even imagine. Thank you for letting me share a few pages of it with you.

This isn't the end.

With the God who makes you amazing, it's always only the beginning.

Go Deeper Guide
(for Individuals and Groups)

In addition to the questions below, visit www.holleygerth.com for more tools, encouraging content, and even life coaching opportunities.

Chapter 1:
A Heart-to-Heart Talk

1. If you had coffee with a close friend today and she asked how you were *really* doing, what would you say?

   > I would probably say, "eh,
   > I'm alright. Sorta stragglin'...
   > I don't know, you?"

2. Which story at the beginning of the chapter did you relate to the most (the friend at lunch, counseling client, or woman sending the email)?

   > counseling client

3. The "it girl" is thought of as a woman everyone wants to be like in our culture. Do you ever feel pressure to be like women in the media? Share one example.

We see images of women w/ perf. bodies...
But for me, I compare myself w/ real
people that I know.

4. In contrast, through Scripture God says you're an "is girl." He looks at you and says, "She is _____." Fill in the blank with a few of the words your heart most needs to hear today. (Example: She is <u>loved</u>.)

loved , mine , enough

5. We sometimes feel shame about who we are or what we do. We tell ourselves, "Most people don't . . ." But those very things can be important parts of the unique way God has created us to make a difference in the world. What are those for you? Finish this sentence below: "Most people don't, but I . . ."

Mine is diff... but...

hurt themselves, love others, cry 24/7,
feel so crazy,

6. We all have brokenness in our lives, and that can keep us from seeing who we really are in Christ or believing he can use us. Write a short prayer asking God to heal your heart and make something unexpectedly beautiful out of your hurts.

Lord, right now I can't find the words
to pray, but help me thru this. Guide me.
use my everything - my brokenness for Your
glory.

One of my FAVS.

7. One of the most powerful passages of Scripture about who God made us to be and how intimately he knows us is found in (Psalm 139). Read it and write a short prayer that includes a few phrases from it below (if you're in a group, take time to pray for each other too).

(song of Psalm 139 = 😊♡)

Lord, I too often make my
bed in hell, but You
can still lead me home.
I can't believe the thoughts
You think of me. I will never understand,
but thank You.

Chapter 2: Who Am I, REALLY?

1. Look back to the strengths you circled on the list in this chapter. Write your top three here.

   encouraging, friendly, responsible

2. If you haven't already, put them through the STRENGTH test below.

Service	*Does it help me serve God and others?*
Time	*Has it been present throughout much of my life?*
Relationships	*Do others see this?*
Energy	*Do I feel energized when I'm living this way?*
Natural	*Does this come naturally to me most of the time? Or do I know God has intentionally developed this in me even though it doesn't?*
Glory	*Does God ultimately get the glory from it?*
Trials	*Even in hard times, does it usually come through somehow?*
Heart	*Does this really feel like a core part of who I am?*

3. We often think of weaknesses as a negative thing. But research shows that having weaknesses in certain areas actually helps us to be stronger in others. God also says that his "strength is made perfect in weakness" (2 Cor. 12:9 NKJV). What's a weakness you wish you didn't have? In what ways could it actually help you be who God created you to be? (Example: Being weak at details helps make you strong at seeing the big picture.)

   lack of perseverence @ times...

   Makes me rely on HIM!

4. Look back to the skills list in this chapter. Write your top three here.

Cleaning, leading, speaking

5. Skills circles can help us see how our skills support our core strengths. Try drawing one here (look back to the example in the chapter if you need help).

cleaning

leading — *encouragement* — *speaking*

6. Social circles help us understand who is in our life and how we're connected to them. You began thinking about that in this chapter; now you have time to actually write some names in each of the circles below. (If you need a reminder of what each circle means, look back to the definitions in the chapter.)

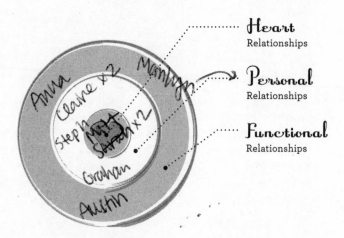

Heart
Relationships

Personal
Relationships

Functional
Relationships

But how can I pray that, if I can't accept it myself?

7. Look back to the "Find Your Who" exercise in this chapter. If you haven't already, fill in the blanks. When you look at your answers, who does it seem God most wants you to use your strengths and skills to serve? Write a short prayer asking him to use you in new ways (if you're in a group, take time to pray for each other too).

(hurting people ...)
Lord, help me serve those who are hurting. Help me to show them Your love and Your grace.

complete

Chapter 3: Why Is It So Hard to Believe I'm Amazing?

1. Lie #1: "I have to be perfect." How does knowing "by one sacrifice he has made perfect forever those who are being made holy" (Heb. 10:14) change that for you? What does God want us to pursue instead of perfection?

We don't have to be perfect, because He has made us holy + blameless...
(Pursue HIM.)

2. Lie #2: "I need to be more like her." Who do you tend to compare yourself to? What helps you focus on who you are in Christ instead?

My friends / siblings... / His Word + my Christian friends show me my identity in HIM...

3. Lie #3: "I don't have anything to offer." What keeps you from "putting your truffles on the table" for God and others? If you had no fear about the worth of what you had to share with the world, what would you do?

being judged or not being the best... Also, a lot of the time I don't believe I can + so I don't want to...

203

If I had no fear? I would do all I could...

4. Lie #4: "Being confident will make me prideful and selfish." What's the difference between insecurity and humility?

When we're confident in Christ, we'll know we're loved + want to serve others...

5. Lie #5: "I am who others say I am." What have others said to you that has impacted the way you see yourself? What does God say about you instead?

"It's always you're falt. You're STUPID, and hateful + selfish." // He says in him, I am not.

6. Are there any other lies you've become aware of that you need God to replace with the truth? Write them below.

I'm fat, I'm screwed up, I have to punish myself...

7. Write a short prayer asking God to continue revealing any lies in your life and to lead you into the truth about who you really are in him (if you're in a group, take time to pray for each other too).

Lord, God, Jesus, my Savior... Reveal the lies that I believe to be truth. Make them flee from my brain + heart + fill it up Your truth and love.

Chapter 4: Why Do I Feel This Way?

1. Are you dominated more by your head or heart? Look back to the descriptions about both and write a few phrases that sound most like you.

"I feel...";

"How I feel affects every part of my life"

2. Emotions make great messengers but bad bosses. What helps you make sure you're ultimately obeying God rather than your feelings?

Conviction

3. Which description most fits your family growing up—stuffers, screamers, or surfers? What parts of your emotional history still fit you well and which ones have you outgrown?

4. We talked about having an emotional range and how if we don't allow ourselves to experience negative emotions, then we limit our ability to experience positive ones as well. Are there any experiences in your life that have caused you to shut off part of your heart? If so, write a short prayer sharing them with God and asking him to heal you and free you to feel again (if you're in a group, take time to talk to God together and pray for each other).

I try and cut out some neg. feelings b/c they cause sin... but I'm killing myself / robbing myself of Gods joy!

5. Look at the list of emotions in this chapter. Which ones are you most comfortable expressing? Which ones are you least comfortable expressing?

6. Read the story of Joshua and Caleb in Numbers 14:1–9. They chose faith over feelings and were the only ones to see the Promised Land. What's one thing they did that you can apply to your life?

7. "Above all else, guard your heart, for it is the wellspring of life" (Prov. 4:23 NIV 1984). What's one specific way you can guard your heart this week? Write a short prayer asking God to help you do so (if you're in a group, take time to pray for each other too).

I need to have a talk w/ Matt about boundaries. LORD, help me do that. You know my thoughts and feelings...

Chapter 5: Where Am I Going?

1. Egypt: Are there any areas in your life where you feel like you're in Egypt? What is God prompting you to do so you can move on from that place?

2. Encamped: Are there any areas in your life where you feel like you're encamped? Review the reasons in the chapter why God sometimes has us stay put for a while. Which one did you identify with and why?

3. Setting out: Which one of the profiles in this section (settler, explorer, traveler) did you relate to most? What's the next step God is asking you to take in an area of your life?

4. The Promised Land: Are there any areas in your life where you feel like you're in the Promised Land? What are you doing to possess, defend, and enjoy it?

5. If you didn't do so in the chapter, fill in your Life Map below:

· · · · · · · · · · · · · · **My Life Map** · · · · · · · · · · · · ·

Under each section draw a dot and write the areas of your life that fit in each one.

> Egypt
>
> Promised Land
>
> Encamped
>
> Setting Out

6. None of us are intended to go through life alone. Who encourages you on your journey? Who else might be willing to do so?

_____

_____

7. Based on where you are now, write a short prayer asking God to help you take the next step in his plan for your life (if you're in a group, take time to pray for each other too).

_____

_____

Chapter 6: Who's with Me?

1. Do you ever feel lonely or out of place? What are the lies the enemy tries to whisper to your heart when that happens, and what's the truth?

yes... youre diff." judgemental, annoying."

2. The word for "helper" in the Bible that describes Eve is the same word often used when God helps us. When you thought of Eve being called a "helper" before now, what did you think it meant? How does seeing that word in this context change that?

She helped Adam w/ "chores"... //
I see her as loving, supporting

3. What makes you afraid that you won't be loved? Do you ever hide from others? Describe a time when you overcame your fear and found the courage to reach out instead.

I'm afraid of being "un-loved";
lied to; I'm afraid of
expectations.../

4. "Love all. Please One." What's the difference between loving someone and trying to please them?

When you try to please someone, you're
only trying to please them, not God..
(idolatry?)

5. There's a "Safe Person Checklist" in this chapter based on 1 Corinthians 13:1–8. Take a moment to read that passage. Who are the safe people in your life?

Sarah Holbrook, Annye Carlisle,

6. As daughters of Eve, we all struggle with the desire for control—we just display it in different ways. In the descriptions of internal and external control, which one could you most relate to? What helps you let go of control and trust God so that you can freely love?

I love the fact that I cannot
change His will for my life...
Ultimately He is in control...
I can love!

I've been this prayer for a while now!

7. This quote by C. S. Lewis is powerful:

> To love at all is to be vulnerable. Love anything, and your heart will certainly be wrung and possibly broken. If you want to make sure of keeping it intact, you must give your heart to no one, not even to an animal. Wrap it carefully round with hobbies and little luxuries; avoid all entanglements; lock it up safe in the casket or coffin of your selfishness. But in that casket—safe, dark, motionless, airless—it will change. It will not be broken; it will become unbreakable, impenetrable, irredeemable.[1]

If loving is so risky, why does God ask us to do it? Write a short prayer asking him for the courage to love (if you're in a group, take time to pray for each other too).

LORD, help me love like you love. Love that never ends; love that points to you. Love that's not selfish, love that doesn't envy. Love that doesn't boast. LORD, I love because you love.

Chapter 7: How Do I Connect?

1. Have you ever thought of the ways you connect with others as strengths God has given you? What are some ways that others frequently describe the way you connect with them (for example, outgoing, compassionate, fun, kind)?

2. Which setting (one-to-one, one-to-few, one-to-many) are you most drawn to? Describe your favorite way to spend time with other people.

3. Which structure seems to fit you best (leading, partnering, serving)? Describe a situation in which you used this to help others.

_____

_____

4. When it comes to sight, are you more internal or external? Write down some phrases in the description that sound most like you.

_____

_____

5. Which sphere of needs does your heart feel called to most (intellectual, relational, emotional, practical)? Describe a time when God used you to meet a need in that way.

_____

_____

6. We are all part of the body of Christ. Read 1 Corinthians 12:12–31. If you were to choose a part of the body that you feel best represents you, what would it be and why? (Example: "Hands, because I love to reach out and serve.")

_____

_____

7. Good news: we don't have to rely on ourselves to live in our strengths or deal with our weaknesses. "For God did not give us a spirit of timidity, but a spirit of power, of love and of self-discipline" (2 Tim. 1:7 NIV 1984). What's a specific way you can apply this verse in your life this week? Write a short prayer asking for God's help to do so (if you're in a group, take time to pray for each other too).

_____

_____

_____

Chapter 8: What Does God Want Me to Do with My Life?

1. Most of us have busy schedules. What's the difference between "life to the full" and simply "a full life"?

   _____

   _____

2. If you have not done so already, take time to write your LIFE statement here:

   I am created and called to express my faith through love, especially by

   _____

   (verb ending in "ing" + what + who + how)

   If you've already written it, make any changes that come to mind.

3. Expectations are like laws we place on ourselves. "You are not under the law, but under grace" (Rom. 6:14). Write some of the expectations you feel below:

   I must_____ or this
   will happen: _____ .

   I must_____ or this
   will happen: _____ .

   I must_____ or this
   will happen: _____ .

   Where are those expectations coming from? What does God want to replace them with instead?

   _____

   _____

4. If you knew you would be completely loved and accepted no matter what, then which items would you cross off your (mental or actual) to-do list?

5. When you read your LIFE statement, what would you like to add to your to-do list instead?

6. In Matthew 22:34–40, Jesus shares what matters most to God. Read that passage and paraphrase it in your own words below.

7. Write a short prayer asking God to help you live your LIFE statement more fully (if you're in a group, take time to pray for each other too).

Chapter 9: What Are My Next Steps?

1. "Let us throw off everything that hinders and the sin that so easily entangles. And let us run with perseverance the race marked out for us, fixing our eyes on Jesus, the pioneer and perfecter of our faith" (Heb. 12:1–2). What tends to hinder and/or entangle you?

2. What did you think of the "Do What You Can Plan"? Which aspect stood out to you most? Describe a time when God prompted you to make a change in your life and you did it. What helped you?

_____

_____

_____

3. If you didn't fill out your "Do What You Can Plan" in the chapter, you can do so now:

Change God wants me to make:	Small next step:	How I'll celebrate:

4. How will these changes help you live your LIFE?

_____

_____

5. What's your strategy for dealing with slipups and setbacks in your plan?

_____

_____

6. Which organizational personality sounds most like you? Write down some phrases that stood out to you in the descriptions.

_____

_____

_____

7. Write a short prayer asking God to help you make these changes and move forward in all he has for you (if you're in a group, take time to pray for each other too).

_____

_____

_____

Chapter 10: Is It Okay to Take Care of Myself?

1. Write down more deposits/withdrawals in your emotional bank account:

Withdrawals (things that take emotional energy in my life right now)	Deposits (things that increase/restore my emotional energy in my life right now)
Example: Conflict with my teenage daughter	Example: Coffee with a dear friend

2. Why is it so hard for many women to receive? Which of the common reasons listed in this chapter did you most relate to personally?

_____

_____

3. What fills you up and brings you joy?

_____

_____

4. Think of the people in your life. Who encourages you the most?

_____

_____

5. We receive so that we can invest in the kingdom and others. Try starting to make a receive/invest plan below:

I will make a deposit in my emotional account by

_____

_____

so that

_____

_____

Ask yourself:
Why am I doing this?
Who will it benefit in the end?
How will I make sure it happens?

6. It's important to be intentional about receiving just as we are about giving. If you haven't already done the Personal Investment Plan in the chapter, do so here. If you have, add a few more ideas.

_____

_____

In each of the areas below, brainstorm more ways to be renewed. Here's an example in each area to get you started:

- Emotional—Watching a movie that makes me laugh
- Mental—Reading a book I really enjoy
- Spiritual—Writing a page in my prayer journal
- Social—A "girls' night out" with friends
- Physical—Walking the dog

"Love the Lord your God with all your heart and with all your soul and with all your mind and with all your strength.... Love your neighbor as yourself." There is no commandment greater than these. (Mark 12:30–31)

7. Write a short prayer thanking God for all he's given you and asking him to help you receive from him and others all that you need (if you're in a group, take time to pray for each other too).

_____

_____

_____

Chapter 11: What God Really Wants Your Heart to Remember

1. As you think about making changes in your life, what is your greatest fear or obstacle? What can help you with it?

_____

_____

2. What are the "loaves and fish" you want to offer Jesus? What would you like to see him do with the gifts and strengths he's given you?

3. What's one new truth you've learned about how much God loves you through this book?

4. Do you ever feel "I was made for more than this"? What do you think of the idea that those thoughts are intended to point us toward heaven?

5. What helps you make the most of every moment in this life? What would you do if you knew you couldn't fail?

6. How do you see yourself differently now than when you started this journey?

7. Write a short prayer expressing your heart to God and asking him to show you what's next on your journey with him (if you're in a group, take time to pray for each other too).

Notes

Chapter 1 A Heart-to-Heart Talk

1. Angie Smith, "Past and Pitcher," *Bring the Rain* (blog), May 24, 2008, http://angie smithonline.com/2008/05/the-past-and-the-pitcher.

Chapter 2 Who Am I, *Really*?

1. Marcus Buckingham and Donald O. Clifton, PhD, *Now, Discover Your Strengths* (New York: The Free Press, 2001), 51.
2. Ibid., 51–52.
3. Janet Kornblum, "Study: 25% of Americans have no one to confide in," *USA Today*, June 22, 2006, http://www.usatoday.com/news/nation/2006-06-22-friendship_x.htm.
4. Lisa-Jo Baker, e-mail message to author, March 17, 2010, used by permission.

Chapter 4 Why Do I Feel This Way?

1. Jennifer Warner, "No Joke: Laughter Is Universal," WebMD Health News, January 25, 2010, http://www.webmd.com/balance/news/20100125/no-joke-laughter-is-universal?src=RSS_PUBLIC.
2. Peggy, February 12, 2010, comment on Holley Gerth, "The Rest of Your Story 28: How Do You Feel?" *Heart to Heart with Holley* (blog), February 11, 2010, http://www.holleygerth.com/heart-to-heart-with-holley/2010/2/11/the-rest-of-your-story-28-how-do-you-feel.html#comment13223794.

Chapter 5 Where Am I Going?

1. Karen R., September 1, 2010, comment on Holley Gerth, "Two Little Words That Will Change Your World," *Heart to Heart with Holley* (blog), August 29, 2010, http://www.holleygerth.com/heart-to-heart-with-holley/2010/8/29/two-little-words-that-will-change-your-world.html.

Chapter 6 Who's with Me?

1. C. S. Lewis, *The Inspirational Writings of C. S. Lewis* (New York: Inspirational Press, 1994), 278–79.

Chapter 8 What Does God Want Me to Do with My Life?

1. Marion, November 4, 2010, comment on Holley Gerth, "When You Want Life to the Full," *Heart to Heart with Holley* (blog), November 3, 2010 http://www.holleygerth.com/heart-to-heart-with-holley/2010/11/3/when-you-want-life-to-the-full.html.

2. Jennifer Stout, November 4, 2010, comment on Holley Gerth, "When You Want Life to the Full."

3. Bernice, November 7, 2010, comment on Holley Gerth, "When You Want Life to the Full."

4. Adrian Rogers, "Love Worth Finding," Adrian Rogers' Daily Devotional, March 23, 2010, http://www.crosswalk.com/devotionals/loveworthfinding/11627838/.

5. Bonnie Gray, "God's Love Is Perfected in De-Perfection," *Faith Barista* (blog), September 24, 2009, http://www.faithbarista.com/2009/09/gods-love-is-perfected -in-de-perfection.

Chapter 9 What Are My Next Steps?

1. Wayne Cordeiro, *Leading on Empty: Refilling Your Tank and Renewing Your Passion* (Minneapolis: Bethany House, 2010), 78–79.

2. Deidra Riggs, "Baby Steps (For Us Big Picture People at the Start of a Brand New Year)," (in)courage (blog), January 6, 2001, http://www.incourage.me/2011/01/baby-steps-for-us-big-picture-people-at-the-start-of-a-brand-new-year.html.

Chapter 11 What God Really Wants Your Heart to Remember

1. Ann Voskamp, *One Thousand Gifts: A Dare to Live Fully Right Where You Are* (Grand Rapids: Zondervan, 2011), 68.

2. Judy J., January 29, 2010, comment on Holley Gerth, "The Rest of Your Story 14: What Would You Edit?" *Heart to Heart with Holley* (blog), January 27, 2010, http://www.holleygerth.com/heart-to-heart-with-holley/2010/1/27/the-rest-of-your-story-14-what-would-you-edit.html.

3. Priscilla Shirer, *One in a Million: Journey to Your Promised Land* (Nashville: B&H Publishing Group, 2010), 172.

Go Deeper Guide

1. C. S. Lewis, *The Inspirational Writings of C. S. Lewis* (New York: Inspirational Press, 1994), 278–79.

Hello, friend!

Thanks again for sharing this journey with me. I truly wish I could have a cup of coffee with you today and hear your heart. Until then, I hope we can stay connected in some other ways!

I'd love for you to stop by my place online, **www.holleygerth.com**. When you subscribe by email, you'll get free encouraging messages from me sent right to your inbox. I'm also on Facebook as Heart to Heart with Holley and Twitter as @HolleyGerth.

I'm thrilled that the Bloom (in)courage book club featured *You're Already Amazing* for spring 2012. So if you'd like to join some girlfriends in exploring this book, you can go to **www.incourage.me** and then to the book club section.

You can also find cards and gifts I created with DaySpring at **www.dayspring.com** and your local Christian store. I hope you'll discover some encouraging ways to share this message with the women in your life as well.

(Psst—I feel a little shy telling you all of this. But that's what friends do, right? Big gulp. Little smile. Thank you for letting me share with you!)

With Jesus you really are amazing, my friend. Keep believing that's true and living like you do!

Love,

Holley Gerth

PS: Together we can help women all over the world know they're amazing. A portion of author proceeds from this book will go to the Compassion International Leadership Development Program. To find out more about the program, visit **www.compassion.com**.

You're Made
for a
God-Sized
Dream

*Opening the Door
to All God Has for You*

For the

God-sized dreamers ~

you know who you are

1

The **"More"**
You're Made For

She whispers it into the phone, almost too softly for me to hear.

"I just . . . have this desire in my heart that won't go away."

She lists off reasons why it won't work, why this isn't the right time, and how she feels odd for even thinking about it in the first place.

When she pauses for a deep, unsure breath, I slip in these words: "It sounds like you have a God-sized dream."

"A what?" she responds with a bit of wonder in her voice.

I smile and share more about desire and hope, what it means to make it to your personal Promised Land, and how everything is going to be different now.

I understand God-sized dreams because I've lived them. And once you have a taste, there's no going back to life as you knew it before.

You may say, "But I don't have big dreams."

Exactly.

The size of the dream isn't what matters.

I believe everyone has God-sized dreams. It's not about how big or small they are, because he creates each one to perfectly fit the size of *your* heart.

Your dream might be to move across the world and start a nonprofit organization that cares for orphans—what looks like a grand adventure in the world's eyes.

Or your dream might be to stay right in your small town and raise your kids so that they grow into strong men and women— what looks like something fairly ordinary in the world's eyes.

Both matter equally.

And both are God-sized dreams.

It's not about what you do as much as *how* you do it. It's about pursuing life with passion and purpose and going with God wherever he leads.

It's about not settling. It's about tenaciously believing *you're made for more.*

Not as in "bigger house, fancier car, more luxurious lifestyle."

No, my friend, I mean "more of Jesus, more of what he's created you to be, more of what he's called you to do." Less of you, actually, and more of all he is and all he has for you—which is beyond what you can even imagine.

I'm thinking of you right now, wherever you are—perhaps holding this book in your hand in the aisle of a bookstore, curled up on your couch, or on a long flight—and I wish I could be right beside you. I'd like to pour you a cup of coffee or tea and listen long and hard to the things you're afraid to tell anyone: the hopes that feel silly, the dreams that seem like dares, the quiet longings of your heart that get especially loud sometimes.

I'd nod, look you in the eyes, and say, "Don't let that go. Don't hide it away. That's real. And, yes, you really can see it come into being in your life. You have what it takes to see those dreams come true because you have a limitless God living in you. He has given you all you need and made you all you need to be."

Then I'd get you a cookie too (because believe me, you'd feel like you need one by then), and we'd talk through all the fears, how it really can happen, what to do next.

You might ask me, "What makes God-sized dreams so important to you?"

I'd tell you that I've lived my share. Some have come true—like being a writer, counselor, life coach, and speaker. Others, like my desire for children, have led me to places of heartbreak and then healing without ever turning out the way I imagined. Through it all, the happy and the hard, I've discovered that the places I feel closest to Jesus, the moments when God is most real in my life, always seem to come when I'm on an adventure with him. And once you've learned that, you can't ever go back to life as you knew it. I'll share more about my God-sized dreams as we go along.

I'd also say that what I've experienced has been echoed by thousands of women on my blog, through emails and life coaching, at my church, and in many other ways. Do you feel like you're alone in your dream? You're not, my friend. I'm right beside you now on these pages. And because I'm passionate about God-sized dreamers, I also do e-coaching for women like you online (find out more at www.holleygerth.com). Many, many of your sisters are on this God-sized dream journey with you too. You'll even hear some of their stories in the following pages.

So consider this book that conversation we'd have over coffee or tea. What I've written is a gift from my heart to yours, from one dreamer to another. I believe with you, for you, and most of all—I believe in the God who lives within you.

You really are made for more.

And this is your time.

Right here, right now.

How Dreaming Begins

I sit in the backseat of a pickup truck with my nieces and nephews. Scrawny legs and arms restlessly swing back and forth as they try to pass the time. To distract them, I ask the question all adults do: "What do you want to be when you grow up?"

The answer comes swiftly and universally: "We want to work at Chuck E. Cheese's!" For those of you not familiar with Chuck E. Cheese's, it's an establishment full of pizza, games, and far too much sugar—the perfect spot to start your career, in the eyes of a six-year-old.

Fast-forward a few years and we're standing in the kitchen around the holidays. Those scrawny legs and arms have grown into tall teen bodies, and I check to see how the professional ambitions are going. "Do you still want to work at Chuck E. Cheese's when you grow up?"

I get laughs and quizzical looks as if I've gone crazy. "Aunt Holley!" they exclaim. "Why would we ever want to do that?"

When we start dreaming as children, it's a lot like practice. We learn to ride bicycles, and we also become more skilled at turning the wheels in our minds. We tell people we want to be astronauts or queens and to find ponies under our Christmas trees.

It's a fine line between reality and what's possible when we're children. Like for my nieces and nephews, most of those dreams disappear through the years, and that's okay. As we mature, so do our desires. Yet in those early dreams, we often find the seeds of the *something more* God has planted within us. If I'd asked you the same question I posed to my nieces and nephews, what would you have said?

(Note: Throughout the book you'll find interactive tools like the one below. If you'd like to download a printable version, go to the "Books & More" page at www.holleygerth.com. You can also download a printable version of the Go Deeper Guides that are at the end of each chapter.)

What were some of your childhood dreams?

_____

_____

_____

_____

_____

I vividly remember perching on the edge of my parents' bed as a child. I squeezed my eyes tight, took a giant leap, and flapped my arms as hard as I could. Landing on the ground, I ran to my mom and dad to declare, "I flew!"

As I got older, I realized that as much as I felt like it was true, I hadn't actually become the world's first flying child that day.

"Flying is an impossible dream," some would say. Yet I have flown across the country and even across the world—many times.

Sure, as I grew up I realized I needed a plane to make the dream happen. But few things thrill me like staring out the window of a jet at twinkling lights below and thinking to myself, "I'm flying." I feel like that kid at the edge of the bed all over again.

Imagine I said, "I can't fly with my arms, so I'm not going to fly at all. What a silly dream. I need to grow up, face reality, and forget that ever even crossed my mind."

You'd probably say, "Holley, you might want to reconsider. Don't you ever want to go to Hawaii, visit Paris, or even just be able to visit your family without spending hours in the car? You're giving up so much!"

Yet we often do the same with our dreams. As children we let our imaginations go wild, and as time passes we begin to understand more of what's reality and what's fantasy. Rather than seeing those outlandish desires as a natural part of childhood, we convince ourselves that we're irresponsible dreamers. We need to settle down. Face the facts. Forget about flying and keep our feet on the ground.

Says who?

Who told you to stop dreaming? Maybe it was a teacher who told you to sit still in class and stop drawing those pictures. Maybe it was an overly cautious parent who wanted to keep you from getting hurt. Maybe it was the bully on the playground who yelled to the whole class that you were weird.

What if they were wrong?

Oh, of course there are dreams that we do need to let go. Like the Chuck E. Cheese ambitions of my nieces and nephews, sometimes a dream is more of a wish, and it blows away like a dandelion in the winds of time.

But if someone said or did something that made you stop dreaming altogether, then, my friend, I can assure you that wasn't from Jesus.

Dreaming is a core part of who we are. True, not all of our dreams come from God and not all of them are his will for our lives (more on that later), but the capacity to use our imaginations, to have visions, to nurture desires is inherent in who he has created us to be. "A longing fulfilled is a tree of life" (Prov. 13:12).

Dreams and desires propel us forward. In many ways, they keep us moving toward heaven—they don't allow us to get too comfortable here, to settle in ways and places God never intended.

As long as you are alive, God wants you to go further, dig deeper, and draw closer to him. And I believe dreams are one of the primary ways God makes that happen. *Every dream or desire you have that comes from God is an invitation for more intimacy with him.*

Did you catch that?

You can stop feeling guilty about dreaming and hoping.

And if life has diminished your capacity to dream, here's your permission to start again.

Really.

Five Lies That Keep Us from Dreaming

Ever since Eden, the enemy has come at us with a million different versions of the same question, "Did God really say . . . ?" And many times those questions are aimed squarely at our dreams.

Did God really say you have what it takes?

Did God really say that's what you're supposed to do?

When you follow your God-sized dreams, you'll face many external obstacles. But the biggest threats are from the inside. So let's start there.

Lie #1: "Dreaming Is Selfish"

She sits on the edge of her chair and stares at the corner of the room. I watch her fidget and run her fingers along the edge of her jeans. I can tell she's thinking of the husband and children and laundry waiting for her at home.

"I want to follow this dream," she says. "But it just feels so selfish."

From all the women I've talked to about God-sized dreams, this is the lie I hear most often. Women are a generous gender. We care deeply, passionately. We'd do anything for the ones we love. We serve selflessly. That is good, beautiful, and true.

But you matter too.

So do your dreams. The enemy knows that it's often one little word that can stop our dreaming in its tracks: *selfish*. We come to a screeching halt and say, "I'm not going within ten feet of that possibility." But if we tiptoe closer to that lie, we can see it for what it really is—a mirage.

Let me cup your lovely face in my hands and whisper this loud enough for your heart to hear: "Your dreams, your desires, your hopes are not selfish when they are from God's heart and in his hands."

"God is love" (1 John 4:16). Everything he does is loving. Everything he places within you is loving. That includes your dreams.

Now, if your dream is to run off to Tahiti with the pool boy and live on a two-hundred-foot yacht, then honey, that's a whole different story.

But if you have yielded to God and you have this nagging desire within you that just won't go away, then most likely it's from him. And if it is, then he has a way that you can live it out that isn't about selfishness but instead is about service.

Oh, the dream may look different than you imagined. You might be speaking at local women's ministry meetings instead of jetting across the country every weekend. But there is a way for that longing in your heart to be fulfilled that will be a blessing to those around you too.

The people in your life may not always like that you're following your dream. They may even whine about it from time to time. But not pleasing people isn't the same as being selfish. You don't have to make everyone in your life happy—the only thing you must do is be obedient.

Lie #2: "I Don't Have What It Takes"

She sits in the back row with me as the speaker takes the stage. Powerful words pour forth, and it's clear the women in the audience are touched. During the applause my friend leans over and says, "See, I could never speak. She's so much better than me."

It seems as soon as we give ourselves permission to dream, comparison is nipping at our heels. We look around and see others who are better, skinnier, more eloquent than us. Before we even get started, we disqualify ourselves. We vow to hold back until we're "as good as they are." Before we know it, time slips by and our dream still waits for its turn.

This lie is ultimately rooted in the belief that our God-sized dream is the same as someone else's. When we decide that's true, it means we're competitors because there aren't enough dreams to go around. But the reality is, even if someone else's dream looks, sounds, or even feels like yours—it's not the same.

God has a dream for you, your talents, your one life that has never been and never will be duplicated by anyone else.

He doesn't want you to be a "me too" when it comes to your dreams. He wants the one, original you whom he created to do exactly what he made you alone to do. No one else can fulfill your purpose. No one else can make that dream happen. There is no plan B for what God has destined to come into being through you.

It doesn't matter if you think you're not as good as someone else. You have what it takes to fulfill the dream God has for your life, and no one else does.

If the person you view as being the "top" in the area of your dreams were to trade places with you, it wouldn't work—even if it seemed like they were better at it than you. That's because God isn't interested in "better" or "the best." He can use sticks and stones to do his will if he wants! What God cares most about is

We're talking of God-sized
   dreams.

About how they are messy, imperfect, glorious, and flawed.

Because we are too.

And one phrase keeps reverberating through my being:

   If not for grace . . .

   If not for grace . . .

If not for grace, God-sized dreams would never come true.

Because I can tell you from experience . . .

You will cry at the wrong time.

You will say that awkward thing.

You will forget what to do in that most important moment.

And God, in his stubbornness, will carry on with his plan anyway.

   You will fail at least once,
      and probably more.

You will think you are incapable.

And sometimes you will be.

   But God, in his audacity,
      will use you anyway.

You will miss opportunities.

You will take steps you shouldn't.

You will walk through the wrong door and shut the right one.

And somehow, inexplicably, God will get you there anyway.

You will be hard to live with sometimes.

You will fall short.

You will forget to stand tall.

And God, unconcerned about what's cool, will say, "That one's mine" anyway.

You see, God-sized dreams don't make sense.

Not a bit.

Because they come from the heart of the One whose ways are higher than ours.

They flow from the One who stubbornly believes in grace.

If not for grace . . .

we wouldn't take a step

because it's grace that paves the road to God-sized dreams.

And we walk it, unworthy,

utterly broken,

and entirely loved!

your relationship with him, your obedience, your ability to hear his voice and say yes when he asks you to take a step of faith.

You are the only you we have. That means your God-sized dream either happens through you or not at all.

Lie #3: "It's Too Late"

She stands with a baby on her hip, and three others are causing chaos in the background. Above the noise she declares, "Well, I once had dreams, but now all I've got is diapers. It's too late for me." I've heard retired people, those with chronic illness, and many facing difficult circumstances say the same thing—that it's too late. Perhaps this is the hardest lie of all. It locks our dreams into a time bomb, and once we think it's exploded, it seems there's no picking up the pieces again.

It's true that our original vision may not come to pass. The "happily ever after" we pictured in our minds as little girls may have veered off course. But like I said before, I believe as long as we're alive, our dreams are too. God doesn't plant desires within our hearts to let them wither and die. Yes, they may be dormant for a season. And yes, when they finally push through the ground, they may look nothing like what we anticipated—but they're still possible.

I once knew a couple who longed to have children for years, but it never came to pass. The desire never went away, and in their sixties God called them to be "parents" to many children in a country far away. Now their family is bigger than they ever could have imagined. Like for Abraham and Sarah in the Old Testament, the answer to their prayers seemed a long time coming ... but it did come. And that wouldn't have been possible unless they kept their hearts open to dreaming.

My grandpa Hollie (yes, I'm named after him) is ninety years old. Almost every time we're on the phone, he tells me of another place he'd like to visit. Then he finds a way to make it happen. He's an example to me that God decides when we're done. It's not up to us to say, "That dream is over. It's just not possible anymore." With God all things are possible (see Matt. 19:26).

It's only too late for our dreams when we decide to write "The End" on our stories and close the book. As an anonymous quote my mom has on her refrigerator reads, "Never place a period where God has placed a comma."

Lie #4: "I Don't Deserve to Dream"

The tears trickle down her face, and she reaches for a tissue. "But you don't understand," she says with a sigh. "I've messed up so much. The life I have now is a consequence of the choices I've made. I don't get to have the desires of my heart—I'm paying for what I've done."

I reach out my arms to her and try to wrap her up in words of grace too. "Your dreams aren't about you," I say. "They're about what God wants to do in his kingdom through you. And he'll use anyone—just look at some of the characters in the Bible! If adultery, murder, and deception didn't stop him, then what you've done isn't going to either!"

She laughs and looks up with a smile and perhaps just a bit of hope too.

Yes, you should pay for what you've done. So should I. But that's the beauty of the cross: Jesus took that payment for us. We may live with consequences, but we're not sentenced to a life of unfulfilled dreams and desires. Jesus said, "It is finished" on the cross so that we don't ever have to say the same in our lives. We are never finished—only fallen. If you've made mistakes, then do what you can to make them right, ask forgiveness, and get back up.

Listen closely, my friend. You have not been disqualified from dreaming. No matter what you've done. No matter what choices you've made. No matter what's in your past. Dreams are about the future. We can say these words with the apostle Paul, a man who had murder, persecuting Christians, and a long list of other sins in his past: "But one thing I do: Forgetting what is behind and straining toward what is ahead, I press on toward the goal to win the prize for which God has called me heavenward in Christ Jesus" (Phil. 3:13–14).

Right here, right now, take back your God-given permission to dream and to follow the desires of your heart.

Lie #5: "I Don't Have Time"

I bump into her in an aisle of the local grocery store. I ask, "How's that dream we talked about going?"

She brushes a stray hair from in front of her eyes and sighs. "I really want to move forward with it, but I'm just so busy. Maybe when things get back to normal." I nod my head with understanding since I've said the same thing many times too. And it can certainly be legitimate.

Yet at some point we have to decide that the time for our dream is now—no matter what. Because in today's world, normal never comes. There's always more to do, another "when I . . ." to check off the list, another urgent demand to be met.

If the enemy can't make us deny our dreams, then it seems his next tactic is to make us delay them. Yes, there are seasons for waiting and being still because that's what God has asked us to do. I'm not talking about those. I'm speaking of the seasons when we let procrastination get the best of us (and we all do sometimes). It's a great way to hold back the fear that inevitably comes when we actually pursue our dreams rather than just talking about them.

So, ladies, let's have a little heart-to-heart confession time. Because the truth is, as the old saying goes, "There is always enough time in our day to do God's will." If that dream in your heart really is from him and his timing is now, then somewhere in your schedule there's space to make it happen.

Hard? Always. But so is living with regret.

You don't have to pursue your dream perfectly. You only have to do what you can. Efforts that fall short of your expectations are still always better than none at all. God can fill in the gaps.

Only you know if this really is the season for your dream, and only you can decide to truly pursue it. I love the biblical phrase "for such a time as this" (Esther 4:14) because it says so much about right here, right now. It's not "for such a time as then" or "for such a time as that." It speaks to today and the moments passing us by that will not come again.

You have time. I have time.

If it's not the season for your dream, then embrace that and focus on what God has in front of you now. That's honorable and faith-filled too.

But if it's your moment to take that step, make that leap, birth that dream, then go for it with all your heart and don't let anything or anyone block your way (or your schedule).

The Truth That Sets Us Free to Dream

She walks through the door with a smile on her face. It seems like she's standing a bit taller, moving a bit faster, glowing with an inner light. "The lies were so loud," she confesses. "But I just kept pressing in to Jesus until his voice was even louder."

The lies don't ever go away. Every step of your dream, they will chase you. It doesn't mean that you're not spiritual enough or you're on the wrong path. It just means that "our struggle is not against flesh and blood, but against the rulers, against the authorities, against the powers of this dark world and against the spiritual forces of evil in the heavenly realms" (Eph. 6:12). You are in a battle—expect opposition.

But remember this too: You have already been promised victory. Nothing can separate you from God's love. And when you're following hard after his heart, nothing can separate you from his will either.

As I write this, I'm looking at a small print by Dee at Red Letter Words that says, "She knew that many were the plans in her heart but that God's purpose would prevail" (paraphrased from Prov. 19:21). I need that plaque every single day. It reminds me that my role isn't results—it's obedience. It's the willingness to take the risks and let God do the rest.

You, my friend, are a dreamer. Whether you know it or not. Whether you're at the beginning of your journey or sitting exhausted in the Promised Land after battling to possess it.

You, my friend, are an Esther—chosen and placed in your generation *for such a time as this.* Your life matters even more than you know, and you are making a difference even more than you see.

You, my friend, are a warrior. Every day you dare to dream, you fight back the darkness and add a little more light to the world. When you keep your heart open, the kingdom wins.

And you, my friend, are on an adventure that's going to take you to places beyond what you could have even imagined. Places with joy, tears, glory, grace, and most of all, *more of Jesus* with each step you take.

The "more" your heart has always hoped for is what God has wanted to give you all along.

So let's get going.

Go Deeper Guide

(Download a printable version with lines for writing at www.holley gerth.com on the "Books & More" page.)

1. What were some of your childhood dreams?

2. What messages were given to you about dreaming (both positive and negative) as you were growing up?

3. "Every dream or desire you have that comes from God is an invitation for more intimacy with him." Do you agree or disagree with this statement? Why?

4. What's one of your God-sized dreams?

5. Which of the lies listed in this chapter did you most identify with? What's the truth God wants to speak to your heart instead?

6. "Our struggle is not against flesh and blood, but against the rulers, against the authorities, against the powers of this dark world and against the spiritual forces of evil in the heavenly realms" (Eph. 6:12). What's one thing standing between you and the dream God has placed in your heart right now? What's a way to overcome it?

7. Think of someone in your life who is pursuing a God-sized dream. What's their story? What have you learned from them?

— *Dream It. Do It.* —

Create a vision board that expresses your God-sized dream visually. You can use photos, clippings from magazines, or images you find online. It can be any size or shape—just as long as it inspires you as you look at it.

2

You Might Have a
God-Sized Dream If . . .

"But how do I know it's not just me? What if I'm just making this up?"

These are the most common questions I hear about God-sized dreams and chasing "more" in our lives. We want to please God. We want to be purposeful. So we worry the whisper within our hearts is somehow not really from him after all.

Is there a way to be sure?

Perhaps not 100 percent. But after talking with thousands of women about their God-sized dreams, I've found there do seem to be some filters you can put yours through to be more certain than before.

You Might Have a God-Sized Dream If It Fits with Your Strengths

She describes the new opportunity that has suddenly appeared in her life. "I really want to do this, but I'm just not sure. What should I think about when I make this decision?" she asks.

I respond, "Well, first let's look at who you are and how well this fits with the way God has made you."

"Really?" she replies. "I always thought about the external aspects—pay, location, opportunities for advancement—but not about the internal ones like who I am. That sounds better!"

The God-sized dreams in our lives usually fit pretty tightly with who he made us to be. Just think of Jesus telling Peter, "Don't be afraid; from now on you will fish for people" (Luke 5:10). What was his current occupation? Fishing. Yes, Peter applied his skills in a completely new way on a totally different adventure, but the core characteristics (tenacity, risk taking, making it through storms) would serve him well when he answered yes to this God-sized dream.

You are who you are for a reason. God could have designed you in any way that he wanted. After all, he spoke the world into being. Customizing you wasn't a challenge. So why would he create you in a way that *didn't* match up with the biggest dreams he has for your life?

One of the myths that tends to derail us from our dreams is the idea that to truly be spiritual we shouldn't really enjoy what we're called to do. We sit in church and hope God doesn't "call me to a poor tribe in Africa." Well, most likely that isn't going to happen. And if it does, you're probably the kid who sat enraptured by the stories of overseas missions in Sunday school, who loved learning about different cultures, who had a knack for making friends in unlikely places. The apostles weren't the only ones whose callings remained consistent with how they were created.

David the shepherd went on to guide the flock of God's people.

Saul, a zealous leader for the Jews, turned into Paul, a zealous leader for Jesus.

Moses, raised in the house of Pharaoh, eventually stood before royalty and rescued the Israelites.

Why would God be motivated to put you in a position where the way he wired you isn't utilized?

Your strengths aren't always arrows pointing directly to your God-sized dreams, but many times that is the case. If you read my first book, *You're Already Amazing*, then you should already be familiar with your strengths. If not, then let's take a quick look again here. Even if you have done this work already, it can be helpful to review it again.

A strength is a personal characteristic that can be used on behalf of God in service to others. Usually they're present throughout our lives but can be enhanced through experience or training. Strengths are part of *who we are* while skills are more about *what we do.*

— *Find Your Strengths: 5 Minutes* —

Circle three strengths that apply to you.

○ Adventurous	○ Fair	○ Organized
○ Athletic	○ Flexible	○ Positive
○ Brave	○ Forgiving	○ Protective
○ Calm	○ Friendly	○ Reflective
○ Capable	○ Frugal	○ Reliable
○ Caring	○ Funny	○ Resilient
○ Cheerful	○ Gentle	○ Resourceful
○ Considerate	○ Gracious	○ Responsible
○ Courageous	○ Hardworking	○ Sensitive
○ Creative	○ Helpful	○ Servant-hearted
○ Dedicated	○ Honest	○ Spontaneous
○ Determined	○ Hospitable	○ Supportive
○ Devoted	○ Imaginative	○ Talented
○ Easygoing	○ Intelligent	○ Thoughtful
○ Efficient	○ Kind	○ Trustworthy
○ Encouraging	○ Loving	○ Warm
○ Energetic	○ Loyal	○ Wise
	○ Mature	○ *Add your own...*

If you're still wondering if the words you circled are strengths, then you can put them through the STRENGTH test:

Service	*Does it help me serve God and others?*
Time	*Has it been present throughout much of my life?*
Relationships	*Do others see this?*
Energy	*Do I feel energized when I'm living this way?*
Natural	*Does this come naturally to me most of the time? Or do I know God has intentionally developed this in me even though it doesn't?*
Glory	*Does God ultimately get the glory from it?*
Trials	*Even in hard times, does it usually come through somehow?*
Heart	*Does this really feel like a core part of who I am?*

What are the parts of who you are that consistently bring God glory and bless others? What are the moments in your day when you find yourself saying, "This is why I'm on earth"? In the busyness of life, we can miss those clues or dismiss them as not being valid. We tell ourselves that surely a God-sized dream has to be more spiritual, be harder, or resemble what our neighbor is doing.

But like we talked about earlier, God-sized dreams aren't one size fits all. You and your God-sized dream are perfectly paired by the One who created you both.

You Might Have a God-Sized Dream If Your Skills and Experiences Have Prepared You for It

She describes her life to me—work, family, church. At the end I smile and say, "You always find a way to teach wherever you are, don't you?" She pauses and then softly laughs. "Yes, I guess I do! So starting a new class for pregnant teen moms makes a whole lot of sense, doesn't it?"

Just as God crafts who we are in specific ways, he also gives us certain skills and experiences. Think of them as practice for your dream. They may not be exactly the same. For example, the woman above didn't have a career as a teacher, but she found herself stepping into that role every chance she got. The skills and experiences she gained as she did so provided preparation for the God-sized dream she was now considering.

When we hear Sunday school stories, they often begin at the "big moment" of a hero's life. Yet when we look back over his or her life, it becomes clear that God has been laying the groundwork for years. For example, we've all heard of how God spoke to Moses from a burning bush in the desert and asked him to lead the people of Israel out of slavery. It seems that's where the story begins. But by that time Moses is quite old! What has he spent his life doing so far? He grew up in Pharaoh's household and then he became a shepherd—both involved skills and experiences that would serve him well in this new mission.

A skill is a strength expressed in a specific way that builds up others and benefits the kingdom.

What are some of the skills you consistently use?

— *Find Your Skills: 5 Minutes* —

Circle three skills that apply to you.

○ Acting	○ Decorating	○ Persevering
○ Adapting	○ Empathizing	○ Persuading
○ Administering	○ Encouraging	○ Planning
○ Advising	○ Evaluating	○ Prioritizing
○ Analyzing	○ Expressing	○ Problem-solving
○ Appreciating	○ Growing	○ Protecting
○ Assembling	○ Guiding	○ Relating
○ Believing	○ Helping	○ Responding
○ Building	○ Imagining	○ Risk taking
○ Challenging	○ Influencing	○ Serving
○ Cleaning	○ Initiating	○ Sharing
○ Collaborating	○ Leading	○ Speaking
○ Communicating	○ Listening	○ Supporting
○ Connecting	○ Maintaining	○ Teaching
○ Constructing	○ Managing	○ Training
○ Cooking	○ Motivating	○ Writing
○ Coordinating	○ Negotiating	○ *Add your own . . .*
○ Counseling	○ Nurturing	
○ Creating	○ Organizing	

Whatever skills you use that seem to be lining up with your God-sized dreams are the areas where you should continue seeking to grow. Yes, we have some natural ability in these areas, but research has shown that practice, education, and experience help us hone our skills so that we can do more than just use them—we can master them. You have been entrusted with certain ways of making a difference in the world, and it's up to you to make the most of them during your time on earth.

Our experiences allow us to apply our strengths and skills. They also show us more about what we're *not* called to do. What are some of the significant experiences in your life that have brought you to this God-sized dream? What do they tell you about your God-sized dreams? Write your answer below (examples: education, jobs, significant turning points, lessons learned).

_____

_____

_____

When we have a God-sized dream on our hearts, it can be easy to hurry past where we are now. What we're doing may seem like a "waste of time" when we can see the vision ahead so clearly. Yet where you are today may be exactly the training you need for the place where God wants to take you tomorrow.

If you think, "I don't have any skills or experiences related to this dream," then take some time to consider whether it's wise to get some before you step into this new phase. Yes, there are times when God wants us to simply go for it, but more often, he prepares us for what's ahead.

Most likely you have already been doing something related to your dream. Maybe in a different place. Maybe in a different way. Maybe with different people. Look for the threads of God's work in your life and how he's tying them together into your dream.

You Might Have a God-Sized Dream If You Can't Think about Anything Else

She rubs the sleep from her eyes, yawns widely, and grins. "I had a new idea last night, and I got so excited I could hardly sleep!"

"Tell me all about it," I say with a smile.

God-sized dreams make their way into our hearts, homes, nights, and every other area. Sometimes they feel like an insistent knocking on a door within us. We can't get any rest until we let them inside.

While this can be a bit bothersome at times, it's also a tremendous gift. God-sized dreams take lots of energy. And energy comes from passion. This isn't a feeling of "Well, one day I might want to. . . ." My friend and fellow writer Lisa-Jo Baker described it this way in a conversation once: "I wake up every morning, and it's like Jesus has his hand on the back of my neck, and he's gently pushing me forward and saying, 'Go, girl, *go.*'"

We all have ideas that cross our minds. But this is much deeper, wilder. It doesn't feel like we have a choice but rather that *we have been chosen.* Someone is calling our name deep inside, and ignoring that voice is almost impossible.

Yes, sometimes we may bury that calling for a season or try to walk away. But in the quiet moments, it keeps coming back. It pulls at us and demands our attention. Few places in life are as miserable as where you find yourself when you are actively running away from your God-sized dream. Remember Jonah? Called to preach in Nineveh, he hightails it out of town in a different direction. He winds up in the belly of a whale for three days. We may not find ourselves in such extreme circumstances, but the feeling of discomfort is one to which anyone who has tried to sidestep a dream can relate.

Why are God-sized dreams so compelling? Because we powerfully experience God's presence in our lives through them. It's not about the destination. It's not what we will get if we complete the dream. It's about a relationship.

As the Israelites crossed the desert, the cloud of God's presence hovered above the tabernacle and led them along the way. When the cloud moved, they moved. When the cloud stayed, they stayed.

If God is calling you to a dream, then that's where his presence is in your life. You are not being drawn to the dream—you are being drawn to the giver of it.

The pursuit of any God-sized dream is ultimately the pursuit of the One who placed it within you. It's like a homing beacon for your heart.

You Might Have a God-Sized Dream If You're Scared Silly

She sends me an email that says, "I want to move forward but I'm totally scared. Maybe I should wait until I feel a bit more courageous."

I click the keys in response. "Friend, if this is what God is calling you to, then do it now. The fear is never going away."

As human beings, we were wired by God in a wonderful way for survival. Our bodies automatically tell us, "If there's a threat, then you should fight it or avoid it." In most cases, that works really well. But when it comes to God-sized dreams, it's very different. We'll spend a whole chapter on fear later, but for now I just want to dispel the myth that fear means your dream isn't from God. You are human, and when you decide to take a risk (and every dream is a risk), then you will always feel fear. You have a choice about what to do in response to that fear, but feeling it in the first place is often more of a confirmation of your dream than a sign you should walk away from it.

I would even take it a step further and say that if you don't feel any fear at all, then it's probably not a God-sized dream. Our God is big, wild, and far beyond our understanding and limits. He tells us, "My thoughts are not your thoughts, neither are your ways my ways" (Isa. 55:8). That means whenever he asks us to do something, it is almost always out of our comfort zones. It usually doesn't make sense ("Hey, Noah, build an ark"). It most often involves a lot of change ("Hey, disciples, leave everything you know and follow me"). It always stretches our faith ("Hey, Esther, go before the king to save your people even though it may cost your life").

What makes you afraid? I don't mean the "Eek! A spider!" kind of fear. I mean the idea that pops into your mind that makes your heart start to pound and your skin begin to sweat, *and yet* you are strangely drawn to it anyway. That just might be your God-sized dream.

The moment that changes everything is when we decide to fear God more than we fear what may happen.

You Might Have a God-Sized Dream If People Think You're Crazy

My cell phone rings. "Can you meet me for dinner? I just shared my idea, and everyone looked at me like I'm out of my mind. I need some encouragement!"

I reply, "Sounds like it went great! I'll tell you why when we get to the restaurant."

When our heart beats with passion for an idea, we quickly assume that everyone else feels the same way. We have a vision and we believe that all those around us should be able to see it just as clearly as we do.

At one point in my life, I had a God-sized dream that I longed to bring into reality. I needed an entire team of people to get on board in order for that to happen. I would share a few sentences in a meeting and get blank stares. I felt frustrated and alone. My life coach, Denise Martin, gently corrected me. "Holley, they can't see what you do. You are the vision carrier. You have to share it with them in a way they can understand. Don't assume that they have this dream too. God has given it to you." When she said those words to me, a lightbulb went on inside. I hadn't been effectively communicating because I thought that everyone else must know and see what I did. Once I changed my approach, people did get on board—although throughout the process I still remained the one with the most passion. That didn't mean I failed. It simply meant God had entrusted that particular dream *to me*.

If you have a God-sized dream, it's natural to want everyone around you to "get it" in the same way, right away. But that probably isn't going to happen. If your idea takes some explaining, that's a good sign. As we talked about before, God's thoughts are not our thoughts. God-sized dreams often don't make sense in our world.

Ask yourself, "Who has to be completely on board with this dream?" This should be a *very* small list. Carefully and intentionally communicate the dream to these people. Then go ahead and let everyone else think you're crazy. You don't need buy-in from all your co-workers, your entire Bible study, your high school friends on Facebook, and the checkout girl at the grocery store. Sometimes we delay our dreams because we think that everyone's approval is confirmation. (*Psst—it's not.*)

If you have prayed, planned, and sought wise counsel from a small group of people in your life, then go ahead and move forward. Expect the blank stares. Anticipate the questioning of your sanity or stability. Be prepared for the questions—and even opposition. Then smile, nod, and move ahead anyway. It's not your job to make your God-sized dream make sense to everyone. They'll see it soon enough when God brings it into being.

You Might Have a God-Sized Dream If It's Bigger Than You Are

"I just have this sense that it's not really about me at all," she says softly. "I get to play a part, but I'm not the main character in this story."

We eat, sleep, breathe our God-sized dreams, and yet in many ways they have very little to do with us. As Rick Warren famously said at the beginning of *The Purpose Driven Life*, "It's not about you."[1]

God-sized dreams are not about your personal fulfillment.

God-sized dreams are not about making you happy.

God-sized dreams are not about filling the empty spaces in your soul.

Yes, all along the way you will be tempted to make your dream about those things. That's just part of being human. But ultimately you know that the calling in your soul is about more, so much more than anything you might hope to gain from it.

If those are the *only* reasons you're pursuing the dream, then it's time to hit the Pause button. Sometimes what we think are God-sized dreams are actually neon signs flashing an unmet need in our lives. Let me tell you a secret: *your dream will not fill you up inside*. Yes, there will be some wonderful moments. Yes, there will be joy along the way. But it will also be hard, even exhausting, and push you to your limits at times.

If you're thinking, "When I _____ (fill in the blank with your dream here), then I will be _____ (fill in the blank with your unmet need here, such as 'happy')," then you may have some more work to do within your heart. Because your dream is not about you.

It's about the God who gave it to you.

It's about the kingdom he's building in this world.

It's about the body of Christ.

His plan is for you to benefit as well—everything he does is for your good. But the dreams he places within our hearts are always about a bigger picture, the grander story he's writing all through history.

If your dream sometimes makes you feel very small, that's a good thing. God-sized dreams can feel like gazing up at the stars at night. We are reminded that in this great big universe, our little world is just one piece of an endless, eternal puzzle.

The good news is that you don't have to be big to have God-sized dreams, because in him you are enough. It's not the size of the dream or dreamer that matters. Those stars that make us feel small were spoken into being by the One who walks beside you, lives within you, calls your name, and dares you to dream beyond yourself.

You Might Have a God-Sized Dream If It Aligns with God's Purposes

She sets the Bible on the couch and leans back. "I know we're studying something else, but all I can see when I look in here is my God-sized dream!"

We've been using the word *if* to talk about these possibilities. But when it comes to this one, it's a must. God-sized dreams always align with his purposes. And Scripture shows us what those are and how we can live them out in our generation.

Does it talk about your dream specifically? Probably not. You're not going to find a page that says, "I want you to open a cozy bakery so that you can feed the hungry hearts of women at the same time you're feeding their bodies too." But when we look at the broader principles that dream embodies—service, reaching out, loving God and people—then it clearly can be something that advances the kingdom of God.

Not all God-sized dreams are super-spiritual. Many are practical. Some are loud and out in the open. Others are quiet and hidden. Yours might keep you at home or send you to the farthest corner of the earth. It may involve face-to-face interactions or clicking the keys on your computer.

Just look around you. Creation is full of variety, and each new dream is another aspect of what God is expressing in the world. Yet all those different expressions point back to the same purposes, the same desires of his heart.

God-sized dreams always align biblically. If your desire takes you outside the boundaries God has set, then it's not from him. But within those boundaries, we have so much freedom! Jesus tells a parable of a master who leaves his servants in charge of different amounts of "talents," which was the word for money in those days (see Matt. 25:14–30). You're probably familiar with how all three use what they've been given differently and get varying responses from the master as a result. What intrigues me about this story is that the master doesn't give specific instructions. He doesn't leave a detailed to-do list.

Sometimes we want to know exactly what God wants us to do before we move ahead with a dream. And yes, he does promise to guide us through his Holy Spirit. Yet there also seems to be an element of letting us choose how we will invest our lives. He has given you certain things—strengths, skills, experiences. What will you do with them? As long as what we do honors the Master, then most likely we have the freedom to pursue it.

If we make the wrong decision, there is grace and God is able to redirect as well as redeem. What's more dangerous is doing nothing at all, as the third servant who buries his talents quickly learns upon the master's return. Doing nothing isn't the safest or most godly option. God never rebukes anyone in Scripture for making a mistake when their sincere desire is to please him.

If what you long to do fits with what God wants too, then you have freedom to move forward in faith. He will get you where he wants you to go in the end—even if you take a few detours along the way.

You Might Have a God-Sized Dream If It's Harder Than You Thought It Would Be

She sighs. "I know this is what God wanted me to do. But nothing is turning out the way I imagined. Did I mess up?"

I give her a hug and say into her ear, "You, brave and beautiful girl, are right where you should be."

When we first discover our God-sized dream, all we can see is the perfect vision, the desired reality. We don't know about the desert in between where we are and the Promised Land. It catches us by surprise when there are delays, difficulties, obstacles to overcome. This is where most God-sized dreams fall by the wayside. When we hit the hard part, we want a fresh start. But there will *always* be challenges.

We're living out our dreams in an imperfect, fallen world and connecting with imperfect, fallen people along the way (including ourselves). Something is bound to go wrong. We're going to goof up. The plans we so meticulously created will sometimes not come to pass. *And that's okay.*

If you're in a place where it feels like what you've undertaken is much harder than you imagined, take heart. If God has called you to this, then he will get you through it. Here's a secret: *God-sized*

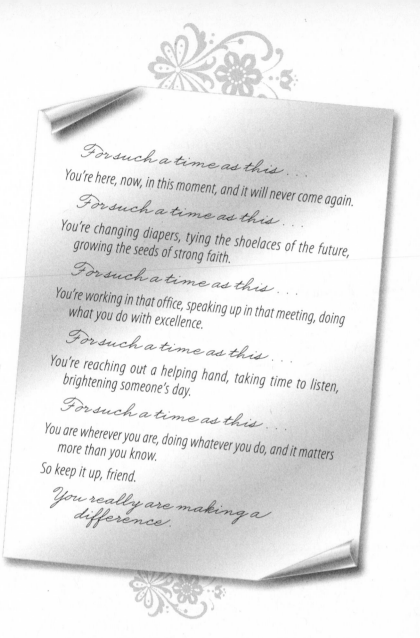

For such a time as this . . .
You're here, now, in this moment, and it will never come again.

For such a time as this . . .
You're changing diapers, tying the shoelaces of the future, growing the seeds of strong faith.

For such a time as this . . .
You're working in that office, speaking up in that meeting, doing what you do with excellence.

For such a time as this . . .
You're reaching out a helping hand, taking time to listen, brightening someone's day.

For such a time as this . . .
You are wherever you are, doing whatever you do, and it matters more than you know.

So keep it up, friend.

You really are making a difference.

---

dreams are invincible when we're obedient. He always wins in the end. Does that mean the result will look like what we had in mind at the beginning? Most likely not. But whatever purpose God has for your dream, he will bring to pass. *Your job is to not quit no matter what happens.* God will take care of the rest.

You Might Have a God-Sized Dream If It Leads to Joy

She's talking so fast I can hardly understand her. "We did it!" she declares. "After all that time and struggle, it actually happened!"

I clap my hands and we clink our coffee cups together in victory. *At last.*

Yes, God-sized dreams are hard. But they are also full of joy. Not the "everything is sunshine and roses" kind of happy but the deep satisfaction that comes from knowing you're doing what you're called to do.

When you make it to the Promised Land, there's simply nothing like it in the whole wide world. It makes everything—all the trials, detours, hard moments—fade into the background. You are here. You finished well. You completed the task.

There's joy along the way too. You'll see God coming through in ways you never could have imagined. You'll find out you're stronger than you ever thought possible. You'll see you're loved and supported more than you could have known.

Your God-sized dream is meant to bring your soul joy. It's intended to be a place where you experience deep intimacy with God and rejoice with him.

If you don't ever feel joy when pursuing your dream, then it may be that another motivation is actually prompting you to move forward. When we try to use our dreams to get rid of our insecurity, to earn love, or to meet needs in a way God never intended, then we don't feel joy—we feel desperation, hopelessness, and endless frustration. God will not let us be satisfied with anything but him. If there's no joy in your dream, ask him what your heart is really looking for instead.

When those times of joy do come, it's important to celebrate them. Those of us who are dreamers can rush on to the next adventure so quickly. But there's time for stopping, savoring, looking back on the journey, and reveling in what God has done in and through you.

God-sized dreams lead us to joy—and to the Giver of it.

Final Thoughts

God-sized dreams are mysterious. We catch a glimpse of where we're headed only to have the vision disappear like a mist on an early morning. God-sized dreams don't cooperate with checklists or agendas. They defy our timing and often our logic. The more we seek to control them, the quicker they slip beyond our grasp.

And yet we can't let them go. We're compelled to continue the pursuit.

I believe God lets it be that way, even makes it that way, because it draws us closer to him. Our dreams may be elusive, but he is ever-present. Our dreams may challenge our sense of safety, but he is our ultimate security. Our dreams may catch our interest, but he's the One who relentlessly chases our hearts.

You don't have to be sure about your dream before you move forward. You only have to be certain of the One who is whispering to you that it's time to come with him to a new place. Just take the next step. And then another.

Do you really have a God-sized dream?

Only God knows.

And sometimes the only way you'll know is to go with him.

It turns out most dreams aren't delivered to our door—they're discovered along the way.

Go Deeper Guide

(Download a printable version with lines for writing at www.holley gerth.com on the "Books & More" page.)

1. What are three of your strengths?

2. What are three of your skills?

3. Describe a moment in your life when you found yourself saying, "This is why I'm on earth."

4. Draw a time line of your life showing significant experiences that have helped bring you to where you are now.

5. What else might you need to do to prepare for the God-sized dream in your life?

6. Which of the "You might have a God-sized dream if . . ." statements from this chapter did you identify with most? Why?

7. "The joy of the LORD is your strength" (Neh. 8:10). What brings you joy, energizes you, and makes you feel closest to God? How is that a part of your God-sized dreams?

— Dream It. Do It. —

Sometimes those around us can see our strengths more clearly than we do because we tend to be so hard on ourselves. This week ask at least one other person in your life to share three strengths they see in you. You can do so face-to-face, on the phone, or through email.

The **Heart** of a Dreamer

I've met thousands of dreamers. Some are so quiet you can barely hear them in a crowded room. Some are so loud that as soon as they speak, everyone turns their way. Some are young, just starting the journey of their lives. Others have experienced decades of dreaming and are looking forward to leaving a legacy. Some are stay-at-home moms. Others are world-traveling businesswomen. Some don't wear makeup and love the rugged outdoors. Others have every nail done to perfection and think a day at the spa is the ultimate adventure. Some are right-brained, creative types. Others are left-brained, practical thinkers. Dreamers show up in every personality profile, economic level, geographic location, and every other variable you can imagine.

God loves variety.

And yet after meeting all of these dreamers, all of these wonderful women, I've noticed one aspect of who they are is remarkably the same.

Their hearts.

I have a strong feeling that if you've made it this far in this book, your heart is much the same too. So let's talk about you, dear dreamer, and what lies within you that makes you so different and yet so similar to many of your sisters.

God-Sized Dreamers Are Faithful Where They Are

In the Old Testament, God sent the prophet Samuel to anoint a new king (see 1 Sam. 16:1–13). Samuel arrived at a household with lots of sons. Good-looking ones. Tall ones. Impressive ones. But as each passed by, Samuel sensed that he had not yet found the one God sent him for. "Don't you have any more sons?" he asked. The father was dismissive. "Oh yeah, there's one more. But he's the youngest. Not even worth meeting. He's out in the fields with the sheep." Samuel demanded that the final son be brought, and it turned out he was God's choice all along. The shepherd boy David became the king. And God showed us this truth: "People look at the outward appearance, but the LORD looks at the heart" (1 Sam. 16:7).

David, the overlooked one, captured the gaze of God. Under seas of stars, out in the desert with no one around but a few sheep, he learned to pray, be brave, and dream with God. I wonder if he had any sense on those starry nights of what was coming, what God was preparing him for in the vastness of that quiet place. He learned to be faithful right where God had him, and that enabled God to place him exactly where he was supposed to be.

Where are you today?

Maybe you're in a place where it seems no one sees you and it feels like what you do doesn't matter. Maybe you feel like your potential isn't being used. What are you doing taking care of a few sheep when you sense inside that you're made for so much more? But you're being faithful anyway. You're serving, learning, loving, growing.

You aren't settling for the status quo, and yet you are choosing to thrive where you are today as well. Dreams can be seductive. They can make us trade our today for an unknown future. They can turn our thoughts away from what's right in front of us.

But not you. You're a God-sized dreamer, and that means you can make a difference anywhere. When Jesus said, "Whoever can be trusted with very little can also be trusted with much" (Luke 16:10), he meant folks like you. Listen, my friend, you are seen. You are watched by the One who spoke the world into being, who numbers every hair on your head and knows each care in your heart. If all those details matter to him, don't you think what you're doing right here, right now does too?

What you're doing isn't small if it's what God has for you. It's big. And it just may lead to something even bigger.

Make the most of where you are right now. Give everything you have. God has so much in store for you. And he has so much for you right here too.

You are a God-sized dreamer, and you are faithful right where you are. In case you haven't heard it lately, thank you. Thank you for what you do. Especially when it seems no one sees. Especially when you wonder if it matters at all. It does. And you do too.

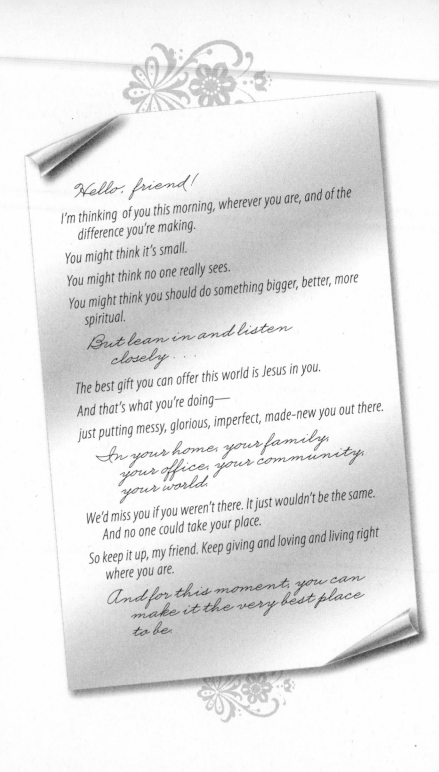

Hello, friend!

I'm thinking of you this morning, wherever you are, and of the difference you're making.

You might think it's small.

You might think no one really sees.

You might think you should do something bigger, better, more spiritual.

But lean in and listen closely . . .

The best gift you can offer this world is Jesus in you.

And that's what you're doing—

just putting messy, glorious, imperfect, made-new you out there.

In your home, your family, your office, your community, your world.

We'd miss you if you weren't there. It just wouldn't be the same. And no one could take your place.

So keep it up, my friend. Keep giving and loving and living right where you are.

And for this moment, you can make it the very best place to be.

God-Sized Dreamers Keep Their Hearts Open

I flip on the television and yet another tale of woe spills into the living room. I see crossed arms, bitter faces, sharp glances that cut like swords. If I could peer into these hearts, I would most likely see a Closed sign hanging on the door.

I switch to another channel in time to catch the story of a woman in her eighties. She tells of a hard life, deep needs, hurts that would stop many of us in our tracks. But instead she beams. She tells of God's goodness and of her dream. She's feeding 150 people a day with what she's prepared with her two hands. And what she'd love more than anything in the world is to be able to do so for twice as many. The sign on her heart says Open in neon, glittering joy.

"In this world you will have trouble," said Jesus (John 16:33). And we do. No one escapes this life without times when tears slip down our cheeks and hope flees from our hearts. We all face loss, disappointment, and failure. That's why Jesus followed those words with three more: "But take heart!" In other words, keep the Open sign up no matter what. Don't let this world make you shut down and lock up what you're meant to share.

If you're a God-sized dreamer, that's the choice you've made. Maybe no one has ever said this to you, but I want to do so now:

If you have gone through hurts in this life and you have kept your heart open, then you are a remarkable person. And if you are reading this book and daring to still dream, then that's exactly what you've done. You are brave, strong, and beautiful. You have made a choice that few do. In the face of difficulties, you have managed to guard what matters most and to press ahead with a resilience that makes you a force to be reckoned with for the kingdom. Thank you for making that choice. Thank you for keeping your heart open. The world needs more people like you.

It's easy to decide to look out for number one. It's easy to push aside our dreams and settle for what's safest. It's easy to plaster a smile on our faces and never let anyone really get close to us. But it's hard to keep your heart open for a lifetime. It's hard to really let love be part of who you are each day. It's hard to keep risking, hoping, and praying even in the face of the impossible.

You might do all of those things without pausing to consider what a miracle it is that you do. It's not "normal" to live that way. In our world, it's much more common to close down and become cold, cynical, and bitter.

You are a light, my friend. Because when your heart is open, it's Jesus who shines out. And that glow illuminates the path to the dreams he's given you too.

God–Sized Dreamers Encourage Others

Caught up in the moment, she didn't notice the little girl behind her. As the woman's hands moved skillfully to combine flour, sugar, and eggs into a delicious confection, small eyes watched and little hands mixed the same invisible ingredients in a toy bowl. Years later, that little girl now grown would stand at her kitchen counter and think of the woman who inspired her to learn to cook.

Who's watching you?

If you're a dreamer, I can guarantee there are eyes on you. You may not see them, you may not even know, but you are encouraging and inspiring someone. In a world where dreamers are rare, you stand out whether you want to or not. You help others to listen harder to Jesus, to take leaps of faith, to live with passion.

You do this without words by the choices you make, the desires you pursue, the joy on your face.

Maybe you do the same with words too. I wouldn't be surprised a bit to learn that you have the spiritual gift of encouragement. Many dreamers do. If so, you're probably verbally helping others along. You cheer them up, cheer them on, and help them take another step when they feel like they want to quit. You notice the desires of their hearts, and you care about seeing them come true. God-sized dreaming is contagious, and you'd love for everyone around you to catch it.

You may think, "Oh, that's just who I am. And everyone else is like that too." Listen here, girl: you offer a rare gift to the world by being an encourager. Kind words are becoming an endangered species. A friend who will rejoice in your successes as much as her own is a treasure indeed. A woman who will say, "Yes, with God you can do this" is a beautiful and hard-to-find wonder.

Being a God-sized dreamer isn't just beneficial to you. It makes a difference to so many around you too. Meredith marketing group did an intriguing study about "Gamma Women."[2] They explain that there's a shift in our society from "Alpha Women" (think prom queen) to "Gamma Women" (think Miss Congeniality). Rather than seeking to try to climb the ladder, Gammas are the hub in a center of relationships. They influence by loving, not by leaping to the top. When they experience success, they take others with them each step of the way. Does that sound like you? I imagine it does. I think all God-sized dreamers are Gammas.

You encourage others. You do so through your life, through your words, through the passion you show in pursuing your dreams. The word *encourage* actually means to give someone courage. When you're a God-sized dreamer, that's exactly what you do. When you take risks, get up from failures, seek God even when it's hard, and eventually make it to the Promised Land, you make others want to do the same.

Someone is watching you today.

God is too.

And I've got a feeling there's a lot of joy happening as they do.

God-Sized Dreamers Are Positive People

We peer at the glasses on the dinner table. In the middle of a lively conversation, the old question has come up: "Do you see the glass as half full or half empty?" One responder adds a new twist: "I don't think it's about the glass at all but instead who is filling it."

Ah, I thought. *That sounds like a God-sized dreamer.*

God-sized dreamers aren't fixated on the glass. Reality is only a part of the equation for them. What matters most is the potential—and the limitless God who lives within them.

That means God-sized dreamers can be optimists. Not the pie-in-the-sky-everything-is-perfect kind. Not the slap-on-a-silly-grin type. I mean *true optimists*. The kind who can maintain a realistic, resilient belief even in the middle of difficult circumstances.

You are one of those people. You may even have had others tease you a bit about it. But let me tell you, being a true optimist in the world today is no small feat. Negativity is far easier than perseverance. Criticism is simpler than encouragement. Saying the world is going to end can be far more convenient than daring to make a difference in it.

That doesn't mean you believe life is all sunshine and roses. You've seen your share of hard times. You can bet there are more to come. But in the middle of it all, you keep holding on to the

God who will not let you go. You trust that he will come through for you. You don't let the embers of your dreams die but instead fan them into flame again and again.

Optimism doesn't come naturally to any of us. We're simply not wired that way. If you choose to focus on what is good, true, and lovely, then you've made a deliberate, difficult choice to do so. Others may think that you're one of those "naturally happy" people, but I imagine underneath it I would find some serious faith backed up by hard work and self-control.

Thank you for being a true optimist. Thank you for continuing to believe even in the face of doubt, criticism, or discouragement. Thank you for not sitting in the dark cave of despair but instead choosing to mine all of the diamonds out of where you are.

Research has shown realistic optimists make more of a difference in the world than pessimists. They also tend to be more successful. As Theodore Roosevelt said:

> It's not the critic who counts, not the man who points out how the strong man stumbled, or when the doer of deeds could have done better. The credit belongs to the man who is actually in the arena; whose face is marred by dust and sweat and blood; who strives valiantly; who errs and comes short again and again; who knows the great enthusiasms, the great devotions and spends himself in a worthy cause; who at the best, knows in the end the triumph of high achievement; and who at the worst if he fails, at least fails while daring greatly, so that his place shall never be with those cold and timid souls who know neither victory or defeat.[3]

Keep believing. Keep fighting. Keep dreaming.

Because when you do, your glass isn't just half full—it's overflowing.

God-Sized Dreamers Don't Do It All

I slumped in my chair at church. Looking around the room, I could see women who were feeding the hungry, raising kids, reaching out in our community, and leading Bible studies—just to name a few. I felt small and inadequate. I mentally began listing ways I could compensate: *If I volunteer at the shelter once a month, join another small group, up my goals....* I quickly felt exhausted and thought perhaps God was simply fed up with me. Have you ever felt that way? I whispered a prayer for help.

About halfway through the message, our pastor pointed out into our very large congregation exactly to the place where I was sitting. "You are not the church," he said. "We are the church. You don't have to do it all." It was one of those moments when it seemed a heavenly spotlight shined on my soul, and I knew those words were for me. A smile broke out across my face, and the heaviness on my chest lifted again.

Our pastor went on to explain that we are each a part of the body of Christ and none of us can do everything. Instead we connect with each other and the Holy Spirit so we can all do exactly what we're called to. With all of us serving together, the needs get met.

If you are a God-sized dreamer, then you are saying no to some things in your life. They may be very good things. Even great things. But they are not for you. In our world today, saying yes can be so much easier than saying no. When we focus on what God has truly called us to do, we can face guilt, criticism, and misunderstanding. It's a brave choice.

Maybe no one has ever told you thank you for making those hard decisions. Thank you for not simply giving in and signing up or settling for someone else's agenda for your life. Thank you for keeping God first and listening to what he has called you to do. I know there are other voices. I know there are other opportunities. I know you could walk away. And you haven't. Good for you.

Good for us too. Because if you don't fulfill your role in the body of Christ, then no one else will. Sure, we may limp along and make it work, but it won't be the same. Like we've talked about before, you and what you contribute matter in an irreplaceable way.

God-sized dreamers don't do it all. They only do what God asks. I'm cheering you on in the yes you've said to what God has for your life. But I'm also cheering for the no you've had to say too. It's just as important and perhaps sometimes even more difficult.

Not doing it all means we can give our all to the One who matters most.

God-Sized Dreamers Feed Hungry Hearts

We carry slow cookers into the kitchen and set them on the table. Soup is ladled into bowls. Bread is neatly placed on plates. Dessert stands ready on a counter nearby. Outside hungry people wait. My community group is serving those in need tonight.

And aren't we all in need?

We wipe down the last of the surfaces a couple of hours later. I think of smiles as spoons are lifted to lips. I remember the laughter of children as they break off a piece of cookie. I recall the looks of satisfaction and fullness as folks lean back in their chairs when they're done.

Where have I seen all of that before?

I realize then that I see it every day. I see it when a co-worker pauses to offer a kind word to someone having a hard day—a little morsel of encouragement that's gobbled up with gratitude. I see it when my friend wraps her arms around her oh-so-tired little one and sees past the crankiness to the silent request for comfort and rest. I see it when a stranger on the street flashes a smile like an unexpected bit of chocolate tossed my way.

If I were with you now, I know I'd see it there too. You're feeding someone today. *Who is the hungry heart in your life?* Oh, what you do may feel small. It may feel unseen. But it matters. It's noticed by the one who said, "And if anyone gives even a cup of cold water to one of these little ones who is my disciple, truly I tell you, that person will certainly not lose their reward" (Matt. 10:42).

Just in case no one has told you lately, I want to whisper this: *Thank you for what you do. Thank you for feeding the hungry in your life in your own amazing way.*

We carry the Crock-Pots back to our cars. The fall wind feels like a whisper around us. Every last bit is gone. We didn't even get to eat, but I don't feel hungry. It turns out those whose bodies we fed did the same for our hearts in return.

And so it goes—round and round. Giving, receiving, in need, meeting needs too.

Until we're all so very full.

God-Sized Dreamers Pursue a Different Kind of Ambition

It's easy to get caught up in the comparison game. We live in a society that tells us bigger is better, more is more, and getting to the top is the ultimate achievement.

I know that kind of ambition.

She calls my name. She tells me I'm not enough yet.

She blurs my perspective so that I can't see the goodness right in front of me.

She tells me that I must try harder, work longer, go further than I am right now.

But then these words: "Make it your ambition to lead a quiet life," says the apostle Paul (1 Thess. 4:11).

What?

I don't know *this* ambition.

It sounds so much more like my Savior.

The One who calls me to smallness, to stillness, to peace and life.

The One who whispers, "You are enough in me because I am enough in you."

The One who stops me from striving, who gives me permission to slow down, who tells me my worth is already won forever.

Yes, this is the ambition I want to live with, to live *for*.

A quiet life ... *especially on the inside.*

Where all the demands and lies have been silenced, and all that's left is ambitious, outrageous, scandalous Love calling my name.

God-sized dreamers know that we're not called to be the biggest and best. We're not called to strive. Yes, in the journey of our dream we may be called into the spotlight. We may find ourselves in a position of tremendous influence. But we don't ever have to pursue it.

Our role is obedience. God's role is results. So thank you for being faithful in the quiet and small, in the unnoticed and ordinary. What you do is a beautiful sacrifice. Your life that may feel so insignificant at times may be just right for the kingdom and have an impact far beyond what the world (and you) can see with your eyes.

God-Sized Dreamers Trust His Love

God surprised me the other night. Does he ever do that to you?

As lights in the sanctuary flickered low, we paused for a moment to pray. My pastor said, "Ask God to show you what you need to see in your heart."

I waited to hear a flaw, a struggle, a secret sin unknown even to me. But the words that drifted into my heart were the last ones I expected to hear.

"Stop doubting my love."

My head snapped up.

Stop doubting my love?

Could that be right?

Yet as I glanced at my husband sitting next to me, I knew it was true. The moments in our marriage that grieve him most deeply are when, for some reason or another, I find it hard to believe he really loves me. It's not about him—it's about me. Insecurities. Past wounds. Believing I have to be perfect.

I began to understand. After all, I'm the bride of Christ, say the sacred pages. Wouldn't doubting his love grieve him too?

I whispered a prayer of repentance of receiving the love that's already mine, of opening my heart more fully to the One who pursues me relentlessly. And you too.

You are loved.

More than you know.

More than you see.

More than you've even dared to dream.

We can stop doubting.

We can be secure in Love.

"And so we know and rely on the love God has for us" (1 John 4:16).

By the time the lights went back up in the sanctuary, I felt all lit up on the inside too.

Full of joy.

Fully loved.

God-sized dreamers know they don't have to work harder and strive more to earn God's love. Instead they rest in it. Draw life from it. Let it be the fuel for their dreams and all they do. You can risk as a dreamer because you are secure in God's love. Thank you for daring to believe that what he says, he really means. Faith is believing in God, but it's also believing—only because of Jesus—that he also believes in us.

God-Sized Dreamers Embrace Enough

I sometimes look in the mirror or at my life, see all I am, then say, "Not good enough."

You too?

And yet . . .

God saw all that he had made (that means people too), and then he said, "Very good" (see Gen. 1:31).

It seems scandalous to believe that's true. Yet who am I to argue with the One who spoke the stars into place, who spread the seas as far as we can see, who numbers every hair on my messy, imperfect head?

It's not because of who we are but Whose we are.

Not because of what we've done but what Love has done for us.

Not temporary but forever and ever because he doesn't change.

I'm going to try to stop saying "not good enough" and instead dare to agree with the Love that will not let me go.

Want to join me?

I believe that this is the heart, the foundation of God-sized dreams. Because the temptation is to make our dreams about proving that we are enough, and then they become about us. But when we begin from a place of love, belonging, and acceptance, our dreams are about the One who calls us. We can move forward from a place of inner peace no matter how busy our lives may be. We can trust that what we do is also enough because we understand our part is obedience.

Thank you for being a dreamer who doesn't always try to prove her worth. I get credit card applications all the time that declare, "Preapproved!" The same is true of you. God has already approved you for your God-sized dream. He has already given you all you need and made you all you need to be. He will make everything unfold in his way, his time. What you're doing today may not feel like enough. But if you're simply saying yes to Jesus and whatever he asks, then it is more than enough—it's world changing. And so are you.

Your Heart

Your most valuable asset as a God-sized dreamer isn't the plans you can make or the connections you have. It's not the talents you possess or the experiences you can list. It's your heart.

That's where the One who gives you dreams and makes them come true dwells. It's where you hear his voice and learn how to follow faithfully. It's where you love, which is the most beautiful dream of all.

Guard your heart like you would a priceless treasure. It's of great worth and can't be replaced by anyone or anything.

You are a gift to this world, my friend. We need more God-sized dreamers like you. Carry on with a smile on your face, joy in your steps, and your heart held high, because you belong to One who loves you more than you can even imagine.

Go Deeper Guide

(Download a printable version with lines for writing at www.holley gerth.com on the "Books & More" page.)

1. Describe a God-sized dreamer in your life. What stands out most about them to you?

2. Where does God have you right now? How can you be faithful where you are today so you're ready for where he wants to take you tomorrow?

3. What helps you keep your heart open to God, those around you, and the dreams he has for you?

4. Who are you encouraging? We all have a circle of influence in our lives (for example, family, friends, church). Who is in yours?

5. Would you describe yourself as naturally a "glass half full" or "glass half empty" type of person? What impacts your attitude most?

6. What hard no have you said in order to pursue a God-sized dream? Are there others you might need to say too?

7. "Make it your ambition to lead a quiet life" (1 Thess. 4:11). How do these words make you feel? If you described your ambition in words, what would you say? "My ambition is to . . ."

— Dream It. Do It. —

Draw your circle of influence and write in names as well as how each person is connected to your God-sized dream.

4

What Comes Next for You?

In the movie *While You Were Sleeping*, actress Sandra Bullock plays the role of Lucy—a single young woman who carries around a passport without any stamps. She sits in a toll booth dreaming of faraway places until falling in love changes that forever. As the movie goes along, Lucy begins to realize that dreaming isn't the same as doing. She eventually faces her fears, opens her heart, and discovers that there's more to life after all.

It's tempting to hide our dreams away. We tell ourselves we'll pursue them later or that we need to feel safer first. But the reality is, later may not come and living out a dream is risky no matter when we decide to do it. Like Lucy, we all have to come to a point when we're ready to stop simply dreaming and begin *doing*. In other words, "Faith without deeds is useless" (James 2:20).

Most dreams never see the light of day. But not yours. You are brave and determined. You are going to say yes to whatever it is God is asking you to do. I just know it.

Even when we decide to truly pursue our dreams, it's still challenging to know what to do next. We wonder, "What steps do I take?" The transition from blue-sky thinking to the solid, practical ground can be bumpy. But it can be done, and that's when the fun really gets started. It just takes time, intention, planning, and lots of prayer.

Defining Your Dream

At first we catch just a glimpse of our dream. It's vague and blurry. Perhaps a conversation draws our attention or a surprisingly compelling idea pops into our minds in the shower. Slowly that outline begins to fill with more color and detail. Over time we begin to see it, really see it.

It's tempting to charge ahead at this point. But now is the time to stop and study your dream carefully. One way to do that is to define your dream in one to three sentences.

Those sentences need three distinct parts. First, the "what" of your dream. This is exactly as it sounds—a description of what you want to accomplish. For example, "My dream is to transition out of my job and be a stay-at-home mom with my kids." Or you might say, "My dream is to get promoted to partner in my company."

It can feel scary to write this down. Up until now, your dream may have been something you liked to take out, hold, look at, and then tuck safely back within your heart. But now you're putting it out there. As you do this, a thousand reasons why this dream is ridiculous, you're not qualified, or the time isn't right will come rushing into your head. Ignore them. They're just a sign that you're on the right track—the resistance that we all encounter as we actually begin to take steps forward. Those words can't hurt you, and with Jesus you are far stronger than those lies.

Write the "what" of your dream here:

_____

_____

_____

_____

_____

After you put your "what" in place, it's time to take a look at the "why" of your dream. God-sized dreams take too much time, effort, and passion to do them "just because it sounds like fun." This journey is going to take commitment, tenacity, and a stubborn willingness to be obedient no matter what happens. The "why" behind your dream is essential.

Start by writing down the first thing that comes to mind. You might say, "I want to be promoted to partner in my company because I can have more influence than ever before with my coworkers." Or you might say, "I want to be promoted to partner in my company because I'm competitive and I can't stand it that the woman who sits next to me might beat me to it." Whatever the reason, it's okay to admit it. God already knows.

Once you put your "why" out there, it's time to ask God if your agenda matches his. Is this a "why" that resonates with his heart too? Has he given you the reason behind this dream, or does it come from a place that might not be healthy or happy?

A little disclaimer: We are human, and having 100 percent pure motives is impossible for us. We will always struggle with our flesh as we pursue our dreams. There will always be a "little bit of me" mixed in as you move forward. If you wait to have all of that resolved, then you will never pursue your dream. What we're talking about here is your *primary* motivation, not your *only* motivation. Whenever you do anything, you will have a thousand different reasons behind it. Don't let that make you feel guilty or deter you. Just be honest about it, deal with any part of it that you need to, and keep moving forward anyway.

Write the "why" behind your dream here:

_____

_____

_____

The "why" behind your dream should fit with who you are overall. In my book *You're Already Amazing*, we walked together through a process of creating a LIFE (Love Is Faith Expressed) statement. If you haven't done that already, I'd encourage you to do so. Even if it's not through the book, think about what your mission or purpose statement might look like. The simplest way to do so can be using this approach.

We all start with a common foundation based on Galatians 5:6:

I am created and called to express my faith through love . . .

Now you'll finish that statement with your unique way of doing so in the world. That part will have this structure:

. . . especially by (verb ending in "ing") + (what) + (who) + (how)

Here's my LIFE statement:

I am created and called to express my faith through love,

especially by bringing <u>hope and encouragement</u>
(what)

<u>to the hearts of women</u> <u>through words.</u>
(who)   *(how)*

Another one might be:

I am created and called to express my faith through love,

especially by <u>meeting the practical needs of</u>
(what)

<u>my family, friends, and community</u> <u>through service.</u>
(who)   *(how)*

Try yours here (this is just a start—you can think and pray about it more later):

I am created and called to express my faith through love, especially by

_____

_____

(verb ending in "ing") + (what) + (who) + (how)

The sentence structure above is just a suggestion. You can write your LIFE any way that you'd like. It can be shorter, longer, or in an entirely different format. *There is no wrong way to do this.*

Think of this statement as your umbrella. Everything you pursue in life should fit under it. Especially for those of us who are visionaries, what looks like a dream can actually turn out to be a distraction. We love what's new and shiny. It seems so appealing—surely that's what we should be doing! I remember my wise mentor in college, Beth English, used to say, "Holley, the hardest choices in life are not between bad and good. They are between good and best." You will have many opportunities and options in your life. You will even have many God-sized dreams. But I believe you will only have one primary purpose. Yes, you will live this out in very different ways throughout the varying seasons of your life. But at the heart, it will remain remarkably the same.

If your dream and your purpose don't align, then it's time to take a step back. One of three things could be happening. First, maybe the purpose you thought fit so well actually needs to be expanded. Sometimes dreams can shine a light on your soul in a new, deeper way. Or it may be that this dream is worthwhile, but it's not for you. It may be appealing for a variety of reasons—a new adventure, money, prestige, or the people you get to connect with along the way. But every yes is a no to one or more things too, and following this dream could lead you away from what you're truly called to do. Finally, it may be that God is asking you to take a specific detour from your primary purpose for a certain season.

You have a unique mission, and whatever God calls you to do will fit with that in some way. A line in a popular movie says, "I don't know where we're going, but we're making good time!" Before you move forward, make sure you're headed in the right direction.

Know Your Destination

As I just described, knowing your direction is important, but so is understanding the destination for your dreams. What is the end result you have in mind? What does it seem God is asking you to accomplish?

I have to admit this is tricky for me because I'm not much of a specific goal setter. The good news is, you don't always need a ten-point plan for everything you do. We are all wired differently. If you get a thrill from writing out detailed lists and checking them off, then go for it. But if you're more of a free spirit who needs wide boundaries, then that can work out well too. Corporate culture in particular can be very focused on goals that are attached to numbers. That can spill into our God-sized dreams too. We have to sell X books or have X profit. Again, if that kind of goal setting works well for you, great. But if it makes you want to hyperventilate, then just realize you don't have to pursue your dream in that way.

What you do need, however, is an idea of your ultimate destination. Imagine getting in a car and saying, "I'm just going to drive until I run out of gas." If what you want is a spontaneous, flexible experience, you'll probably be fine with wherever you end up. But if deep down you actually wanted to make it to the beach, you may be disappointed when you wind up in a fast-food restaurant parking lot in the middle of a rural highway.

It can seem presumptuous to decide on a destination. We pray, "Lord, I'll go wherever you want me to go." Then we sit in a car with the gear in neutral and our hands locked on the steering wheel, waiting for further instructions. A few times in Scripture, God speaks to people when they're in this position. *But most of the time he meets them along the way and redirects them.* Think about the apostle Paul on the road to Damascus. Moses in the desert with the burning bush. The disciples in the middle of their everyday work of being fishermen.

They were all doing *something*.

Then God stepped in and radically changed their course.

Most of us know the verse in Isaiah that says, "But they that wait upon the LORD shall renew their strength; they shall mount up with wings as eagles; they shall run, and not be weary; and they shall walk, and not faint" (40:31 KJV). What's interesting to me is that this Scripture has so many verbs. And it doesn't say sitting! Walking and running, yes, but staying in place isn't there.

Perhaps our idea of waiting is too limited. We think we have to be still and do nothing at all. But what if waiting is more about the attitude of our hearts? We move forward with a sense of expectation and are open at any moment to God redirecting us.

Yes, there are times to truly be still. For example, we often quote the verse, "Be still, and know that I am God" (Ps. 46:10). In looking at the context for that verse, it's in a time of war and great trouble. God is reassuring his people that he will defend them. Sometimes it's the same in our lives. But usually when we have a God-sized dream, it's a time for offense and not defense. Ask God specifically, "Do you want me to be completely still?" If not, then it's okay to start taking steps as long as you keep an open heart and open hands along the way.

It can also be intimidating to actually say, "Well, this is the outcome I'd like for my God-sized dream." As soon as we do, fear is there to start whispering, "But it might not work and then you'll look like a failure." The reality is, we don't know what will happen. Most likely what we decide as our destination won't turn out to be where we end up. *And that's okay.*

My youth pastor's wife once gave me a bookmark that said, "Shoot for the moon. If you miss, you'll still land on a star." Dream big. Write down crazy things. Go wild with your imagination. Bust down the wall of fear by thinking up something so impossible that it takes your fear by surprise and you slip right past it.

Say that thing you would never dare to admit out loud.

Know where you want to go.

Then lay it down. Surrender that goal to Jesus and tell him, "This is where I think you want me to go. So I'm moving forward.

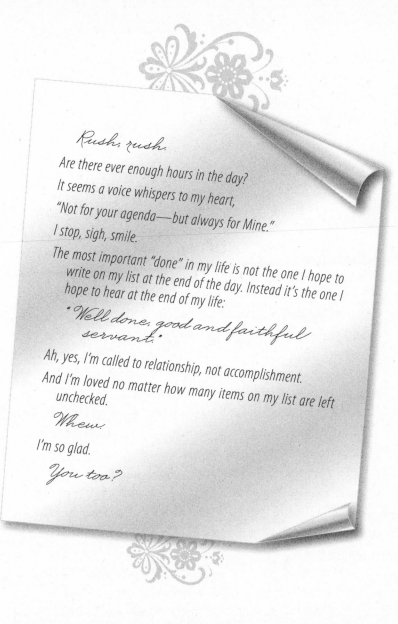

Rush, rush.

Are there ever enough hours in the day?
It seems a voice whispers to my heart,
"Not for your agenda—but always for Mine."
I stop, sigh, smile.

The most important "done" in my life is not the one I hope to write on my list at the end of the day. Instead it's the one I hope to hear at the end of my life:

Well done, good and faithful servant.

Ah, yes, I'm called to relationship, not accomplishment.
And I'm loved no matter how many items on my list are left unchecked.

Whew.

I'm so glad.

You too?

But you are Lord of my life, and you can change my path at any step along the way. What matters most to me is that I'm obedient to you."

Then go.

What's your destination? Where do you want to end up with your God-sized dream?

_____

_____

_____

Figure Out How to Get to Your Destination

After you decide to move forward, it's time to map out where you're headed. Every kid knows there's only one question that matters when you're on a road trip: "Are we there yet?" Kids ask that question because they can't look out the window, see the sign for mile marker 108, and say, "Ah yes, we are 15.2 minutes from Grandma's house." When we don't know how to tell where we are along the way, we become frustrated. Planning in advance can help us avoid feeling lost and confused.

Sometimes God deliberately chooses to keep us guessing. We're not sure where he's taking us or what route we'll end up on along the way. But most of the time there's room for strategy when it comes to our God-sized dreams, and it's part of being a good steward.

Strategy can sound like a big, intimidating word, but really it just means "how we'll get from here to there." It's the mental equivalent of pulling out a map and charting your course from one point to another. Sure, there may be road construction and you get rerouted. Or perhaps you go out of your way to check out the quaint little restaurant in the middle of town. But overall, you know which roads are likely to lead you to your desired destination.

A little heads-up: creating a strategy can cause fear at first because it feels like there has to be *one right way*. But there isn't. Any destination has multiple paths to arrive at it. Some might take a little longer or be a bit more complex, but eventually you get there. Sometimes we delay starting at all because we're just not sure that we've found the perfect path. But the most important part is simply moving forward.

When you look for guidance, you'll quickly discover there are tons of books on how to think strategically. Most involve complicated systems, project maps, and long lists. Can I make a confession? Those things make me want to hide under a table.

My approach to strategic planning? I use an unlined journal and draw shapes with lots of lines connecting one thing to another. Then I transfer any specific tasks to my calendar. Done.

About every month or so, I draw a new version of what's going on and make updates as needed based on what's happened. Often my strategy looks like this:

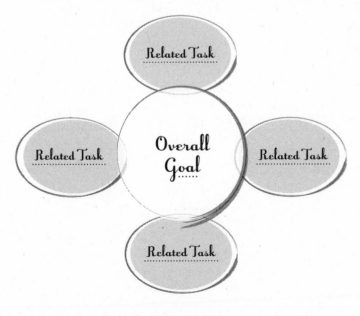

Long lists stress me out. Intricate systems distract me. Maintaining things feels boring to me. Yet I'm productive and most often reach my goals. I even scored very high on "Strategic" in the test from the book *Now, Discover Your Strengths.*[4]

I say all that simply to dismiss the myth that there is one right way to do goal setting and strategic thinking. The best strategy is one you'll actually do because it fits with who you are.

Think about how God wired you. Are you an outgoing, social person? Then having other people highly involved in your God-sized dream along the way should probably be part of your strategy. Are you motivated by details? Then you might want to get one of those very specific books on strategy and map out your plan. It is up to you and the Holy Spirit to decide how to best pursue your God-sized dream.

I do believe having some kind of strategy in place, however formal or informal it may be, is important because it will make you intentional. Life is busy. Other priorities pop up. We're all vulnerable to the urgent overshadowing what's truly important. Strategy makes you focus and also lets you know if you're making progress.

If you need a starting place, you can use the template below as a basic beginning for your strategy.

My God-Sized Dream

○ **Step One**

What I will do: _____

When I will do it: _____

How I will know it's done: _____

○ **Step Two**

What I will do: _____

When I will do it: _____

How I will know it's done: _____

○ **Step Three**

What I will do: _____

When I will do it: _____

How I will know it's done: _____

You can add as many steps as you need. You might feel a bit of panic looking at this section, because this is where the rubber meets the road. This is where the dream starts making the transition from your heart into the world. And that, my friend, is always scary. You will feel resistance when you get serious about putting your dream on paper. You will begin to think that it's not the right time, there's more you need to research, or maybe you're not prepared. *Do it anyway.*

Like we talked about before, God can and will reroute you if needed. And most likely the steps you write above as well as the destination will change. That's okay. What you're looking for here is momentum and progress. Have you ever tried to steer a parked car? It's a tough proposition. Just get in gear and start heading down the road. The rest will work itself out as you go.

Know What You Need to Take with You

After you've scoped out a destination and plotted your course along the way, you'll have an idea of what to pack for the journey. Swimsuit? Parka? Raincoat? Every God-sized dream is different, and it's important to be prepared.

Some people might say, "Well, God will just provide what I need along the way." Yes, that's true. But I also believe he gives us wisdom to know how to plan and prepare as well. Knowing what you may encounter along the way helps you get ready before you find yourself in a tough situation that could have been avoided.

For example, you may know that starting a blog is going to be part of reaching your God-sized dream. If so, then it's time to do some research about what technology you need. If you know you'll require child care for a few hours a week, then it's time to start asking friends about who they recommend. If your dream involves something physical, then it's time to get off the couch and go for a walk each evening.

What do you *not* have right now that you will need along the way?

Look ahead and ask yourself that question. Then go about getting it. Sure, that doesn't seem super-spiritual. But Scripture is also full of really practical advice, especially in Proverbs. The world is set up to work in certain ways, and when we ignore that and go running ahead without wisdom, we shouldn't be surprised at the consequences.

Here's the reality: *God-sized dreams are a lot of work.* It can seem like because we have this grand vision, it will all just fall into place. But that never happens. Ever. You have to be prepared to do the work. Over and over again.

You "reap what you sow," and in order to get a lot out of a God-sized dream, you'll have to put a lot into it. There's just no way around that truth. Yes, God is the one who makes the results happen, but we are clearly called to put in effort. This isn't "works" in the sense that we are trying to earn God's approval by what we do. Nor is it "striving" where we feel the burden is on us to make everything happen. It's simply good, honest, hard work to pursue what God has put in front of us with excellence.

Be prepared. Work hard. Persevere. God-sized dreams are many things, but "easy" is not one of them.

Don't Quit, No Matter What

At some point in pursuing your dream, you will get tired. You will sit down on the side of the road and say, "For crying out loud, if I knew it was going to be this hard and take this long, I never would have started down this path."

Your job in those moments is simply this: don't quit.

Because just over the next hill, just around the next bend is the breakthrough you've been waiting for, and you will miss it if you stop now.

I've pursued enough God-sized dreams to know that's almost always the case. Just when you feel like you're done, just when you think you can't go on, that's when the door opens and unexpectedly you're there.

When we think that there's only one path to our God-sized dreams and it doesn't work out, then we can assume that we have to go back and start over. But that's not true. Just find another way. It doesn't mean you've done anything wrong. It doesn't mean you messed up. It simply means that we live in a fallen world and there will always be obstacles and detours.

The key is to not keep beating your head against the same roadblock. As quickly as you can, pull out your strategy and rewrite it. Don't feel guilty, beat yourself up, or get mad at whoever put that roadblock there in the first place. Just say, "Well, I found one more way that didn't work. That means I'm closer to finding a path that does get me there. I learned some things on that detour, and I'll be wiser as I move ahead. Now I'm going to get back at it again."

We all know the saying that goes, "Where there's a will, there's a way." I'd revise that just a bit to say, "Where there's *God's will*, there's a way." As much as it may seem like we're up against the impossible, there's nothing God can't do. Anything is possible with him. That means if this God-sized dream is truly one he's planted in your heart, he will make it happen *no matter what*. Your God-sized dream is invincible in his hands.

What's most likely to defeat you isn't external circumstances or challenges, it's *you*. Don't give in to discouragement, doubt, or fear. Don't let the enemy tell you that you've goofed this up for good and it's over. Just keep going.

You will get there, one way or another.

Keep Your Dream in Front of You

Most God-sized dreams aren't discarded; they're simply overcome by distractions. The pile of laundry stares us in the face while our dream waits quietly in a corner. A stack of bills that needs to be paid demands our attention while our goal of writing a book silently sits somewhere on our hard drive. In one way God-sized dreams can be very loud, but in another way they don't ever demand to be heard. If you push them away or quiet them down, eventually they'll comply.

It's your job to give your dream a presence and voice in your life. Keep it in front of you. That might mean hanging a reminder on your fridge, making a task list on your computer, writing notes on your calendar, or even having a friend call you once a week to ask how it's going. Whatever you need to do, keep your dream and strategy in front of you.

Be aware of what pulls you away from your dream. How do you procrastinate? What do you choose instead? What are the "When I . . ." statements that place your dream somewhere in the future rather than right here, right now?

Because God-sized dreams feel so powerful, we often take it for granted that they will happen someday. But that's not true. In several studies, older people were asked what they regretted most. The answer? Not what they did but *what they didn't do.*

No matter how passionately you feel about your dream, that is not enough to make it a reality. There have to be actions attached to your emotions. Talking about your dream doesn't count either. Yes, that's an important part of the process. But at some point you've got to shift from your lips to your hands and just do the work. Don't be fooled into believing that saying something is the same as getting it done.

You will have to fight for your dream. There will never be the "right" time. There will never be the "perfect opportunity." There will never be the "easy way." If your dream is going to come into being, it's going to take a lot of hard work, perseverance, and leaps of faith with Jesus that you never thought you could complete.

But you will.

I know it.

I feel it.

You are going to make this happen. You're not going to quit. You're going to keep that dream in front of you and keep the One who gave it to you right beside you all the way.

Remember and Celebrate

The funny thing about dreams is how much they shift our focus to the finish line. But it turns out that the most satisfying part of a dream is often the journey along the way. Author Gretchen Rubin expresses it this way: " 'Happiness,' wrote Yeats, 'is neither virtue nor pleasure nor this thing nor that, but simply growth. We are happy when we are growing.' Contemporary researchers make the same argument: that it isn't goal attainment but the striving after goals—that is, growth—that brings happiness."[5] It turns out that the completion of our dream is simply the cherry on top. But most of the goodness, most of the growth, happens long before what we desire ever becomes a reality, because along the way to our dream, we intimately experience God's presence in a powerful way. We're created to know and pursue him. In doing so, we find joy, meaning, and purpose.

So make time to celebrate along the way. Rejoice in each step completed. Take time to notice what is happening. Share those moments with those you love—and the God who loves you.

In the Old Testament, God often had the people of Israel stop and set up physical markers to remind them of what he had done in their lives. As humans, we're all tempted to just "move on to the next thing." But it's important to stop and reflect on how far we've come and how much God has done on our behalf.

Yes, we're to work hard, plan, and move forward diligently—but not to the extent that we become driven by our dream. I know what that's like. I also clearly remember a moment when it seemed God whispered to my heart, "If you're driven, you can't be led."

It's a fine line that we walk. We take responsibility for what God has entrusted to us, and yet in the end it's ultimately simply about obedience, about taking the next step of faith. The most important thing you can do for your dream? Pray, pray, and pray some more.

Pray words of praise when things go well.

Pray for wisdom when you're not sure which way to go.

Pray with thanks when God comes through beyond all you could have imagined.

Pray that in all you do, his purposes will prevail.

Even if you don't build an actual physical reminder of what God has done, let prayer be like stones you place in the path along the way to remind you of where you've been, where you're going, and who is walking with you.

Conclusion

You've done a lot of hard work in these last few pages. You've dared to define your dream and even to take steps to achieve it. Your heart may be pounding and your head spinning, but you are on your way. Your dream is no longer just an idea or a quiet whisper in your heart. It's becoming reality.

You can do this, my friend.

Keep going.

Keep believing.

Keep pursuing the God who never stops pursuing you.

Go Deeper Guide

(Download a printable version with lines for writing at www.holley gerth.com on the "Books & More" page.)

1. Finish this sentence: My God-sized dream is to . . .

2. Why do you want to pursue that God-sized dream?

3. What's your LIFE statement?

4. What do you specifically want to accomplish through this God-sized dream?

5. "Many are the plans in a person's heart, but it is the LORD's purpose that prevails" (Prov. 19:21). What are three goals and/or next steps that will help you move forward with this dream?

6. What do you not have right now that you will need along the way to your dream?

7. How will you celebrate as you take steps forward?

— *Dream It. Do It.* —

Create a one-page strategy for your dream. Include what your God-sized dream is, what you specifically want to accomplish, and the steps you'll take as well as a due date for each one. Keep this strategy in a place where you can clearly see it. It's not set in stone and God can change it at any time, but having it in front of you will help you stay focused.

5

A Guide to
Overcoming **Your Fear**

Here's a little secret: it's not the work that's the hardest part.

Oh, we tell ourselves that's true—that the most difficult part of the dream will be writing the book, launching the business, making the decision. But it's one four-letter word that turns out to be the biggest foe of our dreams, the enemy of the "more" we long for in our lives.

Fear.

It growls at us in the dark. It whispers to us in the daylight. It tries to tell us that this is too much or we're not enough.

Fear is a bully who doesn't fight fair.

But like most bullies, fear doesn't stand its ground when you decide to turn and face it. And you can, my friend, *you can.* Let's talk about how to do that together.

Calling Fear's Bluff

She sends a note over email. "I'm stuck," she says. "I keep trying to take the next step, but every time I do I feel so much fear."

I softly smile when I read her words. She doesn't know it yet, but this is a *good* thing.

I place my fingers on the keyboard and type, "Fear camps out right next to whatever it is you're most called to do. That means the closer you get to your calling, the louder fear sounds. You must be headed in the right direction. Keep going—fear is a Chihuahua that sounds like a Doberman."

A few days later she wrote back that she'd pushed past the fear, and yes, when she looked fear in the face, it wasn't at all the intimidating beast it appeared to be from a distance.

You will face fear. Fear is a response to a threat. It means there's risk and something you value is on the line. If you don't feel that way about your dream, then it's not close enough to God's calling for you.

So why do we resist fear so much? There are many reasons, but one of the primary ones is a myth that holds many of us back: *fear is a sin.*

I've heard that my whole life. So for a long time I sidestepped anything that caused me to feel fear because I assumed it must not be God's will. But as I dug deeper into Scripture, it became clear that fear itself isn't a sin any more than other emotions we have, such as happiness, anger, or grief. All emotions are just messages about what we're experiencing. Imagine if you couldn't feel fear. You'd be vulnerable in a lot of ways. The initial fear response is a gift from God that tells us, "Hey, be alert and pay attention to this," or perhaps even, "Do something!"

God wired our minds in beautiful ways. Fear comes from our amygdala, the area of our brain that controls the "flight or fight" response. When we feel fear, our body releases chemicals that direct us to do one of those two things—either get out of the situation or get ready for a rumble. In our modern world, that "flight or fight" isn't often triggered by actual physical threats like a lion on the side of the road. Instead it's more often set off by the lion described as the enemy of our souls (see 1 Pet. 5:8), waiting to pounce on our hearts when we're hot on the trail of God-sized dreams.

When we feel fear, God understands, because he's the one who made us that way. In many ways, that first response is involuntary. He designed our minds that way so we could react quickly in dangerous situations without being slowed down by the rational thought process, which takes much longer.

Surprise: fear is not a sin—it's a gift.

All throughout Scripture God does talk to his people about fear. As I dug into those verses, two primary phrases appeared. God says, "Do not fear" or "Do not be afraid" almost one hundred times. That may make it seem like fear is a sin. But if you look closely, those phrases are almost always in contexts where the audience God is addressing is *already* feeling fear.

"Do not be afraid" appears more than any other place in the story of the Israelites going to the Promised Land. God says, "Do not be afraid," and then he gives instructions about what to do next—commands, like going into battle, that he knows will cause even more fear to spring up. In essence, he's telling his people, like a father would tell his kids when they're scared in the dark or about to jump off the high dive for the first time, "Don't be afraid. Go ahead and jump. It will be okay."

I love that the word *be* is in that phrase. God doesn't say, "Don't feel fear." Because he made us, he understands that would be impossible. Instead he says, "Don't *be* afraid." In other words, don't *live* in fear or make it part of your identity.

You will feel fear. More than once. But you don't have to live in fear. You don't have to make that Chihuahua your pet and carry it around in your bag like a socialite. You don't have to pet it, give it treats, and let it sleep in your bed at night.

I mentioned before that fear is a response from the area of our brains called the amygdala that bypasses our rational thought. But after that first surge, the other parts of our brain do kick in, and that's when we have a decision to make.

Our amygdala says, "Ack! A threat! Fear alert!"

Then the rest of our brain starts searching for evidence to support or disprove that initial response. Is the monster we thought we saw in our closet actually the vacuum cleaner? Is the loud noise that sounded like a gunshot actually just a car backfiring?

With examples like those above, it's easy to shoo away the fear with physical evidence. But when it comes to the heart, it becomes much harder. Because most of the time there isn't a black-and-white answer to that fear. We have to respond by faith.

One of my pastors, Matt Newman, likes to say, "When David saw how big Goliath was, he could say either, 'He's too big for me to ever win' or 'He's too big for me to miss—and my God is even bigger.'"

Pick the first option and fear takes over, David runs for the hills, and history changes forever. Pick the second and you get a boy with a slingshot who chooses to stand boldly in faith and goes on to become the most well-known king of Israel.

This is the place where we get to choose obedience or rebellion. It's a myth that all fear is sin, but it's quite true that *fear can lead us into sin*. We can say no to what God asks of us. We can listen to the lies more than the truth. We can compromise our calling.

Most of us already know that's true. So we say, "Hey, fear might get me in trouble. So I'll avoid anything that makes me afraid." But saying that is a bit like saying, "Hey, water is kind of dangerous—I could drown—so I'll just never go near any kind of water." A better solution? Learn to swim.

The same is true of fear. And unlike avoiding water, which you possibly could do, getting around situations that make you feel afraid is impossible in this life. The cost of doing so is also much too high. If you decide never to feel fear, then in essence you are saying you will not complete God's purpose for your life, because doing so always involves fear in some way.

The first step to overcoming fear is to stop avoiding it. If avoidance is your only plan, the Chihuahua of fear will chase you down the street and nip at your heels forever. You will spend all your time and energy trying to escape fear when you could be using it to pursue your dreams instead. Stop and face the fear. Say, "Yes, I'm afraid. But fear isn't going to kill me. It's not even going to maim me. Fear has no power in my life. It's all bark and no bite. I'm going to move forward in faith. Fear may come my way, but I am not going to let it control me."

Facing your fear also lets you get a good look at it. Because we tend to avoid it, we often don't even know much about our fear. Where did it come from? What's it really saying to us? We've been talking about fear like it's a single Chihuahua. But really there's a whole herd. There might be the one wearing the pink collar that's the mean girls from high school yapping, "You're never going to fit in," or the one wearing the cute little sweater your grandma knitted barking, "That dream of yours just isn't practical."

Pause and write down your fears. Picture in your mind a Chihuahua for each one and name it. (Yes, I realize this is pretty ridiculous—but sometimes making your fear look silly is just what's needed. How many times has it threatened to make *you* look silly? Well, it's time to turn the tables. Take that, fear.)

My fears:

_____

_____

_____

After you've written down your fears, look closely at them. Denise Martin, my life coach, went through a similar process with me when fears seemed especially loud in my life. After I wrote out my fears, she asked me questions about each one until eventually I realized the fears that seemed so real to me now were actually just echoes of lies from years ago.

So what do you do with that herd of Chihuahuas? You probably want to donate them to the local animal shelter. But it doesn't work that way. Each one of those fears is attached to something important in your life. To completely get rid of the fear would mean letting the other part (like a dream) go too. Your Chihuahuas are here to stay. You might decide you'll just swat them with a newspaper every time they nip at your heels. So whenever you feel fear, you spout out a cliché or slap a quick verse on the situation. But that's exhausting and ultimately not very effective.

Those puppies need to go to obedience school. Because here's the thing—fear always thinks it's the master. Sometimes it convinces you of the same. But it's not true.

You are the boss of fear and God is the boss of you.

That fear has got to learn to sit and submit.

Sure, it may still bark when someone rings the doorbell (that initial brain response we talked about). But you can teach it to behave nicely when you open the door.

Is this hard to do? Yep, especially at first. But over time fear learns who holds the leash, and while those fears may still be in your yard, they will no longer be wreaking havoc on your life and dreams.

How to Train Your Fear

You may have heard of Cesar Millan, the "dog whisperer" with an uncanny ability to alter the behavior of pups. I'd like to step in and be your own personal "fear whisperer" for the next few pages. I'm thinking that would look pretty awesome on a business card or T-shirt. Yes, ma'am.

Here are a few little things I've learned about fear.

Fear Responds to Truth, Not Commands

When we're not busy running from it, we like to boss our fear around. We throw commands at it. We tell it to go away, sit, fetch, or whatever else might make it settle down and let us get back to business.

But fear is a rebellious beast. It doesn't listen to commands *at all*. In fact, it's more likely to turn around and bite you on the toe than do what you say.

However, fear does respond to truth. When God is speaking to his people about fear, he often follows the directive not to be afraid with a promise about who he is and what he will do. For example, "Do not fear, for I am with you; do not be dismayed, for I am your God. I will strengthen you and help you; I will uphold you with my righteous right hand" (Isa. 41:10). We can grab hold of these truths and repeat them when fear comes at us. David does just that when he says, "The LORD is with me; I will not be afraid" (Ps. 118:6). He goes on to finish the psalm by listing what God has done for him.

Like we talked about, our rational minds need evidence to know how to proceed once the initial fear response has passed. David is giving his heart and mind evidence so that fear backs down. If he said, "Go away, fear!" then nothing would happen. But when we speak truth, fear responds and settles down. This usually doesn't happen on the first try. Because fear causes our minds to respond automatically, really pushing past fear means building another automatic response that comes after the initial fear. That means creating a habit. You are training your fear—not just forcing it to obey in the moment. That takes time, patience, and lots of practice.

Fear Is Lazy

My husband and I often go for walks through our neighborhood in the evening. On the corner of our street, there's a pint-sized dog that has learned to squeeze through the fence so it can run after unsuspecting pedestrians. The first few times it happened, I jumped and started to run—which, as you might guess, only made that little dog chase me. My husband, on the other hand, simply kept walking calmly. That turned out to be the right approach, because before long the dog got bored and tired, so it slipped back under the fence to take a nap.

Fear is much the same way. When it comes after you, it seems like it has a ton of energy. It's barking, bouncing, bristling the fur on its back. But it doesn't have any stamina. Sure, if you run from it, then it has motivation to chase you. Walk calmly, steadily, in the direction you're called to go instead, and fear will opt for lying down in the grass almost every time.

Speak truth to fear as a start. If it listens, great. If it doesn't, then just ignore it and carry on with whatever God has told you to do.

Fear Needs a Leash

Sometimes fear is persistent and keeps walking beside you. In those cases, it's time to put that fear on a leash and remind it who's boss. I love the story of Queen Esther (see Esther 4). She has the opportunity to go before the king on behalf of her people. But she also knows that doing so uninvited could lead to her death. She's afraid, but in the end she says, "If I perish, I perish." Then she keeps walking forward in faith.

I can almost guarantee that as she stepped before the king and waited to see if she would be accepted or executed, her heart was pounding. Big dream. Big risk. There's no way she could have done that without anxiety.

If you can't get fear to obey or go away, then put it on a leash and bring it with you. Just remember that you are in control—not fear.

Fear Gets Bigger When You Feed It

Fear has enough food to survive on just by living in this world. But sometimes we fatten it up even more by giving it treats. Every time we believe a lie, it's like throwing a bone to fear. We indulge it with insecurity or offer it a bit more of our attention to nibble on. Fear eats it all up, and then we're surprised when it grows.

Sharon Wooten, who blogs at *Hiking Toward Home*, says:

> I have a fear, I know in the depths of my heart, I really need to get over.
> Fear of failure.
> Fear that it will be more messy than beautiful.
> But can't the messy be beautiful too?
> It is to God. Isn't it?
> Because if not for the messy there would be no need for grace.[6]

By changing her perspective, Sharon is learning to nourish her creativity instead of nurturing her fears.

An old story goes that a little girl asked her grandfather which dog would win if they happened to get into a fight. The grandfather replied, "The one you feed the most."

Don't feed your fear. Feed your faith.

Fear Has a Muzzle

Our town has a farmers' market on Saturdays. As we stroll through it, we see an abundance of all shapes and sizes of dogs with their owners. A few of the more ferocious-looking ones usually have muzzles. They may let out a bark that startles those standing nearby, but they can't do any real damage.

Fear is the same way. In the end, it can't directly harm you. The way fear causes damage in our lives is indirect. It scares us away from the door God wants us to knock on that day. It convinces us that we're not as strong or brave as God tells us we are. It chases us in the opposite direction of the dream we're called to pursue.

You can tell fear that the jig is up and it can bark as much as it wants, but you know it can't really get to you. If you don't let fear control you, then there's nothing it can do to hurt you.

It's time to take your fear to obedience school, my friend. Show it who's the master—and who's the Master of you.

Make Fear Work for You

If you've ever felt a surge of panic and slammed on the brakes just before you hit the car in front of you, then you know that fear can be your friend. Like I talked about earlier, fear is an emotion and emotions are neutral. They're not good or bad—they're just a way our brains relay messages to our bodies about what's going on in our world.

Now that you've trained your fear, you can go one step further and actually make it work for you. That's especially true when you're pursuing a God-sized dream. You may not like having fear around, but it actually has an important role to play as you take steps of faith.

Let Fear Warn You about Risks

When fear starts barking, it usually means there's a perceived risk around. It might turn out to be the neighbor's cat, or it could be a burglar in the backyard. Stop and listen to your fear. What is it directing you to pay attention to? Look closely and then decide if the threat is valid or not. For example, if fear says, "You don't have what it takes and you're going to fail," then respond with the truth that God has given you "everything you need for life and godliness" (see 2 Pet. 1:3). If fear says, "You haven't prepared at all for this speech, so you may not do as well as you could," then that's a legitimate warning and it's time to go practice a bit more.

How do you tell if fear is giving you a false alarm or if you really should pay attention? Helpful fear is about something specific that you can take action to correct. For example, you might be afraid to start a blog because you don't know much about the internet. But you can do some research and quiet that fear down. Harmful fear is general, often about your character, and is usually not something you can control. For example, "No one is going to like you at that conference" is sure to evoke fear, but it's not based in reality. In those cases, it's time to speak truth and then press on in spite of the fear.

Let Fear Tell You What's Important to You

Like I mentioned at the beginning of this chapter, if you don't feel any fear about something, then it's probably not a true area of passion in your life. Think of your biggest fears. They most likely involve what matters most to you. Your family. Your friends. Your calling. When it feels like there's a risk, ask yourself, "What am I afraid of losing?" If the answer is, "I might look foolish and lose a little of my pristine reputation if I don't do this speech perfectly," then it's probably worth making the leap. If the answer is, "If I take this new job and have to work eighty hours a week, it could destroy my marriage," that's a whole different story.

Whatever you value most will cause the most fear in your life. What does that mean? When we're making decisions about risks and we understand that fear points to what matters most, then we can make a plan to protect those things while still moving forward. For example, if you know God is calling you to take that job that may end up with eighty hours of work a week, then a serious conversation about boundaries with your potential boss might be in order. Let fear show you how to proactively guard what's sacred in your life, but don't let it paralyze you into inaction because there's a possibility of loss.

Life is risk. There are no guarantees. We also need to ask ourselves, "What might I lose if I *don't* do this?" Usually those answers are more subtle but just as essential. Inaction doesn't equal safety. Doing nothing is much more of a risk than doing the something God has commanded.

Be bold. Step out. But let fear add wisdom to your journey as you go.

Let Fear Energize You

Imagine you're a teenager at an amusement park. You hop on a roller coaster, pull down the safety bar, and begin the slow *click-click-click* to the top. With each passing second the fear grows, but so does the excitement. Your stomach drops at the first hill, but then you put your hands in the air and enjoy the ride. When you get off you exclaim breathlessly, "Let's do that again!"

Physically and chemically, fear resembles another emotion we experience—excitement. Both emotions put our bodies on high alert, make us focused, and get us ready for action. If fear were only negative, then roller coasters, scary movies, and haunted houses would quickly cease to exist. I'm not advocating that you go out and try those activities. I'm simply saying that when we feel in control of fear, it can actually be (dare I say it) *fun*.

Think of a moment when you took an intentional, well-planned, God-ordained risk. Maybe you spoke to a group of people. Perhaps you carried your first baby home from the hospital. Or you accepted a new role at work that stretched you out of your comfort zone. Oh, sure, there was fear. But there were also glorious emotions like anticipation, joy, and the feeling of being fully alive. Believe it or not, you have fear to thank for part of that.

So when you begin to feel your stomach tighten, pretend you're on that roller coaster and embrace the journey. Whee! Then do it again. And again.

Let Fear Lead You to Love

When the little dog in our neighborhood that I mentioned earlier comes racing toward us, I'm not as afraid as before, but I still instinctively reach for my husband's hand. I want to know that I'm safe and secure, that someone bigger and stronger than I am is ready and willing to fight on my behalf. I need to know that love is there and that it will win.

It's the same for our hearts. While our fears show up in various forms, ultimately they all point back to the deepest fear of all: that we won't be loved.

I might fail . . . and I won't be loved.

I could let everyone down . . . and I won't be loved.

I may step out and find myself alone . . . and I won't be loved.

When it comes to that deep fear, there's only one solution. Perfect love. And there's only One who offers it to our hearts. "There is no fear in love. But perfect love drives out fear, because fear has to do with punishment. The one who fears is not made perfect in love" (1 John 4:18). God says that he will take care of the fear in our lives. This isn't a one-time event. He sends that fear out through the doggy door, and the next day it may come sneaking back in. But he promises us that fear will not win. When we get to heaven and stand before him, because of the blood of his Son and his sacrifice on the cross, we will not be afraid. In the most important moment of our lives and the first step into eternity, fear will be completely gone.

Until then, love chases away fear as often as we ask. Think of the moments when you feel the most loved and accepted. Those are probably also the ones when you feel the least fear. When fear comes at you, ask God to hide you in his love, to draw you deeper into it, to whisper to your heart the truth you need to hear so that his voice is louder than anything else.

The more we grow in love, the more fear shrinks. That process will continue until we're safe forever in heaven.

Let Fear Expand Your Faith

Every time we choose to listen to love more than fear, our faith grows. We learn to trust more, to see God act in new ways in our lives, to let him take us places beyond where we could have dared to go before.

The sound of fear can also be an invitation. It can be a signal that God is asking you to go somewhere new with him, to get outside your comfort zone, to be part of an adventure.

As the Israelites approached the Promised Land, twelve scouts were sent to bring back a report (see Num. 13). Ten returned with fear nipping at their heels and influencing their words. Two returned with proclamations of faith. Joshua and Caleb saw the land

We all have times when fear growls at our door,
when doubt creeps in, when we feel so very small.
But those are the moments when God's love can be the biggest,
when he's there with open arms, with truth that reminds us
who we are.

And who are you?

- You are loved. (Ps. 103:11)
- You have a purpose. (Phil. 1:6)
- You are not alone. (Ps. 73:23)
- And you are stronger than you know. (Phil. 4:13)

Nothing can change that—

not this day, that situation, those thoughts inside your mind.
Who you are is secure in the hands of the One who made you,
the same One who spoke stars into being,
whose hands can stretch from one end of the sea to the other,
who counts every hair on your head.

Keep going, my sister.

Press in, press on, and never give up.
We will do this together.
With each other.
With him.

For as long as it takes.

as one with obstacles, yes, but even greater opportunities. We want it to be one or the other. But there's never a time when what God asks us to do feels completely safe. If we wait for the giants to move out on their own, the roads we need to appear, and the opposition to disperse, then we'll never take possession of what God has given us.

Faith without risk isn't faith. It's just facts.

If we want a nice, safe reality where we don't ever feel fear, then we're going to miss out on much of what God has for us.

God is not committed to your safety. He is committed to his kingdom and your ultimate good.

He promises you security, yes, but not a free-from-fear life.

And even if you were perfect, that would still be true.

Jesus was perfect, and God's plans for him still included a cross.

This life is short. You get one shot to fulfill your purpose. There's not a plan B for you.

God's plans for you are good, my friend. Not always safe. Hardly ever predictable. Far from what you imagined. But they are good because he is.

Let fear push you into faith . . . and into the everlasting arms waiting for you that promise to never let you go.

From Now On

You've looked fear in the face. You've seen it for what it is. Now all that remains is to choose what you will do.

In *The Dream Giver*, Bruce Wilkinson says, "My life changed the day I decided to never again run away from my Comfort Zone fears. When you think about it, stepping through fear is a small price to pay for a Big Dream. That one step—that we face many times in our lives—must be the universal price tag God had in mind. I think God wants to know whether we really want the wonderful gift of his Dream in our life."[7]

Over and over the phrase "Do not be afraid" is paired with another one in the Bible.

Be strong and courageous.

God doesn't ever command what's impossible.

So no matter how you feel, no matter how big the obstacles may seem, no matter how loud the fear may sound right now—you can move forward in faith.

And I know you will.

Because you are a brave daughter of the King, chosen and cherished by him. You are an Esther for this generation, and this is your "for such a time as this" (Esther 4:14).

Take that step. Make that move. Seize this moment.

We need you to complete your calling.

You and Jesus are stronger than the fear.

Together you're unstoppable.

So go for it, girl, and know that I'm cheering you on in my heart every step of the way as you do.

> *Lord,*
> *I thank you for the one reading these words right now. You know the fears in her heart and how she longs to step out in faith even more. I pray you will take her by the hand, silence those fears, and lead her into all you have for her.*
> *Thank you for the gifts that you have placed within her.*
> *Thank you for the strength she has through you.*
> *Thank you for the ways she is called to make a difference.*
> *You are greater than our fears. Whatever you have asked us to do is possible with you because you are un-stoppable. And when we are obedient, we are unstop-pable in your plans for us too.*
> *Please take us on a new adventure with you.*
> *Amen.*

Go Deeper Guide

(Download a printable version with lines for writing at www.holley gerth.com on the "Books & More" page.)

1. What are your biggest fears when it comes to your God-sized dreams?
2. What is the truth that tames each of those fears?
3. What risks could those fears be pointing out to you? What can you do about them?
4. What do those fears tell you about what's important to you?
5. How does "perfect love drive out fear" (see 1 John 4:18)?
6. How can these fears expand your faith?
7. Describe a time when you felt fear and pushed through anyway. What happened?

— Dream It. Do It. —

Confront one small fear this week. Maybe you've been putting off a phone call, avoiding a difficult task, or something else. Face that fear head-on, ask for God's help, and get it done. Then celebrate when you do.

6

The **Disclaimers**

I sat on the couch, legs curled up under me. It had been one of *those* days. My husband walked by and asked, "What's the matter?"

I responded, "I don't like my dream today. It's not how I pictured it. Right now it just feels like a bunch of hard work."

He shrugged and said, "All dreams are that way."

As I sat there and considered his words, I thought back over the different God-sized dreams in my life. And I realized there had always been moments like this one along the way. Always.

I remember how before I got married, I watched endless chick flicks and dreamed of happily ever after. No one told me about the hard moments when the laundry needs to be done, you both have the flu, and the dog just peed on the carpet. But that's reality. When it comes to our dreams, we do much the same thing. We have a grand vision in which we ride off into the sunset with the desire of our hearts, and then we're disappointed when just over the next ridge, there's road construction and smog.

Yes, God-sized dreams are beautiful.

Yes, they're worth pursuing.

But they're not all cotton candy and daisies.

There are some things I wish someone had told me about dreams before I got started. And so, my friend, I'm going to share them with you.

Disclaimer #1:
You Will Never Feel Ready

We tend to think in terms of 100 percent in our culture. We like the idea that we can do enough planning and preparing to make whatever outcome we desire a sure thing. It feels less risky that way. The danger comes in that we can delay forever in the name of being "responsible." Sometimes this relates to our circumstances—we want the weather to change, the crisis to pass, the leader to get on board with our idea. Other times it's more about who we are—we need more education, more experience, a better spiritual life. We start those requirements with the biggest dream-killing four-letter word of all: "When . . ."

Here's a secret: most dreams don't die a crash-and-burn death. If you at least try, then you're likely to have some kind of success come out of what you do.

Most dreams just never get born.

One weekend my husband and I visited a local community farm for their first day of planting. The organizers handed out packets of seeds. I dropped the seeds into my enormous purse with good intentions of planting them as soon as I got home. We became busy with other things and the seeds went untouched.

Every few days I would think about the seeds and how I should plant them. Then days turned into months and the opportunity slipped by without me even noticing.

Our dreams can be like those seeds. We carry them around with us and tell ourselves that we're going to plant them. Then life gets busy, distractions come, and we keep putting off what we know God has called us to do.

Yes, there are times for waiting and proactively seeking God's voice. But when we already know what he's asked us to do, it's time to plant. "Sow your seed in the morning, and at evening let your hands not be idle, for you do not know which will succeed, whether this or that, or whether both will do equally well" (Eccles. 11:6).

Don't wait until the time feels right. Don't wait until you feel ready. *You will wait forever.*

You don't have to be ready. Conditions don't have to be perfect. Because it's not about you. It's about God fulfilling his purposes through you, and he has always been able to make that happen in spite of our humanity and the fallen world around us.

If David had waited to feel ready, he would never have fought Goliath as a shepherd boy with a sling.

If Moses had waited to feel ready, he would never have led an entire nation to the Promised Land.

If Esther had waited to feel ready, her people would have perished at the hands of a wicked man.

When we don't feel ready, God has the opportunity to get the most glory.

Now, I'm not talking about being reckless and irresponsible. This is not an excuse not to pray or plan like we talked about in the chapter before this one. You need to put in the work and spend time listening to God's voice. But at some point it's the moment to act. We are to make our plans and step out in faith. Even if we

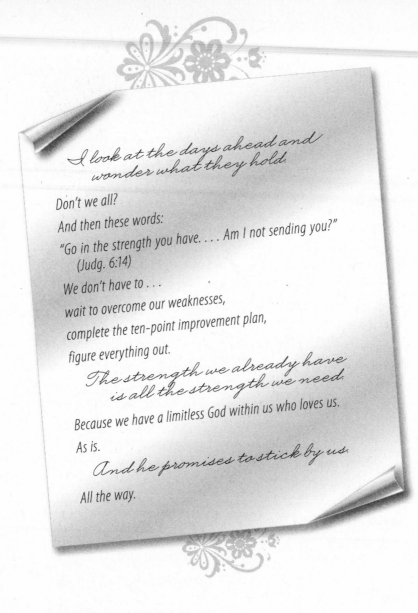

I look at the days ahead and wonder what they hold.

Don't we all?

And then these words:

"Go in the strength you have. . . . Am I not sending you?"
   (Judg. 6:14)

We don't have to . . .

wait to overcome our weaknesses,

complete the ten-point improvement plan,

figure everything out.

The strength we already have is all the strength we need.

Because we have a limitless God within us who loves us.

As is.

And he promises to stick by us.

All the way.

don't fully go the right direction, God can redirect us to end up where he wants us to go.

You don't have to be ready for anything.

You only have to be ready for the next step God has for you to take.

And you are.

Disclaimer #2:
You Will Not Like Your Dream Sometimes

Like that day my husband discovered me curled up on the couch bemoaning my dream, there will be times when you feel like you'd rather be doing anything *but* your dream. When this starts happening to me, I have fantasies about running off to New Zealand to become a Starbucks barista. I can barely make a cup of black coffee, much less a triple-shot grande no-whip mocha, but when I get tired of my dream I become a bit delusional.

Now, feeling like this doesn't mean you don't love your dream. It doesn't mean that it isn't what God called you to do after all. It doesn't mean you messed up or heard wrong or any of the things the enemy would like you to believe.

It's just part of living out a dream in a fallen world.

You see, we're made for two places: Eden and heaven. I'm not sure where you are at this moment, but I can guarantee it's not either of those. While we don't get to live in those places right now, we still have the ability to capture a bit of both in our imaginations. Eden reminds us of *who we're created to be* and heaven reminds us of *where we're called to go*. God said he has "set eternity in the human heart" (Eccles. 3:11), and I think our ability to dream is a reflection of that truth. We can create visions far beyond what's possible in this world. Their beauty pulls us forward, excites us, causes us to press in deeper to Jesus. Believing that there is something more keeps us going when life can be hard.

This near-perfect dream is always the best place to start because it pulls us the farthest and the highest. Yet when we turn that dream into a set of expectations that everything *must* be that way right here, right now, then we're headed for disillusionment.

The most important part of the desires of your heart will come into being. The essential aspects of your God-sized dreams will happen. But they will not look like that picture-perfect vision that you started with in the first place.

I go to a lot of baby showers. Cute little presents like bibs and pacifiers get passed around. Even diapers are built into fake cakes and declared "Adorable!" A few months after the baby comes, the diapers are anything but adorable and that mama is wiping spit-up off that sweet little bib for the tenth time. Imagine if you said, "Well, you look pretty tired and like you're not exactly enjoying this at the moment. That baby must have been a bad idea." She'd promptly kick you out the door and tell you her baby is the cutest thing in the universe, thank you very much.

Yet we don't often extend the same kind of grace when it comes to our dreams. We start out at the "baby shower" stage when it seems everything is going to be perfect. Then we hit the sleepless nights and changing diapers phase and call it quits because surely if this was our dream, it wouldn't be so hard and we'd love every minute.

If you don't love *any* minute of your dream, then that's a concern. But having days when you don't like that dream all that much and you'd like to trade it in for a convertible and a beach house is totally normal.

There's nothing wrong with you.

There's nothing wrong with your dream.

There's just a whole lot wrong with this fallen world. And for now, that's where we get to live out our dreams.

When you have those moments, just remember they will pass. You will get through this time. There will be better, brighter days ahead.

Sometimes we do drift away from our dream in a way that wears us out on a long-term basis. For example, a woman has a great job as a music teacher. She loves the kids and the creativity. She does so well at it that she's offered a promotion to head up a new initiative in the district that will take the music programs in the schools to a new level. She jumps at the opportunity, and six months later she finds herself dreading going to work each day. What happened? No kids and no creativity. This new job seemed to be her dream, but it wasn't. Beware of parallel or imitation dreams. Know the core characteristics of your dream and stay as close to them as possible—even if moving away from them seems enticing because of other benefits.

If you've gotten away from what you're truly called to do, then realign and get back to where you started. This is more than an occasional bad day, frustration, or needing to push through a hard time. And if that's the case, then it's time for some adjusting.

You won't always like your dream. But you will always love it. Somewhere deep inside you, there will still be that whisper that says, "Even if you're tired, even if this doesn't seem worth it, even if you feel like you're crazy, *this* is what you've got to keep doing somehow."

The good news? Just like in a good marriage, wait a bit and the spark will come back. You'll open your eyes one morning and all of those old feelings will be there again. And you'll be so glad you stayed.

Disclaimer #3: You Will Sometimes Feel Alone

She confesses over the phone, "I spent time with some women in my neighborhood last night. They all talked about normal things—the weather, kids, which restaurants were good. Then they asked about my dream, so I took a deep breath and told them my latest idea. It got so quiet you could hear the crickets. Then someone said, 'That sounds exciting!' and changed the subject."

When we're captivated by a calling, it takes over our lives. We eat, sleep, and breathe it. Our passion and energy for it are endless. We're enthralled by every new detail, every little development. It becomes part of who we are. Then if other people don't respond in the way we'd like to what's on our hearts, it can feel as if we're being personally rejected.

But no one will ever love your dream the way you do.

We talked about this a bit in the last chapter, but it's important enough to touch on again. This dream is *your* baby. No one else cares what color its poo was that morning or how many ounces it had at every one of the last ten feedings. Yes, they want to hear some of the stories and hold it occasionally. They want to see the birthday party snapshots and congratulate you when it goes off to college. But you are the one raising this dream.

Don't take it personally when other people aren't as interested or supportive as you'd like for them to be. They love you. They want to be there for you. They most likely have good intentions.

A dream only lives in one heart. "Each heart knows its own bitterness, and no one else can share its joy" (Prov. 14:10). Other people literally can't feel what you do, experience it the way you can, see the vision the way you do.

Because they love you, they will try. Some will try very hard. But at the end of the day, it's unrealistic to expect them to be as excited as you are about this dream.

Sometimes you may even have outright opposition. You might have a "Pharaoh" in your life who refuses to let the dream happen, like Moses did.

But usually that's not what discourages us the most. The moments that can threaten to derail us from our dream completely are usually when we feel simply and quietly alone.

Elijah had a moment like that after a major showdown with the prophets of Baal in the Old Testament (see 1 Kings 18–19). God shows up in a serious way and then Elijah hightails it to the desert, tells God he's done, and declares, "I'm the only one . . ." (see 19:10). While we may vary in the ways we finish that sentence, those four words are a sure sign for all of us that our hearts need some TLC. God tells Elijah that's he's far from the only one, and the same is true for us too. But in those moments, the isolation can feel very real.

You are not alone. I am not alone. We are not alone.

But we will all have moments when it feels that way. That doesn't mean there's anything wrong with you. God didn't rebuke Elijah—he fed him and let him rest. Sometimes feeling alone means we're exhausted and we need to take time to care for ourselves.

Sometimes feeling alone means we're the person God has chosen to carry this out. While we're called to be in connection with others, there are lots of examples of when God gave an individual a particular assignment only he or she could complete. When that happens, we feel weird because we end up doing something like building an ark in the front yard.

One of the most important tests of your dream is your ability to push through those times when you feel alone or strange and finish what God has called you to do anyway.

God doesn't think like we do, and if you're following his plans, there will be times when it seems you are completely out of step with everyone else. Good for you. Just keep going.

We as dreamers can sometimes add to this by not sharing the dream fully or effectively with others in our lives. We spend a lot of time in our own minds wondering about what to do next and how that will work out and picturing the future. We come back from those journeys assuming everyone else in our lives has been on that path too. But they haven't. It's up to us to hone our skill of sharing our dreams with those who are closest to us. If we don't share the vision, they can't join us as we move forward. Yes, there are inherently times when we'll feel alone no matter what, but we can lessen those by intentionally making others part of our dream too.

Sometimes we feel alone not because we need to be with others but because God wants to be with us. Our lives are busy—especially when we're pursuing a dream—and God may want to pull us aside for a bit. We've been going one hundred miles an hour on a racetrack surrounded by other cars, and all of a sudden we find ourselves parked in a quiet corner. That doesn't mean we've messed up. Instead it's often God's way of saying, "I've got something important to tell you" or "I need to prepare you for the next part of the race."

God is always with us, so that means even when it feels like it, we're never really alone. Sometimes the feeling that we are alone is actually an invitation to stop and recognize his presence with us.

You will feel alone at times. But you don't have to be lonely.

You're surrounded by love more than you can see, more than you'll ever fully know.

(A little note from me: I've started doing e-coaching to help God-sized dreamers feel less alone. You can find out more at www.holleygerth.com.)

Disclaimer #4:
Success Will Look Different Than You Think

When we start down the path of our dream, we have an idea of what the "gold medal" we'll receive when we cross the finish line will look like. Maybe we want to write a *New York Times* bestselling book. Maybe we want to have a thousand people attend our event. Maybe we just want to get our kids off to college without any of them going to jail.

We want to know that we did it right.

And for that to happen, we need to have some concrete, clear goals in mind.

But God, in his mysterious ways, hardly ever lets us have that kind of goal. He moves the finish line just before we think we're going to cross it. He changes up the course. He announces that we're doing a triathlon and not just a footrace.

He's not doing that to trick us, discourage us, or make us want to throw our hands in the air and quit. He's doing that so we remember that success is not about results. It's about a relationship. God is not all that interested in your getting things done. If he made the world in seven days, there's nothing he can't check off his to-do list without your help. What he wants on this journey to your dream is intimacy with you.

Success is simply this: obedience.

It's the moments when we forget this that we panic. That's when the parade of "have to's" start marching through our minds. I *have to* get this promotion or I'll be a failure. I *have to* make this company a success or I'll let everyone down. I *have to* reach that family goal or I'll look foolish.

With God, there aren't "have to's" involved. He gave us free will. With him, all of the steps of our dreams are "get to's." I *get to* take this promotion so I can make a bigger difference. I *get to* make this company a success so I'll have more resources to share with those in need. I *get to* reach this goal so I can glorify God.

Saying yes to God at every step is the only true success when it comes to your dream.

I've had a few moments when a really big dream of mine has come true. I feel joy, yes, and yet there's always this little whisper of *"Is this it?"* nagging in the back of my heart. That little whisper used to drive me crazy, but I've learned to recognize it as an important reminder that no, this isn't it. That success you're picturing in your mind might be wonderful, but it will not fulfill you. Only God can do so. And if you decide that the world's definition of success is the only one that you'll pursue, then you will fail even if you attain it because you will miss what matters most.

What fulfills us isn't the gold medal. It's the Maker of the universe.

There's a huge difference between setting goals and creating idols. Serve the One who loves you with excellence. But don't use him to serve your personal agenda. God is not a means to an end. He is the end.

He *is* the success you seek.

He is better than a *New York Times* bestselling book.

He is richer than millions in the bank.

He is the "more" that your heart is looking for in everything you pursue.

He promises, "You will seek me and find me when you seek me with all your heart" (Jer. 29:13). You're not called to pursue goals. You're called to pursue a Person. That's what dreams are really all about—going with God.

When you suddenly find more of him, then you know you've succeeded.

You might be spooning baby food into a little mouth and realize that the dream you prayed for is sitting in a high chair right in front of you.

You might get an email late at night saying, "I never told you that what you did made a difference to me, but . . ."

You might push through that last obstacle in a project to find you've finally broken new ground and now what matters most can grow.

Then all at once you feel his presence with you, a whisper inside your heart that seems to say, "Yes, you are a good and faithful servant." It's an echo and a preview of what we all hope to hear one day when we cross the only true finish line into heaven.

There's something more than a gold medal waiting for us. It's a crown we'll get to lay at the feet of the One who walked with us all the way.

If you don't achieve "success" in the way you imagined, don't despair. Most likely that was never God's goal for you. Whatever he has called you to do, he promises to complete through you. *If you are obedient, then you are successful regardless of the results.*

The most important "done" in your life is not the one you write next to your biggest goal. It's the one that will be spoken over you when you hear "well done" from the Lover of your soul.

Disclaimer #5:
One Day This Dream Will Be Your New Normal

Stop and look around you for a moment. Wherever you are, there's probably a piece of a God-sized dream. It could be that the man sitting on your couch is the husband you asked God for years ago. The chaos in the other room could be the voices of the children you didn't know if you'd ever have. You could be on a flight for a job you asked God to give you. You might be at a church that you spent a long time looking for before settling in to one that felt like home.

When we're pursuing a dream, it feels all-consuming. It seems like this will be *the dream* forever. It's hard to even imagine having what our hearts long for, much less feeling like it's normal for it to be in our lives. Yet most of us are living right in the middle of many of our God-sized dreams from yesterday.

Our culture is big into finding *the* one or *the* calling or *the* dream. But it doesn't seem to work that way as much in the kingdom of God. Our lives with him are a journey, and he's always calling us forward to the next thing. "They go from strength to strength, till each appears before God in Zion" (Ps. 84:7). You will most likely go from dream to dream during your lifetime.

Yes, some dreams will be more meaningful than others. Some will consume years or even decades of your life. But believing that there's just one dream out there for you puts way too much pressure on it. The God-sized dream in your heart right now isn't *the only thing* God has for you—it's simply *the next thing*. He may bring it into being, and you'll get to set your feet firmly on that piece of Promised Land for a season. Or he might redirect you to something new, and you'll find that original dream isn't what he had in mind after all.

If you do make it to your God-sized dream, at first it all feels shiny and new. Every moment is a wonder. Every new opportunity is miraculous. Yet over time it simply becomes normal. Just like when we fall in love, our bodies can't sustain all the adrenaline and other chemicals that get our hearts pumping when we're in pursuit of a dream.

If you're in the phase of the dream when it's exciting and every day is filled with glory, then take time to savor and enjoy it. What many of us don't realize is that one of the best parts of the dream is the journey to it. Sometimes what happens along the way even turns out to be more meaningful and fulfilling than the end result we had in mind because of who we become and what we experience along the way. Savor those moments. Appreciate them. Don't let them be a blur as you zip past to what you think will truly make you happy.

Maybe you've actually achieved your dream and you're wondering why it isn't as exciting as it has been in the past. If so, just know that all dreams become our new normal after we've lived with them for a while. In this scenario, the key is to remember to stay grateful and to continue asking God what else he may have for us. We don't want to become too complacent or comfortable, and yet expecting the dream to always feel new isn't realistic.

You will continue to grow as a person throughout your lifetime, and that means your dreams will grow along with you. What challenged you yesterday may become easy at some point. What you thought you really wanted may turn out to be a stop along the road to somewhere else. The dream you thought would always be your passion may give way to another deeper call that surprises you when it appears.

You don't have to find or achieve "the one" when it comes to God-sized dreams. Expecting that to happen can keep you in a holding pattern forever. Just see each new dream as another step on the journey, another piece of the Promised Land God is calling you to possess. He may have you stay there for a while or move you on more quickly than you imagined. Like we talked about before, the "more" you are looking for isn't the dream itself. It's the Dream Giver.

Each new dream he places in your heart and has you pursue is an opportunity to know him in a different way. Maybe one dream reveals his faithfulness. Another shows you his strength. Then the next one helps you discover his infinite tenderness.

....

Dreams also show you more of who you are too. As you pursue different ones, you stretch, grow, and become even more of who you've always been created to be. Dreams are a sign that you're gloriously, beautifully awake to life. Stay that way even when your dream becomes your "new normal."

Remember how you pursued that dream.

Remember how you longed for it.

Remember that today you are living in the answered prayers and realized hopes of yesterday.

Conclusion

Dreams are unpredictable. We don't know where they'll take us, what will happen along the way, or where we'll wind up in the end. But in all of that uncertainty, there's One who is the same "yesterday and today and forever" (Heb. 13:8). He's the same One who said, "I am doing a new thing" (Isa. 43:19). What God does in your life will always be changing, always surprising. Who he is will always remain the same.

That's what gives us the courage to dream.

The disclaimers are never too much for the One who has claimed you as his own and called you on this adventure with him.

He's even better than happily ever after.

Go Deeper Guide

(Download a printable version with lines for writing at www.holley gerth.com on the "Books & More" page.)

1. What "seeds" of dreams are you carrying around in your pocket? Remember, this may not be the season for them, but at least you know they're there and can be planted in God's perfect timing.

2. Describe a time in your life when you realized a blessing in your life wasn't "perfect" after all (getting married, having a baby, starting a new job). How did you find the joy in it again?

3. Who in your life shares your God-sized dreams? If there's not anyone right now, who would you like it to be (a good friend, business partner, romantic relationship, etc.)? Begin praying for God to bring the people you need for this dream into your life.

4. What's your definition of success?

5. "They go from strength to strength, till each appears before God in Zion" (Ps. 84:7). What's "normal" in your life now that was once a God-sized dream (e.g., getting married, having children, pursuing a creative passion)?

6. Which "Disclaimer" in this chapter spoke to your heart most? What will you remember from it?

7. Are you discouraged about your dream? If so, write that down here. What's the truth you need to hear from God instead?

— *Dream It. Do It.* —

Make a list of the "God-sized dreams come true" in your life. They can be small or big. When has God answered your prayers? What blessings do you see around you that simply seem "normal" now? When we're pursuing a dream, we can lose sight of how many have already come true for us. Remembering can bring joy and encourage our hearts when we need it most.

7

When Your
God-Sized Dreams
Go Wrong

The first drip slips from the sky as thunder claps its hands above us.

We're in a park trying to shoot a video for my next book.

Hours of preparation have gone into this time.

Schedules have been rearranged. Props have been purchased.

Most of all, a vision has clearly been cast. We knew exactly how this was going to work out. We'd seen it in our minds a thousand times—now all that remained was bringing everything into reality.

Or so we thought.

That first drop is followed by another. Then another. Before we even fully realize what's happening, the sky cracks open and pours buckets on us. The water is like an invisible hand, covering everything, overflowing our paint cans, drenching a canvas where we'd been carefully creating.

We dash to our car, grabbing whatever we can to carry with us.

I pull the door tight behind me. *This is not the way I thought it would be,* I whisper to myself.

We take a break until the rain stops and come back to begin filming again. Work is redone. The vision resumes. And then just as it seems we're back on track, once more the sky has other ideas.

Colors run like a rainbow river onto the sidewalk. We take cover under a giant tarp, but as the storm rages on, it becomes clear we're done for the day.

Another dash to cars. Another reckless gathering of whatever we can salvage. My umbrella is small, and in the end I drop it.

I stand in the rain, soaking wet in a red dress, and I lift my hands to the sky. The only words that come to my mind are the last ones I expected.

This is the most fun I've had in a really long time.

Letting Go of Control

God-sized dreams can take over our worlds. That's true even when it's a relatively small dream, like that video. What starts out as a creative adventure full of freedom can quickly narrow down to worry about details, intricate plans, and what we think we must control.

Let me lean in and whisper a secret to you, my friend: *God-sized dreams are not controllable*. To believe any different is to tell yourself that a bucking bronco in the rodeo ring is no different than a sweet pony at the petting zoo.

The reason we can't tame our dreams is because the One who gives them to us is wild. We want God to be more predictable—especially when we're doing what we think he wants. That film was covered in prayers that it would all be "for God's glory and the good of his daughters." And yet it rained. Not just rain—*it poured.*

Why? Heaven only knows. I mean that literally. I have no idea why on a day when we worked so hard, prepared so much, and planned every detail, God saw fit to let all of it turn into puddles on the sidewalk.

If you dare to follow a God-sized dream, dare to try for anything more than ordinary in your life, dare to take a leap outside your comfort zone, then I can guarantee at some point the same will happen to you.

Because we don't have control.

Oh, we tell ourselves we do. Or if we don't dare say it out loud, then at least we live it. We do our best to construct a reality in which we know what happens next in the story. Sure, many times we should do so. It's part of practicing wisdom and stewardship.

But that is not the same as getting to write the story. We get to say yes to what the Author asks of us, yet inevitably we turn the page and what comes next is not what we had in mind at all.

When that happens, our minds quickly search for an explanation or someone to blame. That someone is often ourselves. We question, "What did I do wrong?" This seems to be especially true for visionaries because we can so clearly see what we think should be. When reality and our ideals collide, it always seems like our fault, that we fell short in some way. My friend, let me cup your brave, beautiful face in my hands and tell you that often that isn't so at all. It's simply because you're on a journey not with a tame lion, not with a mild-mannered author but with the One who flung stars into space, who spoke and there was light, who is weaving history together in a way we will never understand this side of heaven.

Let him have control.

....

Because here's the thing: *whoever is really in control is responsible for the results.* And as much as we may stamp our feet in the rain and whine about things not going the way we want, having the weight of what ultimately happens on our shoulders would be infinitely harder.

Our part is not control. It's not results. It's obedience. It's intimacy with the One who asks us to trust him even when nothing makes sense.

We all come to a place when we're standing in the rain watching everything we hoped for wash away. What do we do then? Do we raise our fists at the heavens? Or do we take off our shoes and dance in the puddles because we are standing on holy ground?

It's the choice we all must make. And the choice that ultimately makes us.

Trying Again

So what do you do if your God-sized dream gets derailed? Actually, I should reword that question: What do you do *when* your God-sized dream gets derailed? Because it will. Several times.

An old saying slips into my mind, and somehow it seems wiser as the years go by: if at first you don't succeed, try, try again.

There's nothing romantic about the notion of "trying again." We love the stories of heroes who scale Mount Everest on the first shot, who win the gold medal their first time at the Olympics. Yet even in those grandiose stories, there are thousands of "try agains" behind the scenes.

What I want to have an honest talk about here is the shame we feel in needing to "try again"—especially as Christians.

We place high expectations on ourselves. We feel "called" to do something and therefore certain that all will unfold just the way we imagine. And if it's not right, then we must be to blame.

Oh, that is a heavy load to carry, my friends. One that can weigh us down until we stop in the middle of the road to the Promised Land and say, "I can't do this anymore."

In every other area of our lives, it seems we're able to receive grace, to find freedom, to accept that the work God is doing in us won't be complete until heaven.

But our dreams? We'd better get it right the first time or we're disqualified.

Not so, my friend. The same "try again" grace that lets you get up and restore that relationship, renew that commitment, reach out once more for God's love is the grace that will be with you every step of this journey too.

It seems the enemy tries to keep us away from God-sized dreams in two ways. First, through so much fear that we never even start. But also by telling ourselves that unless we do it perfectly and everything unfolds according to plan, then this must not be God's will and we should just give up.

That's not true.

When we look through Scripture, the paths to dreams being fulfilled are full of zigzags and "try agains" along the way. David was anointed by the prophet Samuel and told he would one day be king. Yet the years that followed were filled with the current king, Saul, chasing him through the wilderness and attempting to take his life. Talk about a detour! Joseph got sold by his brothers and unjustly thrown into jail before becoming second to Pharaoh.

It's all about being faithful where we are and refusing to quit until we see the vision God has placed in our hearts become a reality.

The video that got ruined by the rain? Even as I write this we're trading emails about another shoot on another day. Try again. Will it work this time? I don't know.

What I do know is that there are two kinds of pain in this life: risk and regret. I'd rather live with the first than the second.

The path to your God-sized dream that you had in mind may not be turning out the way you want. You may wonder why God even chose you to walk it. You may feel like someone else should be in your shoes.

Listen closely: If you have heard the call, then you must go. God will make sure you get to where he wants you in the end.

Try, try again.

Changing Your Perspective

Sometimes the storm that comes into our lives isn't a passing summer shower that happens to put a dent in our plans for the day. Sometimes the red that flashes on the radar of our dreams is more like a hurricane, and we're left standing with shattered hopes by the time it passes.

In my first devotional book, *Rain on Me*, I shared about the storms in our lives. Those words came out of the personal storm my husband and I have faced for years—infertility. As I write, that rain has not relented even though it's been almost seven years.

But who I have become and how I respond to that rain is totally different than when our journey began.

We don't have a choice about the rain that comes into the pathway of our dreams, but we can choose what we do with it—*and what we let it do to us.*

When my Nana was twenty-nine years old, she contracted polio. She was barely clinging to life and told she would likely never walk again, and the outlook for her dreams seemed grim. A pastor came to visit her and said these simple words: "Frances, this can make you bitter or better." Years later she'd say with a smile on her face, "I chose better."

Perhaps you're just starting out in your dream and the thought of something going wrong isn't even on the horizon. I'd still challenge you: *decide now*. Decide now that no matter what happens you won't let bitterness in. Decide now that you will guard your heart. Decide now that your response to the rain will be to see that every drop can lead to growth.

Maybe the hard time has already come and you're wondering what to do now. *Press on*, my friend. You are going to make it. What seems like your greatest defeat may turn out to be your most shining victory when you look at it in the rearview mirror.

The day before the infamous downpour on our filming, a friend of mine and I met for coffee. We talked about some upcoming God-sized dreams and the fears that seemed to knock at the door of my heart each day about how it might all turn out.

"What's the worst-case scenario?" she asked.

I looked at her in shock and then slowly began to spill out all I'd been afraid to even think, much less say out loud. In the light, those monsters in the closet didn't seem so scary after all.

Then the next day at the filming, I found myself face-to-face with a real, live worst-case scenario. And it turned out to be just what I needed.

When we finally pulled away, soaking wet, I noticed four little girls laughing and jumping at the edge of the sidewalk, soggy pigtails flying through the air, broad smiles across their faces. I remembered doing the same earlier in life. Rain wasn't a nuisance but instead an opportunity on hot summer days.

I wondered when I stopped feeling that way, how I decided to start fighting the rain instead of realizing that it led to every flower I saw blooming around me.

The girls squealed with unexpected joy.

"It really is a matter of perspective," I whispered.

....

345

Guarding Your Heart

As the rain began to slip from the sky that day, we quickly decided what had to be protected and what could be left in the elements. Cameras, phones, and valuable papers quickly found refuge under a table or tucked into a car before anything else. Other items soaked in the torrent until we came back for them later.

When it seems our God-sized dreams begin to go wrong, we have a similar decision to make. What will we let bear the brunt of it? What will we hide away? In the middle of it all is our hearts.

"Above all else, guard your heart" insists Proverbs 4:23. "Guarding" can bring visions of locked doors and high security safes. But shutting our hearts completely means ceasing to dream as well.

In the time those words were written, guarding was done not by technology or highly sophisticated locks but instead by literal guards. Those guards decided who got in and who stayed out. Guarding was not a one-time, passive process but a proactive one that required being highly alert, engaged, and intentional. It's the same for our hearts, especially when things on the road to our dreams get hard.

As dreamers, we have hearts that naturally tend to swing open. We let in ideas, people, and opportunities. Through all of those, we piece together the vision it seems God has for our lives. Especially when we're young, the guards of our heart may be more like a welcoming committee. Hopefully, over time we learn to use more wisdom and discernment. We begin to ask what really belongs in that sacred space within us and what should be left outside.

Then something happens and we tell the guards to shut the place down. No one gets in, nothing gets out. We've tried to dream and we've learned it's anything but safe. Yet there, alone, in the quiet of our hearts we find that rather than feeling protected we begin to despair. Where is the life and growth? What's new? Where are we headed?

Our dreams can't coexist with absolute security. We can't eliminate risk and still have our God-sized dreams come true. It just isn't possible. A dream coming to pass always requires a leap between what is now and what could be.

So, yes, guard your heart, but don't lock it away—no matter how much you've been hurt, no matter how much it feels like doing so will guarantee your safety.

Learn from your hurt, but don't make it a lock on the door of your life.

To help guard your heart when it comes to decisions about your dreams, ask yourself:

- Does this align with Scripture?
- What do the wise people in my life say about it?
- When I pray about this, what does it seem God is whispering to me?

When the rain comes, protect what's valuable. But don't hide it away so deeply that it never sees sunshine again.

Dreams need light to grow—so do you.

Remembering It's Never the End

For forty days, water floods the earth. Noah and his family float on an ark, wondering what will happen next in the earth's story. Finally, a rainbow appears—a visual promise that God will never again flood the world. Yes, it will rain. But never again will the water overcome.

I believe that promise applies to us too. Standing in the park, it seemed to us that the storm would never stop, that we'd never be dry again. But it eventually blew over, our clothes found their way to the dryer, and we went on with our day. Eventually, we'll go on with our dream of that video being completed too.

Perhaps our rainbow is found in these words: "He who began a good work in you will carry it on to completion until the day of Christ Jesus" (Phil. 1:6). This verse doesn't say *if*, *might*, *maybe*, or *hope so*—it says the good work *will* be completed. Perhaps not in the way we plan. Perhaps not in the time we plan. Perhaps not even until heaven. But those desires in your heart? The ones you know are from God? They will be fulfilled. He's not teasing you, toying with your heart, making you long for something he doesn't intend to provide.

You will not be flooded by disappointment to the point you can no longer keep your head above water. You will not be washed away without God realizing what's happening.

You will make it through the rain. Your dreams will dry off, the sun will come out again, and you'll carry on with what God has placed within your heart. It's still there. It's safe within you. You may be soaking wet, but if you look closely, you'll find the deepest, most sacred part of your dream is still dry.

That's because it's protected not by you but by the One who placed it there in the first place. The Dream Giver is also the Dream Keeper.

I'm sitting in the corner of a coffee shop. Across the room, a group of teen girls are huddled together with their mentor. I look at them, so many dreams and storms ahead for those pink T-shirts and bright eyes.

One says, "Even when we don't understand what God is doing, we can still trust his promises." She's holding an invisible umbrella in the shape of those words. One day when she needs it most, she'll reach for it. The rain will fall, the water will rise, and she will be okay. Maybe she'll even dare to embrace the rain.

Perhaps that's the heart of what dreaming really is—the receiving of what comes and making it part of something more than what we thought could be.

Today's showers into tomorrow's flowers.

The girls laugh low, and it sounds like spring thunder whispering through the skies about good things to come.

I turn my eyes upward, and I remember again how it feels to dance in the rain.

Go Deeper Guide

(Download a printable version with lines for writing at www.holley gerth.com on the "Books & More" page.)

1. Think of a time when you released control of a situation in your life to God. What happened? What's in your life now that you might need to give to him too?

2. When something doesn't work out the way you plan, do you tend to give up or try again? What encourages you to persevere?

3. How are you guarding your heart as you pursue your God-sized dreams?

4. Think of a decision you need to make in your life and put it through this set of questions as practice:
   - Does this align with Scripture?
   - What do the wise people in my life say about it?
   - When I pray about this, what does it seem God is whispering to me?

5. Are you facing discouragement or disappointment in your life right now? What does your heart need from God and those around you to move forward?

6. None of us are meant to go through life's storms alone. Who will walk through the rain with you? Who are you doing the same for too?

7. Write out a short commitment below to never, ever give up on what God calls you to do.

— *Dream It. Do It.* —

Rainy days will come on the way to your God-sized dreams. So start preparing now. Write a letter to yourself with encouragement about what's true. Then seal it up, tuck it away for a rainy day, and open it when you need to remember what God spoke to you before the storms came.

8

How to Stop Sabotaging Yourself

We've talked about how storms will come on the way to our God-sized dreams. But sometimes it's not life's weather that gets to us most—it's what we do to ourselves. God-sized dreams take a lot of energy, strength, and emotion. That means taking care of yourself as you pursue them is not self-indulgence or a luxury; it's a necessity. Believe me, I've learned that the hard way.

I remember a turning point years ago when tears slipped from my eyes. I was utterly exhausted. Working full-time, going to grad school, and keeping up with a heavy writing load had taken their toll on me. I felt as if I couldn't move forward one more step. *I know better*, I silently thought. *How did I get to this place?*

Even being trained as a counselor still wasn't enough to keep me from standing on the brink of burnout. Since that day several years ago, I've realized that most dreamers find themselves at this point at one time or another. *But you don't have to.* I made changes in my life that enabled me to pursue my God-sized dreams with joy, energy, and a full heart. So let's talk about the common mistakes and pitfalls that you can avoid as you're pursuing all God has for your life.

Remember You're Human

When we're caught up in a God-sized dream, we can forget that we all have limits. Our enthusiasm and passion can almost act as painkillers that dull us for a time to the emotional and physical toll our journey is taking on our minds, hearts, and bodies.

Yes, moving toward the "more" God has for you is an exhilarating process. But it also takes more energy and resources than any other season in our lives. My husband is an avid biker. One of the biggest thrills in his life is completing a challenging ride. Yet he knows that if he's unprepared for what's ahead, then his body won't be able to complete what his mind is determined to do. Bikers call this state "bonking." It's when your physical resources have been completely depleted, and even the most experienced and fit athlete can find himself or herself sitting bewildered on a curb with the finish line only a little bit farther down the road.

One of the most important lessons athletes in training learn is not just their strengths but also their limitations. When I first started joining my husband for bike rides, he repeated three words to me often: "Watch your pace." I had a tendency to start off at a high speed, fueled by the fun and exhilaration of the experience, but by the time I climbed the last hill, my mood was anything but enthusiastic. I realized I did much the same thing in other areas of my life. I would start a new dream, project, or strategy full of zeal only to find myself weak and weary before I reached my goal. I've learned the hard way that *everyone has limitations*. That's not a sign of weakness or failure but instead a reminder that we are gloriously and imperfectly human. While most of us roll our eyes and wish we could banish those limitations, they play an important role: to remind us that we're not God.

Actually, many of our limitations are intentionally placed there by him. He's the one who decided we'd all need an average of eight hours of sleep and frequent meals. When you look at humans as a species, it's clear we're not built simply for efficiency. We're not machines that can endlessly perform. We're not robots that are immune to the conditions around us. When God declared that what he made was good, it included the parts of your humanity that may sometimes frustrate you or slow you down.

Know your limitations. Embrace them. Then use them to get to your God-sized dreams. For example, when we work out with weights, there's a natural breakdown of our muscles—a limitation to what we can lift. But when those muscles are given rest after exercise, that tearing down is what enables new muscles to grow. If we take this into account and modify our behavior accordingly, that limitation ultimately leads us to greater strength. But if we ignore it, then we miss out on some gains our effort would otherwise bring.

You are not a superhero. You are not invincible. You are intentionally human. You don't have to be afraid that your limitations will keep God from accomplishing what he wants to do through you. Even Jesus grew tired, got thirsty and hungry, and had other human limitations. What does that tell us? *Being human is not a sin.*

God can and will accomplish all he wants to do in and through you. Your limitations won't prevent that—but pushing yourself to the point of burnout just might. Take care of yourself. Respect what you need. Accept being human.

....

You're loved just as you are by a limitless God who can more than make up for whatever you feel you lack. As Sara Frankl, an amazing woman who spent much of her life homebound and yet made a significant difference in this world, said, "There is such pressure to do everything to its limits, when all you need to do is do everything to YOUR limit ... to the limit God gives inside of you."[8]

Take Care of Your Body

When we're on the journey to "more" in our lives, especially if it's a God-sized dream, the spiritual aspect of who we are can loom larger than anything else. But an important part of crossing the finish line well is purely physical. If you want a better, more fulfilled life and to achieve your dream, then you must take care of your body.

It's an odd thing about humans that we seem to consistently try to divide up parts of who we are. We think of our bodies as separate from what we consider to be the more meaningful parts of our existence. Yet throughout Scripture God consistently reflects the spiritual through the tangible. Jesus is described as "the Word made flesh" and this is just one example of how the physical is tied closely to God's heart for us.

Your physical condition matters when it comes to your God-sized dreams. Do you need to be an Olympic athlete? Nope. Not even close. But keeping up with the basics of eating fairly well and taking some time to move your body will do wonders as you pursue the path of all God has for you.

It's ironic that when we're in the midst of following a passion in our lives, we often grow tired, and the first things to go are usually what could actually make us feel better. Believe me, I know what it's like to skip out on exercise and choose the couch instead or reach for a candy bar rather than something healthier.

Only as I learned how those choices impact not just my waist size but more importantly my mental state did I start making small but consistent shifts in my behavior.

Our brains are fascinating. To me looking at how God has wired us is the equivalent of staring at the Grand Canyon. What he has created within us gives an astounding picture of his brilliance. It's important to know how he made us so that we don't unintentionally trip ourselves up in simple ways that can be avoided.

Like we talked about before, one area of our brains is in charge of emergencies. It takes over when we're in a fight-or-flight situation. God gave us this part of our minds so that when we need to act quickly and think later, we can effectively do so. In modern life we're not often chased by wild beasts, but everyday stresses have the same effect. We trigger this part of our brains and all we hear is "You must do something to feel better now!" So we reach for a doughnut, plop on the couch, or make another choice that later leaves us shaking our heads. As Laurel Mellin describes in *Wired for Joy*:

> Stress hormones affect your motivations, because you are in survival mode. Forget about compassion. Instead, you focus on surviving the moment, doing whatever it takes. In that stressed state, your thinking brain is not functioning well. It is not thinking magnificent thoughts and fueling you with passion to be your most altruistic self. Your emotions, thoughts, and behaviors are decidedly extreme, because even though you are not being chased by a hungry lion, your brain perceives that you are. Survival is the drive, and the chemical cascade is ensuring that you will do whatever you need to do to get what you want when you want it, without

regard to how that affects others. That is the nature of the stress response.[9]

Stress is inherent in pursuing "more" in your life. It's part of God-sized dreams. When it's positive, stress serves as a motivator and pushes us toward growth (exercise is an example). But when we chronically live in stress, it saps us of our strength and we end up in survival mode.

Our brains have another area intended to help us rationally process life and our emotions. Most of the time, this is the part God intends to be in charge. But ensuring that happens means intentionally creating a healthy lifestyle. When we make poor food choices, ignore exercise, and don't get enough rest, then we flip ourselves into living out of a stress response. That makes it much harder to hear God's voice, love those around us, and effectively pursue the God-sized dreams in our hearts.

Again, this isn't about becoming an athlete. It's simply about removing unnecessary obstacles in our paths. Because they seem so ordinary and unglamorous, we can underestimate how much these little changes can impact us.

At a minimum:

1. *Commit to getting from seven to ten hours of sleep a night.* Don't buy into the myth that you don't have time to do what's needed—you always have time for God's will for you, and he created you to need that amount of sleep.

2. *Put a basic plan in place for healthy eating.* Keep it simple. I don't mean an extensive formula that includes fancy meals or extensive tracking. The easier you make it, the more likely you are to stick with it. For example, buy almonds instead of mini candy bars next time at the store. Keep healthy frozen dinners around for emergencies. Little changes can make a big difference.

3. *Get moving a few times a week.* Exercise is important for our physical well-being, but it's also a big part of what keeps us humming along mentally and emotionally as well. Research has shown that moderate exercise can be just as effective as an antidepressant because it releases natural feel-good chemicals in the brain. What exercise is the most fun for you? If possible, do that three times a week. One of my graduate school professors, Dr. Ryan Rana, liked to say that it's important to work as hard physically as we work mentally and emotionally or we get out of balance.

If you find yourself having a tough day, pause and ask, "What does my body need right now?" This may not seem like a spiritual question, but there are examples throughout Scripture like Elijah after the showdown with the prophets of Baal (he needed food and a nap; see 1 Kings 19:1–9), Jesus asleep on the boat with his disciples, and other times when what that individual needed most was something simple and tangible. Start there, because it will help you deal with whatever else may be happening.

Don't be surprised if you ask yourself that question and the answer that comes back is, "I need a triple-shot mocha with extra whipped cream." That's the part of your brain that's in charge of the stress response simply telling you what it thinks will make it all better *now*. Think of it like a toddler and kindly respond, "Thanks for that idea, but I think we'd better go with something different this time." Give yourself, and your brain, grace in those moments. Overall it serves you well—you just can't let it take charge in times of stress.

Think of your body as the vessel for the rest of you. Take care of yourself physically and respect your tangible needs. You're fearfully and wonderfully made, so learning to work with, rather than against, your body makes a big difference when it comes to your God-sized dreams.

Simplify Your Life

In *You're Already Amazing*, I talked about how we all have an emotional bank account. Much like our financial account, we make deposits and withdrawals. In that book, we discussed negative withdrawals and what to do about them. In our conversation now, we're still talking about withdrawals—but this time they're positive.

One of the reasons so many people burn out after being successful or achieving a dream is that they think because they love what they're doing and feel a great deal of passion that it's not going to take a toll on them. But any amount of energy and emotion given out is still expenditure, whether it's something that brings joy or sorrow.

I remember sitting in a class for my graduate degree in counseling and staring at a diagram about change in wonder. Although I don't recall all the details, it clearly showed how negative change (for example, losing a job) and positive change (for example, getting married) both cause stress. Timothy Ferris explains the difference:

> There are two separate types of stress. . . . Distress refers to harmful stimuli that make you weaker, less confident, and less able. Destructive criticism, abusive bosses, and smashing your face on a curb are examples of this. These are things we want to avoid. Eustress, on the other hand, is a word most of you have probably never heard. Eu-, a Greek prefix for "healthy," is used in the same sense in the word "euphoria." Role models who push us to exceed our limits, physical training that removes our spare tires, and risks that expand our sphere of comfortable action are all examples of eustress—stress that is healthful and the stimulus for growth.[10]

The goal isn't to avoid stress but instead to realize that both kinds cause withdrawals from our emotional and energy accounts.

What does this mean for your God-sized dream? You have made a decision to designate emotional and energy funds in a specific way. That naturally means that there is less to go around elsewhere. Just like most of us don't have unlimited bank accounts, our internal resources have limits as well (and as we talked about earlier, God created us this way).

Each time you spend a dollar on one thing, you are saying yes to that purchase and no to many other ways you could have used your money.

When you say yes to a God-sized dream, you are committing to a significant investment in your life. That means cutting back on extraneous emotional and energy expenses in other areas. Because many dreamers are big-picture idealists (which serves us well in many ways), we often underestimate the "cost" of what we're undertaking. Jesus put it this way: "Suppose one of you wants to build a tower. Won't you first sit down and estimate the cost to see if you have enough money to complete it? For if you lay the foundation and are not able to finish it, everyone who sees it will ridicule you, saying, 'This person began to build and wasn't able to finish'" (Luke 14:28–30).

These verses are talking about the cost of being a disciple. And, ultimately, that's what we're talking about too. This isn't just going after the "more" you want in your life—instead this is about saying yes to God and following him faithfully through God-sized dreams. There is always a cost.

Is it worth it? Oh yes.

But being able to finish well means, as Jesus says above, understanding the cost and planning for it ahead of time.

When I work with life coaching clients, I often give them the assignment to "say a hard no" during the week. In other words, to turn down something they feel pressured to do in order to pursue something more significant instead. It always makes them squirm a bit, but when they report back about what they chose to say "the hard no" to, there is always relief in their voice.

What is draining your time, emotions, or energy?

It can be as obvious as clutter in your house.

Or as complicated as a toxic relationship.

Whatever it is, now is the time to deal with it.

Make a list of everything that takes valuable resources that you will need for your God-sized dream. Everything. Put a minus sign (–) by anything that drains you and a plus sign (+) by anything that adds to your inner account by bringing you joy. Then look through the minuses and decide which things have to stay (for example, laundry) and which ones can be decreased, delegated, or eliminated all together (for example, the committee you signed up for that sucks the life out of you but you feel obligated to continue).

Look at the items that remain and begin to make plans for dealing with each one. For example, can someone help you with the laundry, or can you do it on one particular day? As you try to find solutions, you'll hear all kinds of nonsense in your mind: "You're selfish. Everyone else seems to handle this; why can't you?" Recognize those statements for what they are: lies that distract you from God's calling in your life.

You are giving God, those you love, and yourself a tremendous gift by simplifying your life so that you can focus on what matters most. It's actually the most unselfish thing you can do. Start by counting the cost, and you are much more likely to finish well.

Building Your Dream Team

From the very beginning, God made it clear that "it's not good for man to be alone" (or woman either) (see Gen. 2:18). Yet in our culture chasing a dream is often seen as a solitary pursuit. Let's put that myth to rest right now. No one achieves their God-sized dreams alone. Even Jesus had disciples, and he was perfect. We're not intended to carry out God's plans for our lives without the support and encouragement of others.

When it comes to God-sized dreams, it helps to fill several specific roles.

A Mentor

There's nothing new under the sun, and wherever you're going, someone else has already been there. Find someone who has pursued the dream that you have who can offer wisdom along the way. Or, if their journey isn't the same path as yours, at least look for someone who has experience doing what it takes to complete a dream well: taking risks, building relationships, persevering. Even if they're not in the same field as you are, those skills will transfer over to your situation too. Most importantly, a mentor is someone who follows hard after God with all of her heart and will remind you to do the same.

An Encourager

While a mentor is a few steps ahead of you, an encourager is someone who's right by your side. Your journeys are somewhat parallel, and she understands where you are now. You're facing the same kind of struggles, celebrating similar victories, and when one of you has a bad day, the other can be a source of strength. "Two are better than one, because they have a good return for their labor: If either of them falls down, one can help the other up. But pity anyone who falls and has no one to help them up" (Eccles. 4:9–10).

A "Younger" Woman

When Scripture encourages older women to train the younger, we tend to think of it in terms of age. But I think it's really more about the heart. When I use the term *younger*, I'm not referring to years but instead to where each woman is on her journey. She may just be starting out in her dream while you're midway through yours. Perhaps she wants to grow in an area where you have experience. Or her spiritual faith might be just taking root while yours has gone a little deeper. Who can benefit from where you are now?

A Cheering Section

In addition to the individuals above, thriving in your dream also comes from having a group of people you can turn to for encouragement, advice, or prayers. This can take time to build, but you can begin asking God, "Who is in my cheering section?"

As I tackled a challenge, my life coach, Denise Martin, admonished me to set up an "advisory board." These women serve as a team who can review ideas, confidentially pray, and speak the truth to me no matter how hard it may be for me to hear at times. I love that each one brings a different perspective, and their variety of strengths fills important gaps for me.

I communicate with my advisory board primarily through email. You can connect with yours online, over the phone, or face-to-face.

If you think, "I don't know who I would ask to be on my team," you're not alone. Most people don't have a group like this in their lives. And we all go through seasons and circumstances, such as a move, that impact our relationships at times. If you have even two people in your life you can confide in, including family members, that's more than most Americans, according to research.[11] Cultivating these kinds of relationships takes time and intention but is definitely worth the investment.

Who You DON'T Need

Each of the relationships above can help you as you pursue your dream. But before we wrap up this section, we need to talk about the kind of people you *don't* need in your life on this journey too. That may sound a bit harsh, but as we talked about before, the funds in your emotional and energy bank account need to be spent on your dream, and some people will drain away those resources without any real benefit to you or them.

Avoid negative people as much as possible. They will shoot holes in your dream, get you discouraged, and distract you with problems you can't fix. If you're around someone negative, intentionally resist the pull in that direction. Consistently go back to positive topics and tones in the conversation. You can't afford to spend your valuable emotion and energy, and even though they don't realize it, neither can they. You're doing those negative folks a favor by brightening their day a bit rather than joining the downward spiral.

Be ready for the doubters. Many people will tell you that your dream is silly or foolish or will never work. Take those statements as compliments and proof that you're disrupting the status quo—which is what every God-sized dream does. You don't want everyone to like your idea. If they do, it's not out of the box enough.

Change scares people, and the reaction they have is not about you but instead about their discomfort. Smile, nod, and move ahead.

Stand guard against bullies. One step past the doubters stand the bullies—those who intentionally oppose your dream. Again, if you've got bullies, it's a pretty good sign that you're doing something significant. Jesus definitely had his share. In *The Dream Giver*, Bruce Wilkinson says this about bullies:

> Some bullies you absolutely have to convince in order to move forward, especially if it's a boss or a key player in your Dream. . . . Some bullies simply need to know that you have heard them out. Some need to be affirmed for their viewpoint or role in your life. Some simply need to be avoided.[12]

In other words, expect bullies at some point and then strategically address them. It's not fun to engage with them, but ultimately they will help you build your perseverance.

Relationships are at the heart of who we are and all we do. While dreams can seem to be about tasks or achievements, ultimately they are always about people. That's because God is inherently relational. He *is* love, and whatever he calls us to do will be about love too.

Decide to Be on Your Side

What if our thoughts about ourselves were broadcast to the world? Are you getting chills down your spine just thinking about it? Me too! The reality is, most of us are much kinder to others than we are to ourselves. It's easy to offer grace to those who fail us, but when we don't meet our own expectations, we can be unmerciful. But in addition to the folks we talked about above, another essential member of your team is *you*.

A famous quote says, "We have seen the enemy and he is us." While we talked about bullies, it often turns out that we are our biggest opponent. Before we can move forward with all God has for our lives, we have to decide that we will be on our side.

The apostle Paul asks a rhetorical question, "If God is for us, who can be against us?" (Rom. 8:31). It seems the answer is intended to be "no one." Yet as I looked at those words one day, the realization flashed across my mind that there is someone who can be against me. It's *me*. I know that firsthand because I've struggled with being hard on myself throughout my life. I sometimes wonder if that's part of being a dreamer—because we can imagine everything as better (including ourselves), we become frustrated when the ideal isn't met.

So let's have a talk, you and I. It's time to stop coming against us and instead stand with God as we say, "I'm not perfect but I'm deeply loved, made in God's image, and I have everything I need to be all he's called me to be."

Occasionally a life coaching client will make a statement about herself that's so harsh it shocks me. I catch my breath and then quietly ask the question, "Would you say that to your dear friend?"

She quickly responds, "No, of course not."

I gently reply, "Then God doesn't want you to say it to yourself either." There's usually a moment of quiet as what this really means sinks into her heart.

When you wound yourself with your words, it's the same to God as if you were to doing it to someone else in your life. Jesus said to love our neighbors as ourselves. That means all of the "one another" statements in Scripture (i.e., be kind to one another, encourage one another) apply in our relationship with ourselves too.

We often fear that pride will creep in if we start treating ourselves with more kindness. But research has shown that those with a healthy self-relationship are more likely to be loving to others as well. Humility is strength under control. It's knowing who we are, being secure in that, and then choosing to serve.

You will face a lot of tough moments on the road to your God-sized dreams. Obstacles will appear, mistakes will be made, and sometimes you will be staring at the ceiling in the middle of the night and asking yourself, "Why in the world did I ever decide to do this?" It's at these moments when all of your encouragers are fast asleep that you need to be able to be on your own side and push through to what's next. More dreams die by self-inflicted wounds than any other kind.

God is for you ... and it's time for you to be too.

Conclusion

There's only one way for the unique God-sized dream in your heart to come into being, and that's through you. God doesn't have a backup plan. You are here at this time, in this place for a purpose that only you can fulfill.

When we think of our dreams, it's easy to shift the focus outside of ourselves. We plan, strategize, and take steps forward. Yet what's most crucial to our dream is what's happening within. Taking care of yourself is not a luxury when you're pursuing a dream—it's a necessity. It's not selfish—it's the ultimate in self-discipline. You and everyone else in your life will benefit when you proactively address the areas of your life that have the potential to trip you up or slow you down.

You matter. You are wonderfully made. You are the vessel for a God-sized dream.

And that, my friend, is a beautiful thing.

Go Deeper Guide

(Download a printable version with lines for writing at www.holley gerth.com on the "Books & More" page.)

1. How is your pace of life right now? We all have one that's optimal. Does it feel like you're below it, above it, or just right? What changes might you need to make?

2. What are you doing to take care of your body (sleep, exercise, what you eat)? What's one small way you can do so even more? In other words, what does your body need right now?

3. If you haven't already, make a list of everything that takes valuable resources that you will need for your God-sized dream. Everything. Put a minus sign (–) by anything that drains you and a plus sign (+) by anything that adds to your inner account by bringing you joy. Then look through the minus column and decide which things have to stay (for example, laundry) and which ones can be decreased, delegated, or eliminated all together.

4. Who is on your dream team (mentor, encourager, younger woman, cheering section)? Note: if you don't have all of these people, it's okay. Most of us don't. Just begin praying for God to fill in the gaps.

5. What are you most critical of yourself about? What does God want to replace those words with instead?

6. In what other ways could you be sabotaging yourself? What changes can you make so that's no longer the case?

7. "If God is for us, who can be against us?" (Rom. 8:31). The answer to that question is intended to be "no one." Write a

short prayer to God expressing that you will side with him in being for yourself too.

— *Dream It. Do It.* —

Make plans to connect with someone on your dream team this week. Share an update about what's going on with your God-sized dream and let that person know how they can pray for you. Then ask how you can do the same for her too.

9

Why Your Dream Is Worth It

The sun had just begun to slip lower in the sky. I felt traces of sand between my toes as I stepped onto the narrow boardwalk that led to the beach. As I crested a dune, I took in a scene that caused tears to spring to my eyes. Standing on the beach in what felt like a glimpse of heaven were the writers of (in)courage, a website I co-founded. As I looked at them laughing and talking while they watched the sunset, all the hard moments of the last year flashed before me again. I caught the eye of co-founder Stephanie Bryant, and we smiled at each other, silently saying, "Yes, it's all been worth it."

As I reflected on that moment, I realized it was the closest I'd come to experiencing what it might be like to step into eternity and hear those words, "Well done, good and faithful servant." I knew all the struggles and battles of this life would fade away as I looked at the One I loved and whose joy I could now share forever.

God-sized dreams are always worth it for so many reasons—some that we experience in this life and others that wait for us in eternity.

Because God Doesn't Have a Plan B for You

If someone else has a dream similar to ours, we may think that there are other ways this dream can come into being. Surely someone else could take it on or do what you're called to do. But it's clear—there's just one irreplaceable you. God doesn't have a backup plan for your life. Either this dream happens through you or it doesn't happen at all. Yes, he can find another way to accomplish his purposes, but it won't be the same.

You are here at this time in history, with the strengths you have and the experiences you've gained, for a purpose. Every part of your life has been designed so that you can say a loud "Yes!" to God when he asks you to step out in faith with him.

As we talked about before, this isn't about the size of your dream. It may be as small as a mustard seed, but we know that in God's hands even just that much faith can move mountains. It's not what the world thinks, how much recognition we receive, or the amount of applause we hear that matters. More is not better in God's kingdom. Simply being obedient to whatever he asks matters most.

Because you are the only one who can fulfill this dream, there is no one better than you to do it. Resist the urge to compare, and instead embrace that this dream is between you and God. He doesn't want you to change who you are to be someone else. He simply wants you to become all he's created you to be and trust that means you will have everything you need to make this dream come true.

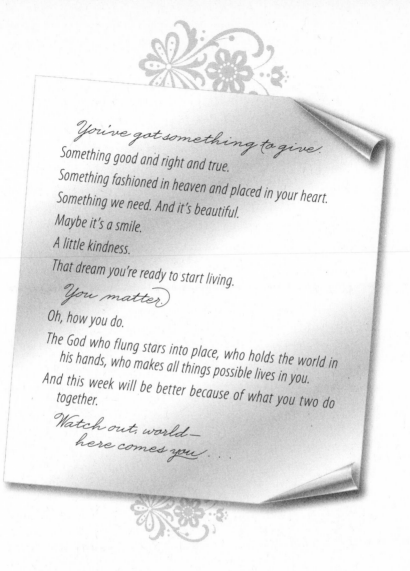

You've got something to give.
Something good and right and true.
Something fashioned in heaven and placed in your heart.
Something we need. And it's beautiful.
Maybe it's a smile.
A little kindness.
That dream you're ready to start living.

You matter.

Oh, how you do.
The God who flung stars into place, who holds the world in his hands, who makes all things possible lives in you.
And this week will be better because of what you two do together.

Watch out, world—
here comes you . . .

We need you, just you, to be who you are. We don't get a second chance at what you have to offer. We never have another opportunity to receive what you have to give.

You are one-of-a-kind wonderful. You are chosen by God for a particular purpose, and he promises to see it through to completion if you'll only say yes to what he's whispering to your heart—and your heart alone.

Because You Will Never Feel Closer to God Than When You're Pursuing a Dream

God-sized dreams are invitations for you to get on board with him and go to places your heart has never imagined. And there's only one way to get there—by being right by his side. The moments in my life when I've sensed God's presence most have always been when I'm taking a step of faith with him. That's true in Scripture all the way back to the Israelites' journey to the Promised Land. God's presence was with them, and their number one job was simply to follow wherever he led.

In our culture, we value learning and thinking quite a bit. We can find ourselves in the middle of a Christian life that's all about knowing. Yet somewhere within us there remains a longing to be *doing* with God. We're created not just for belief but also for action. When you put into practice what God has been whispering to your heart, it's the difference between talking about ice cream and sticking your spoon into the most delicious hot fudge sundae ever imaginable. There's simply no substitute for experience.

If your spiritual journey has been feeling a bit dull, then a deep dive into an adventure with Jesus might be just what you need. Don't wait until you feel like you know everything. You're going with the One who knows it all. He will fill you in as you go, through his Holy Spirit.

When James said, "Come near to God and he will come near to you" (4:8), he offered a powerful invitation. The more we pursue God, the more he chases us right back. We're made to share a life with him that's full of intimacy, excitement, and passion.

You are in a relationship with the God who spoke the world into being, who hung the stars in place, who created that dream in your heart. You may have many opportunities in your lifetime, but none is better than this—to let God take you by the hand and lead you into all he has for you.

In the classic story *Chariots of Fire*, Olympic runner Eric Liddell is planning to go to China as a missionary. But he first competes in the Olympics. When his sister questions this decision, he replies that yes, he will be a missionary, but that God also made him fast and he feels God's pleasure when he runs.

Find the moments when you feel God's pleasure, when you sense him right next to you urging you on, when your dream and your relationship with him intertwine in a flow that feels like what you've been made for all along. Then live in those moments as much as possible.

Because Dreams Make You Come Alive

We all know what it's like to simply go through the motions. We get up, move through our day, and drift off to sleep wondering if there's more to life. And no matter how much we try to silence it, something within us says, "Don't be satisfied with this." We brush it off and tell ourselves we need to be content. But the longing remains.

Then one day we find the courage to say yes to the whisper within us and what we're being asked to do. We take the first step of faith and find that rather than falling, we suddenly feel like we're flying. Parts of who we are that have been dormant, perhaps for years, spring to life again. We discover we can do more than we thought we could in ways we might not even have imagined.

Rather than an obligation, life begins to feel like an adventure. We wake up in the morning and want to know what God is going to do in and through us today. We drift off to sleep dreaming about what comes next. Even in the hard moments, there's still the exhilarating feeling that we are fully engaged in the world around us and we are right where we are supposed to be.

There's a myth in Christian culture today that says the Promised Land is only heaven. When I look through those chapters in Scripture, I just don't see that being true. Yes, the ultimate Promised Land is ours when we step from this life to the next, but I believe God has so much for us right here and now too.

We are made for a purpose, and until we are intentionally pursuing it, we feel half alive. We are dreamers waiting for someone to wake us up so the real adventure can begin.

If you feel numb, depressed, or even just flat-out bored, I don't believe that's God's plan for you. Yes, we all have seasons when we go through grief or experience difficulties. But if we live year after year in a state of just surviving, God has more for us. He didn't put you on this earth just so you could hold on by your fingernails until you get to heaven. He loves you and wants you to thrive. As one of my favorite verses says, "The LORD be exalted, who delights in the well-being of his servant" (Ps. 35:27).

But we have to agree with God that not only is this possible but it's actually what he wants for us. The Israelites wandered in the desert for forty years because they refused to believe God really could give them more. They looked at the Promised Land, saw the abundance, and said that they were better off playing it safe.

Don't settle. Don't give in to fear. Don't stand on the edge of all God has for you and be sent back to the desert.

You're allowed to be happy.

You're allowed to be blessed.

You're allowed to live a full life.

Even more than allowed—this is what God ultimately wants for you. If you believe anything else, then you have been sold a lie. Now let me be clear: all of the above doesn't come through doing whatever we want. That's not the way it works. But obedience is supposed to lead to joy. Even Jesus endured the cross "for the joy set before him" (Heb. 12:2). Don't let the idea that suffering is part of the Christian life trick you into believing that it's the entirety of what God has for you. It's not even the majority. It's only a gateway that he will use to bring you into deeper joy in the end.

And just surviving is certainly not God's plan for your life either. He didn't put you on the earth to be mediocre. He didn't form you with his hands, dream you up in his heart, and place you in this world for a purpose just for you to go through life being "fine."

Oh no, my friends. God has more for you—so much more than you can even imagine. You are made in his image, and the more you display all he has placed within you, the more you bring him glory. And when we bring him glory, we feel joy, freedom, and purpose. Life becomes a gift rather than a chore.

Will you believe that God does have a Promised Land for you? I know that you will, that you do. You are not a grumbler. You are not a doubter. You are not someone who settles for safety. You, dear reader, are a Joshua or Caleb standing on the edge of the Promised Land, seeing all that is good and saying, "Yes, this is possible!" (see Num. 13). Then you take the steps of faith, fight the battles, and go the distance to take possession of all God has for you.

Spend your life being fully alive.

Then spend eternity full of joy.

When God said his plans for you are good, he meant it.

Because Regret Hurts More Than Risk

Imagine you step onto the porch of a retirement home. A few contented residents sit in the sunshine enjoying a peaceful day. You decide to spend some time talking with each one. You ask about their childhoods, their families, and what has mattered most in their lives. Then you ask a single question: What do you regret most? The answers startle you. One by one they share not about epic mistakes, business failures, or family falling-outs. They tell you about what they *didn't do*.

Does that sound far-fetched? As I mentioned earlier in this book, studies have been done asking older people what they regret most about their lives. The overwhelming answer: what they didn't do is much more painful than what they did. It seems that even when you try and fail, you walk away with something, even if it's just a lesson learned that can be applied next time. But if you don't give it a shot at all, you're guaranteed to end up with nothing.

Our brains are wired with what scientists like to call a "negativity bias." It has many different facets, but long story short, it means we pay more attention to the negative. When we're thinking through taking a risk or pursuing a dream, our mind has no trouble summoning up every worst-case scenario imaginable. I believe God gave us this ability to navigate life, to survive, and to make overall sound decisions. But when it comes to our dreams, this normally handy feature of who we are can get in the way.

There's a time and place for your negativity bias to serve you, but it's not when God has just asked you to take a leap of faith. The wonderfully made systems in our minds are much like the computer I'm typing on right now. I'm very thankful the software is there, but I know it's up to me to apply it and even override it when necessary. We've talked about overcoming fear, and that's exactly what we've got to do if we're going to be one of the residents sitting on the front porch of the retirement home telling stories of victory and not tales of regret.

We have one life to live. We have one shot at fulfilling the purpose God has for us. And while we live in a culture that values safety to the extreme, I don't see God doing the same thing. Throughout Scripture he places people in precarious situations and then comes through in miraculous ways. But there is always that moment when they must decide, "Will I choose obedience over safety?" Yes, God promises us security, but safety and comfort are another matter.

Safety is ultimately an illusion, a grasp for control that makes our minds calm down. But none of us are truly safe. A meteor could crash through my ceiling right now, and that would be the end of me in this life. The idea that we can be safe can trick us into avoiding risks that God is asking us to take. And ironically, when we risk with him it's the safest thing we can do. Because he gives us what truly can't be taken away—security. Security doesn't depend on external circumstances. It's invincible. So you may be taking more risks than ever before and feeling more fear than you think you can stand. But actually you're more secure than when you felt safe because you're right in the middle of God's plan.

Your brain will rebel against this idea. It will tell you that survival is paramount (whether that survival is physical or just emotional and social). It will tell you that if you take that step, reach out to that person, push past that limit, your world will come to an end. That's your brain's job, at least the amygdala, which is where the flight or fight response resides. But another part of you (your prefrontal cortex—the reasoning part of your mind) can respond with, "Thank you for looking out for me, amygdala. I'm glad you showed me there could be danger here. And you're right—but the greatest danger of all is missing what God has for me. I serve a limitless God for whom all things are possible, so I'm moving ahead with him."

If you move ahead and nothing works out as you planned, you still have what matters most. And that's knowing you were faithful. Your role is obedience. God's role is results. That's the only way to live without regret. As John Piper explains:

> This is the promise that empowers us to take risks for the sake of Christ. It is not the impulse of heroism, or

the lust for adventure, or the courage of self-reliance, or the need to earn God's favor. It is simple trust in Christ—that in him God will do everything necessary so that we can enjoy making much of him forever. Every good poised to bless us, and every evil arrayed against us, will in the end help us boast only in the cross, magnify Christ, and glorify our Creator. Faith in these promises frees us to risk and to find in our own experience that it is better to lose our life than to waste it.[13]

Before you get to sit on a front porch and talk about your life one day, make sure you live in a way that lets you tell stories of God's glory that will knock everyone else off their rockers.

Because It's Really Not about You

As Rick Warren's infamous line at the beginning of *The Purpose Driven Life* declares, "It's not about you." We read those words with a giggle, a bit of shock, a twinge of guilt. Because really our biggest battle in life is exactly that: not making it about us.

Even our God-sized dreams can become about us. When that happens, the enemy will try to tell you to stop. He'll whisper that you shouldn't be doing this at all, because really it's all about you. Swat that thought away like you would a stray fly buzzing in your ear. You are human, and you will never be able to pursue a worthwhile goal without it being about you at times. The point is not to say, "This isn't about me at all" but instead to say, "This isn't all about me." Of course God wants part of the dream to be about you. The entire story of the gospel is about partnership, intimacy, relationship. The best loves, the best marriages, are not one-sided. They have give-and-take, shared joys, two hearts coming together in a way that benefits them both.

It's the same with the journey we share with Jesus. He wants us to be part of the dreams he's placed within us. What we're to guard against is simply the temptation to put ourselves first, to make our dream an idol, to forget the Giver and cling to the gift.

Feeling guilty? Don't—that's not what this is about. We all face those temptations. Even Jesus did in his face-off with the enemy in the wilderness. Simply realize that they're part of the journey and you will have to address them at some point.

So if it's really not about us, then what is it all about? The answer actually is not "what" but instead "who." Because when it comes down to it, all of our lives, all we do, are simply to be about making much of Jesus. As John the Baptist said, "He must increase, but I must decrease" (John 3:30 KJV). Your dream is a gift God gives to you. What you make of it is your gift to him. You have an opportunity to bring glory and honor to the God who hung the stars in place. Isn't that amazing? He could do anything with just a breath, just a word, and yet instead he chooses to partner with you.

It's all about God.

It's all about his kingdom, his purposes, his name, his plans that stretch throughout eternity. We're all part of a much bigger story. We're invited to play a role in the only real truth. It's an incredible honor.

What does that say about you? It says that you are chosen. You are treasured. You are cherished. You are important to God's work in this generation. It means he has entrusted you with something very meaningful, a piece of his heart reflected in yours.

You are made in the image of God, and there is a part of who he is that will only get expressed through who you are. None of us can possibly contain all of who he is—only Jesus could do that—but who you are reveals a tiny bit of who he is in a way no one else ever will.

Your God-sized dreams are not just about making his purposes and plans a reality. They are also about revealing his character through you. Who you are on this journey is just as important as what you do.

It's a paradox. A mystery. It's not about you, and yet you are right there in the middle of it. Think of yourself as a lightbulb. You're there to shine, and yet really what matters most is simply what you illuminate, what you allow others to see.

The God of the universe has chosen you as his ambassador, his partner, his way of sharing his light with the world. You may not feel qualified. You may not feel ready. You may not think you can do what he asks. Listen, my friend: you are all you need to be to do all he's called you to do. "It's not about you" can be hard words to hear, but in this context they can also bring a profound sense of relief. You do not have to be superwoman to make God's plans happen in your life. Because it's ultimately about him, and your role is simply to let his light flow through you. You're the vessel—he's the source.

I'm smiling as I write these words and think of you. Maybe you're in an office. Perhaps you're curled up on a couch. You could be on a plane or tucked under the covers with sleep coming soon.

Go ahead and shine, my friend.

"But that's not humble."

"I don't want it to be about me."

When I talk to women about living the purpose and calling God has for their lives, I hear those two phrases often (and I've said them myself).

And yet . . .

> You are the light of the world. A town built on a hill cannot be hidden. Neither do people light a lamp and put it under a bowl. Instead they put it on its stand, and it gives

light to everyone in the house. In the same way, let your light shine before others, that they may see your good deeds and glorify your Father in heaven. (Matt. 5:14–16)

In other words, let what you do shine in a way that helps people see who God is.

Yes, people will see you.

That's okay.

You're still being humble.

And it's certainly not about you.

We all know a lightbulb isn't ever the main attraction—it just enables us to see what matters most. So go ahead and shine, my friend. Brighter than ever.

Oh yes, that's beautiful!

I think I can see the glow all the way from here.

Keep it up, friend. Keep making much of the One who made you. You bring so much light to the world and so much joy to his heart when you do.

Final Thoughts

I'm wishing we were together right now. By now we wouldn't just meet at a coffee shop. We'd hang out at my house. I'd pull up a chair for you at my kitchen table. I'd pour you a cup of something warm and cozy. Then I'd raise my mug high in the air and propose a toast: to you, to your dream, and most of all to the God who gave it to you. As our mugs clinked and we sipped, we'd talk of how this journey is going for you. You could tell me about your victories and I'd cheer with you. You could tell me about the hard parts too. Then I'd do the same.

By the time we got to our last drop, I imagine we would both be ready to say the same thing: "It's worth it."

It always is in the end. There will be days in your dream when the fog of fear or doubt descends and you forget. It's okay—the sun will come out again and you will remember. There will be times when you're tired and you just want to stop, but somehow you'll find the strength to keep going. There will be moments when it seems nothing is coming together, and then God will show up and split your Red Sea, and you'll watch in amazement at what he can do.

It's a wild ride, this dreaming. Our role is simply to hang on with all our hearts. And to remember that it's worth it because God is worth it. The One who called us by name, took our place on the cross, fashioned our hearts, and walks with us every day is the ultimate reward. He's the reason we keep going, keep pressing on, and refuse to give up.

As we sat at the table, there would be an empty chair across from us. I'd tell you of how as a little girl I used to have my mom pull up an extra chair for Jesus. We'd both laugh at my innocence. I'd tell you that sometimes it almost seemed as if I could see him sitting across the table, smiling, enjoying our conversation.

And in moments like these, as we talk of dreams and the Giver of them, it still feels that way too.

Go Deeper Guide

(Download a printable version with lines for writing at www.holley gerth.com on the "Books & More" page.)

1. God doesn't have a plan B for you. How does knowing that affect your perception of how much your life matters?

2. When do you feel closest to God as you're pursuing your dream?

3. When do you feel most alive and fulfilled?

4. Regret hurts more than risk. What do you think of that statement?

5. "It's not about you." What helps you get beyond yourself and focus on God's kingdom in your life and dreams?

6. What else makes your God-sized dream worth it?

7. If you don't pursue your God-sized dream, who will it affect? If you do pursue it, who will that affect?

— *Dream It. Do It.* —

Review what you've written in the chapters before this one. What's different than when you started? Take a few moments to thank God for where he's brought you so far and where you're going in the future.

10

God-Sized Dreams
Stories

We tend to think God-sized dreams happen through larger-than-life people. The stuff of legends. The ones who seem to dwell on unreachable pedestals. But that's a myth. God-sized dreams always happen through ordinary folks. People like you, me, and your neighbor across the street.

The stories that follow are about real God-sized dreamers. You might bump into them at the grocery store. You might sit across the aisle from them at church. You might read their blog or be friends with them on Facebook.

None of them would describe themselves as exceptionally brave or outrageously adventurous. But they're all consistently, lovingly living in an obedient way that makes a difference.

I've learned a lot from their stories, and I hope you will too.

One disclaimer: when we read the God-sized dream stories of others, it's always tempting to compare. Please resist that urge. As we've talked about all along the way, the God-sized dream he has for you perfectly fits the size of your heart. *There is only one you.*

What I want you to see in these stories isn't "how to" but instead more of the heart of what it means to be a God-sized dreamer. I imagine I could include your story here too. And who knows? Maybe someday I will.

By the way, these are all women I know in real life. They're not stories from the internet or out of a magazine listing the world's most influential people. They're women I love, celebrate, and have the privilege of cheering on as they pursue their dreams. I tell their stories the same way I would share them with you over a cup of coffee. Because you know by now that's just how we do things around here.

While You're Waiting: Kristen Strong

In fifth grade Kristen chose staying in to do schoolwork before going out to recess. She worked hard and slept little even in high school because she was bent on giving maximum effort so she could shine.

If effort alone could have brought ultimate success in high school and beyond, she would have graduated valedictorian. She did well but was still not the "A" girl she desperately wanted to be. She says, "No matter what I did—or how much effort I expended—I fell into that expansive middle labeled 'average.'"

She shared with me how she couldn't enjoy what small victories she had because her good was never good enough. She thought God worked through and was most proud of those whose life's work and worth were labeled with a big, tangible A. Something everyone could see for themselves. The grade A end result proved their God-sized dreams were realized.

Kristen says that early attitude carried right on into her grown-up years too. "Unfortunately, I have bought into this for part of my adult life too. That the visible results—what I can see right now—determine the success of my God-sized dream."

But then Kristen began discovering that's not how God works. She says, "His God-sized dream in me is taking something I have little patience for . . . time. Like a fitful toddler, I want what I want and I want it now. But God says, 'Listen, girl. I planted this dream in you. Since I planted it, I get to say how long it takes to grow and how tall it's going to be. I'm working on you more through this dream than you realize.'"

Kristen adds that she now knows God first pushed her to work hard as a young girl because it would lay a foundation for going the distance and appreciating a slower path instead of a quick sprint to her dreams. So she's shifting her thinking to look at the journey as what matters most rather than the destination. Kristen says on the journey we can:

- *Build relationships.* Ever try to carry on a conversation while sprinting down a track? It's kinda hard. While slower times of life can be frustrating, they can also be opportunities for meeting folks and nurturing relationships.
- *Improve our skills.* If we want to learn and improve our craft, we need to take the time to study hard so we can learn what God wants us to learn.
- *Fellowship with God.* We want to enjoy his very real and active presence. We will grow and flourish most when we are in regular communication with the One who instilled our dreams in the first place.

Sometimes God-sized dreams seem so powerful we could burst from the excitement and scariness of it all. If God is working on us through the journey and not just the destination, we want to give him some serious glory in the process. Kristen sums it up this way: "I want to get caught up in him rather than results." It's about each step with God along the way and throughout eternity.

> *You make known to me the path of life;*
> *you will fill me with joy in your presence,*
> *with eternal pleasures at your right hand. (Ps. 16:11)*

And you know what else? When God instills a God-sized dream in your heart, he is telling you, "You are enough." You know enough. You have what it takes. You may not think it, feel it, or see anything in front of you that proves it, but it's true nonetheless. Sometimes it may take missing-recess, up-all-night kind of effort, but keep going the distance.

God-sized dreams penetrate deep. So if it seems yours is taking time to bloom, perhaps it means he is still growing it. Don't give up on the fact that his dream for you (and the wait!) is ripe with purpose.

Over the last few years, I've watched Kristen continue to be faithful when it comes to waiting for God's plans in her life. Right now her family is in the midst of waiting to hear if her husband will be deployed to active military duty again. Her dream is for all of them to be a family in one place, but she knows God may have other plans.

Kristen and her husband also recently discovered their young daughter will need surgery to correct a genetic feature in her spine. Another God-sized dream for Kristen is a completely healthy daughter, but it seems there will be some medical hills to climb before that's a reality. As she shared the news with her friends and family on her blog, *Chasing Blue Skies* (www.chasingblueskies. net), Kristen wrote:

> The Lord is always revealing and saving and proclaiming. Sometimes this fact shows up in jump up and down good news, like twin lines on a pregnancy test. Sometimes it shows up real quiet, like on a difficult but certain x-ray. Either way, it shows up because *he* shows up. He doesn't reveal and then take a nap or proclaim and then forget about us. He moves and acts always, even during those dreaded ambiguous uncertain times. Especially then.
>
> Every bit of bad news holds good news because He. Is. Always. Good.[14]

In the good, the bad, and the in-between times, Kristen has learned that God-sized dreams are not about our circumstances but instead about the One who holds our lives in his hands.

I love this beautiful, openhearted God-sized dreamer who lights up the room with her smile and knows how to make anyone's day brighter even if she's having a difficult one of her own. Kristen isn't just waiting—she's thriving. She's daily living by grace as she trades her "not good enough" striving for a "more than enough" God who loves her deeply and shows us all more about how to do the same.

When You Have More Than One God-Sized Dream: Heather Steck

We got married one day apart. We had the same flippy blonde hair. We could sing along to every Amy Grant song. We also both worked at DaySpring, the Christian subsidiary of Hallmark. I wrote cards and Heather made them beautiful with her stunning designs. We ate lunch together, played fun games with our husbands on the weekends, and even shopped at the same stores. I'd never met someone whose heart and life seemed so parallel to mine.

We both talked of having kids one day. My husband and I began that journey first, and seven years later it seems God has called us to focus in other places right now. Heather and Tony quickly became pregnant with their first son, Micah. The day she told me we both hugged each other and expressed joy as well as the sadness of not sharing that experience. It seemed God had different plans for each of us in the next season ahead.

Heather gave me the gift of watching someone become a mother—a wonderful, loving, creative mother. She gave me another gift too. She let me watch her wrestle with what the changes in her life meant for her God-sized dreams.

Heather didn't ever think of herself as a "stay-at-home" mom. She respected and admired women who made that choice. Yet it was clear she had an incredible gift when it came to designing and God had called her to DaySpring. Still, as Micah grew and a daughter, Lily, arrived as well, it seemed she heard a new call too.

She sensed God whispering that for this season, he wanted her to be able to focus more on being a mom. We talked about that transition many times over lunch. Heather wrestled with it intensely. Even when she made the transition, she confessed that it was much harder than she imagined, although it was what a part of her deep inside really wanted too.

She had two God-sized dreams that seemed to be in conflict with each other. Heather says:

> It took some time to adjust to the idea. Those first few months were very hard. Then one day a quote stuck out to me. It said, "You can have it all—but you can't have it

all at once." That changed my perspective. I began to think of my dreams in terms of seasons. For now, I knew that the God-sized dream of being home with my kids was supposed to be my main focus. That was a dream that didn't come naturally to me. My other dream, of fulfilling my creative calling, had always been there, and now it seemed I needed to pursue it differently. For a while I stepped away completely from that dream but then gradually began doing freelance work and finding other ways to express that desire of my heart. In a few years, both of my kids will be in school and my God-sized dreams will change again. I used to think that dreams stayed the same all of our lives. Now I understand that they change right along with us and what God has in each season.

I know many other women like Heather. Some have felt called to be at home like she did. Others sensed God prompting them to continue working. Many have found hybrids of both that fit their families in unique ways.

During the time when Heather and I talked a lot about our dreams and her decision, I came across a quote that I loved. Jill Churchill said, "There is no way to be a perfect mother and a million ways to be a good one."[15] I shared it with Heather, and we talked about those words often. Even without kids, I applied it in other ways to my life. ("There's no way to be a perfect wife, friend, writer ... but a million ways to be a good one.")

It became our little mantra for a few years, and I still think of it from time to time. It's true of God-sized dreams as well. *There's no way to do your God-sized dream perfectly, but there are a million ways to do it well.* Our lives shift and change. Seasons come and go. Our dreams do too. But through it all one thing remains steady: the God who put those dreams within our hearts in the first place.

I'm so proud of Heather because she's a woman who listens to Jesus. She loves him with all her heart. She does whatever is in front of her with creativity and excellence, whether that's being a mom, designing something beautiful, or loving on me as her friend.

Heather is a God-sized dreamer, and she's taught me so much about faith, flexibility, and being willing to let go so God can give me even more.

Do It Afraid:
Keri Lynn

Keri remembers the first time she had to perform in freshman drama class. And every time she does, she also recalls exactly how she came to be in that freshman drama class.

It was the end of her eighth-grade year, and the counselors were explaining that in high school, students were required to take one semester of either speech or drama. Keri says, "Both options made me want to lose my lunch."

She describes herself as the quiet, shy, awkward kid who did everything in her power to avoid the spotlight. Simply being called on in class to answer a question made her break into an instant cold sweat. And now, sitting in the cafeteria, she had just been informed that she would have to spend an entire semester taking a class that would require her to stand up and speak out. Yikes!

Keri decided to take speech, not because she wanted to but because it was the lesser of two evils. But her best friend had other plans. Her friend had heard a rumor that there was only one freshman drama class and concluded that it was the only way to guarantee the two of them would have a class together. "So I caved to peer pressure," Keri confesses.

The following September Keri found herself standing on a stage with twenty teenagers and one teacher watching her. She was supposed to perform. Looking back on that moment, Keri exclaims, "I don't remember what I had to do. All I remember was the absolute terror that gripped my heart!"

Keri remembers telling her teacher she was afraid. His response? "Do it afraid!" He told her fear was good; it would heighten her senses and give her a rush of adrenaline that would help her performance.

Keri says, "I promise you it didn't help. It was awful! The only consolation was that I made it to the ladies' room before losing my lunch. But over the weeks something strange began to happen. I started looking forward to my drama class. I even started feeling excited when it was my turn to perform. Don't get me wrong, I was still scared every time I faced the stairs leading to the stage, but I was learning to manage my fears."

Keri wound up taking four full years of drama. She joined the competitive drama squad and traveled all over the state competing and winning awards, thank you very much. And she loved it!

Years later, Keri reflects on that turning point in her life:

I still love the stage. In fact, I get paid to be onstage—well, it's actually a studio, not a stage. But there is a microphone, and there are people watching (listening). Friends ask me how I can do it. They ask if it's scary to be on the radio as a morning show host for KLRC every day. But for me, honestly, it's not scary. Not now. Because I pushed past the fear. I learned to overcome my anxiety.

Here's the problem with following Jesus. Every time I find myself relaxing . . . I find myself stirred. Every time I think I've arrived . . . I realize that I have further to go. You see, God won't let me quit dreaming. And the dreams just get bigger and scarier. To tell you the truth, it makes me want to run for the hills!

But I can't. The pull to be with him is just too strong. And over and over I hear him whispering, "Do it afraid! Push past the fear! Overcome the anxiety! I'm here. I'll hold your hand. I will catch you if you fall."

I want to settle in and rest here, in this place of comfort. I want to be content. But God isn't calling us to settle; he's calling us to follow.

Follow him into unchartered territory.
Follow him into new relationships.
Follow him into taking risks and chasing dreams.
As Keri learned, he's calling all of us to "Do it afraid!"

Permission to Have Joy along the Way: Bonnie Gray

Bonnie has depended on God since her early years as the oldest girl growing up in a single-parent family with little means. God was the only daddy she knew, so she stuck to him for dear life.

Dysfunctional upbringing? Bonnie sucked up the words of Jesus like they were the last oxygen mask left in a broken plane crashing down.

Dreams of becoming a writer dashed for a practical engineering degree? Bonnie chose to find her joy in serving others instead.

A traumatic stint in missions left Bonnie with years marked by solitude and prayer, while singleness past thirty handed her questions about the gift of singleness.

Even though Bonnie later got the surprising joy of getting married, she's been learning to be content with the story line of her life for a very long time. She got so good at living with the disappointment of yesterday that she had trouble opening up her heart to taste joy in today. Bonnie shares:

> I'd say I'm a happy person who loves to laugh, eat chocolate, and enjoy friends. And I can't describe the thrill my heart feels when I get to encourage others.
>
> As for personal joy, the kind that is God-sized? I like to stick to the kind of joy that comes out of suffering and trials. Not because I'm all that spiritual. That's just the kind I know about.
>
> I'm comfortable with walking through deserts. I'm used to wearing sandals and getting sand between my toes. Trouble is, I was walking along fine until one day I stepped out of the desert and into new waters of healing. Scenes in my life that previously looked void of purpose took on a new shape, color, and sound. I started seeing God in the background.
>
> I realized as hard and painful as my losses have been, Jesus's love for me grew deeper in spite of it all.

Bonnie describes always feeling like an ugly duckling with experiences she wishes had never been written into her life. But since Jesus started showing her how he carried her through it all, she now sees the fruits of love, faithfulness, and gentleness that he's planted in her, along with each sorrow.

She explains, "A new kind of joy has been growing in my heart. It's a growing desire for beauty even though I've experienced the barrenness of dreams. This joy is calling me to embrace abundance and celebrate the opportunities he's placed in my life. Like a new pair of shoes, this joy is very uncomfortable. This joy doesn't feel like it's me. I'm afraid to lean into this joy because maybe it won't last."

Questions Bonnie never asked before are now challenging this new freedom.

How will this joy change me?

Will my friends like this new me?

If I embrace this joy, will I love feeling this way more than depending on God?

Ultimately, all this awkwardness is a question about trusting in God's love.

Bonnie describes the permission she's found to have joy in her God-sized dreams with these words: "I'm used to snuggling in Jesus's arms. Now he wants me to ride on his shoulders. Do I really deserve to be here? God is saying, 'Yes, you deserve to be here. Because I love you.'"

Bonnie continues to write about her journey on www.faithbarista .com. She's moving forward with joy, hope, and the promise of growing into all God has created her to be and everything he has for her to do.

When Your Dreams Are Bigger Than You Are: Kristen Welch

The house was quiet. Kristen's family had been asleep for hours. The night was still, but her thoughts weren't. Kristen says, "I knew if I closed my eyes, I would see her face again."

Kristen never thought of herself as a dreamer. She shares, *"I'm a realist,* I would say to the gleam in my hubby's eye, the one he'd get right after he shared one of his big ideas. I like my feet on the ground. I like to know the beginning and the end. I like safe things."

After returning from a trip to Africa in March with Compassion International, Kristen knew she was being called to a God-sized dream. She was able to push it off during her busy day, hectic with kids, but at night all the suppressed thoughts would surface in her dreams.

The girl was there, feet caked with mud, her eyes distant. Hollow. She was desperately searching for something.

It was hope. And she had none.

When God began dropping the dream of The Mercy House into Kristen's heart and connecting the dots—hers with others who had the same recurring dream—she wanted to run.

She describes that season: "I kept saying, 'It's too big. This is too big for me.' (What I was really saying? 'God, I'm scared. This isn't safe. I can't.') But then I was reminded by this anonymous quote: 'God gives us dreams a size too big so that we can grow into them.'"

God wants us to stretch, to reach beyond ourselves and our own capabilities. It's there that we grow into our God-sized dreams.

Kristen feels clothed in a dream a size too big. She has more questions than answers, more fear than courage. But she has asked him what he required of her, and he answered:

> He has shown you, O mortal, what is good.
> And what does the LORD require of you?
> To act justly and to love mercy
> and to walk humbly with your God. (Mic. 6:8)

Does your dream feel too big for you? It probably is. But God is bigger.

Now when Kristen sees the girl's face in her dream, she doesn't turn away.

Because hope is on its way.

Kristen launched The Mercy House, which exists to provide alternative options for pregnant girls living in the streets of Kenya. The Mercy House aids them in nutrition, housing, prenatal care, counseling, biblical teaching, and job skills for sustainable living. Find out more at www.mercyhousekenya.org.

Building Dreams: Angie Washington

Much like Kristen's, this is a dream come true story for those in need.

Busy streets in a faraway place make it easy to overlook little ones in need. But one day a pair of feet pause and eyes look down to see the children—the ones who curl into their tiny spots on earth. The crowds continue to rush by, but change is coming.

"Somebody needs to do something about the orphans in our city," whispers a Voice.

"Yes, they do" is whispered back with a shake of the head and a shrug as footsteps hurry away. It's hard to embrace the need.

But for three more days this scene and conversation repeat.

"Somebody should do something about the orphans in our city," says Someone persistent, insistent.

The response slowly changes: "Yes, we may not be able to help them all, but we can help some."

Angie's husband listened to Someone, the One, and they started the House of Dreams Orphanage in Cochabamba, Bolivia. This dream began with months of paper trails. Finally a building could be prepared. Staff were hired. Beds waited. Warm clothes and healthy meals sat ready. This House of Dreams would be filled with dreamers, children who needed Someone to be their Father. Children whose flickering hope could be stoked and set ablaze once again.

That was over four years ago.

Now learn from Angie's little dreamers how to dream. She says:

> First, they dream with eyes closed. The pavement they sit on is cold, the scorn on the faces that pass by too harsh. Starving, they lift a weak hand to the air and beg

for help. Heads bow to the ground. They close their eyes and paint beauty in the darkness.

Slowly they begin to dream with their eyes open. They are brought in from the frigid night to safety. They are fed and clothed. Their dreams are coming true. They know the tangible love of Someone real. But wait—that is not the end.

Their eyes open wide, they look around and dream through the eyes of those around us. The goodness that was poured on them, they pour on others. Hands that once reached out begging now reach out healing. The extended arms of Someone made our dreams come true; we follow him. Our arms stretch out in sacrifice and love.

Are you dreaming with your eyes squeezed tight shut today? Don't lose hope. You are not alone.

Maybe your eyes are adjusting to the light of his goodness, of dreams come true. We celebrate with you today!

To those living a dream life, might we invite you to see through the eyes of those around you? You may be a dream come true as you follow the nudge of Someone close.

"Freely you have received; freely give" (Matt. 10:8).

Angie and her husband started the House of Dreams in Bolivia. You can find out more at www.houseofdreamsorphanage.com.

The Art of Dreaming: Dee Kasberger

Right away Dee exclaims, "Red Letter Words is a God-sized dream. There is no possible conceivable way that I could have planned for it to become what it is."

What Red Letter Words is today started as a thought, an idea for Scripture as art, big and plain for everyone to see. Bold and readable across the room. The focal point of a living room. That was 2003. It was a desire of Dee's heart.

Except that the timing was off. It wasn't the right season. Ecclesiastes 3 says that there is a time for everything. And 2003 was busy. Dee says:

> I was too busy doing too many things and not doing any of them very well. We had three young kids, and I was working for my husband, who at the time had two companies, a photography studio and a digital printing lab. I was volunteering at school and at church and at soccer. Whatever spare time I had was spent at the mall or reading gossip magazines. (Now, I am not saying that I don't still enjoy shopping as much as the next girl, but when I was on a first-name basis with every store manager, that was not good.) My worth was tied up in what I was doing.

Fast-forward a few years and Dee is home with their fourth baby. Her husband has sold his photography studio, and she is no longer working for Color, Inc.

They had decided that enough was enough. So Dee stopped working and volunteering so much and concentrated on staying home, raising the kids, and managing the house. Dee describes that season:

> I never thought that I would be so content with the ordinary daily cleaning and laundry and groceries and everything involved with keeping a home.
> I decided to seek first his kingdom.
> God's way of doing things.

> I had always done things my way. But when I sought after his kingdom, I became more and more aware of exactly who I was in Christ.
>
> A sinner saved by grace.
>
> Created in his image.
>
> Blessed and highly favored.
>
> Worthy. Redeemed. Loved.
>
> I was content and happy. And it wasn't until I was content with the ordinary that God opened the door to the extraordinary.

Dee started having small blocks of time during the day that she was so thankful for—spare quiet moments to work on her dream of Scripture as art. Because she had long before decided that whatever spare time she was given was going to be used to bring God glory.

The ideas for Red Letter Words became clearer. The art would look like an erased chalkboard. With big text. With Scripture that had personal meaning to her. After much trial and error, Dee made pieces for her house and started giving them to friends and family members for Christmas and birthdays and baby showers and wedding presents.

In 2008 Dee started an Etsy store. She wrote down the vision. Every month it was the same: "Bring God's glory to lots of people." It is still the same vision, and www.redletterwords.com soon followed. Dee says:

> It is so exciting to see what God's plan is for Red Letter Words. His plan is always for good, and I love walking by the foyer and reading Jeremiah 29:11. Over the years I have held on to and confessed out loud many Scriptures at different seasons of life . . . most of which have been made into Red Letter Words prints.
>
> God is no respecter of persons . . . this is for you too—

You were created in his image.
You are blessed and highly favored.
Worthy. Redeemed. Loved.

God is endlessly creative in the dreams he gives us—and the unexpected ways he makes them come true in our lives!

It's Not Too Late: Mela Kamin

Mela always wanted to be an artist—but singer was someone else's dream.

She was a jock, then a journalist, and then a juice-slingin' mom of three. Sure, she sang—but with the radio and to her kids (easy crowd).

She searched for an activity to pour herself into. Not that she wasn't already busy, but she was looking for "her" something.

Mela wondered, *Whatever happened to the creative, dazzling, big dreamer? What became of the girl who graduated in three and a half years, gave the commencement speech about being an "agent of change," and soared into an exciting career?*

She says, "It turns out she was afraid—afraid, after spending years at home trying to be everything to everyone, that she was gone for good. Afraid she was too old or too ordinary to do anything worthwhile. But a singer . . . really?"

Two years ago, as a middle-aged mom living in the suburbs of Minnesota, Mela was a far cry from the picture of most recording artists. She had no musical training, fan base, or blog readership to support an album. Some people closest to her didn't even know Mela could sing.

God-sized dreams, though, aren't easy, expected, or practical.

No matter her stage of life or missing credentials, what she had far outweighed what she lacked.

She had Holy Spirit power from a God who says that with him, *all* things are possible.

She had a deep-down desire to use her gifts in a bolder way.

And she had just enough gumption to go for it, even faced with Goliath-size fear.

Just call her David.

David wasn't the first (or fifth) choice or the most qualified to fight. When he stood up, *no one* saw it coming. He was unlikely *and* unqualified.

Mela knew her fears could have counted her out. She felt the enemy telling her to keep her head down, go through the motions, and keep her mouth shut.

But as she pushed through, God's plans, and the faith he provides, kicked in. People, events, and songs were placed in her life, on her lap and on her lips.

Mela explains, "I couldn't ignore it any more than David could ignore his call to action. He won, knowing God gave him everything he needed . . . not by being the biggest or best but by being the boldest."

So what got Mela out on the battlefield?

Someone pushed her. A friend helped her put her hopes on paper, and that was the first time she shared her dream to be a singer.

Her friend didn't laugh. She told Mela it was awesome. And Mela finally saw the possibilities.

Once she started writing songs, everything she knew about herself came back into view. Passion resurfaced, confidence came bouncing back, and she couldn't stop smiling.

God had brought her back to life for such a time as this.

Then doors opened and people appeared.

Mela met musician Carl Herrgesell at a women's event, playing keys for Kathy Troccoli. Mela told her story, and as only God can orchestrate, Carl offered to produce her album.

Just. Like. That.

Two months later, Mela was in a Nashville recording studio meeting her coproducer, Dan Needham. He and Carl lovingly guided her through the process and took all the pressure off. Five trips to Nashville and four short months later, that big dream became Mela's debut album, "Summer in My Soul."

Mela exclaims with a smile, "I'm here to tell you—there are no expiration dates on your gifts or your dreams. Start where you are with what you have, and don't be surprised when God makes a way."

"Each of you should use whatever gift you have received to serve others, as faithful stewards of God's grace in its various forms" (1 Pet. 4:10).

Dreams Even in the Middle of the Desert: Ashley Wells

In the midst of the most difficult journey of her life, Ashley rediscovered God was much bigger than she had ever imagined. He was with her and carrying her through her journey. There was Someone to rescue her.

After she had felt hurt and isolation because of infertility, God, by his wonderful grace, opened Ashley's eyes to the fact that he had a plan for her and for her future. He was guiding her through.

Ashley shares, "I didn't know all of his plans for my life (and I still don't), nor do I understand why he had led me through my personal valley. However, in the midst of my journey, God

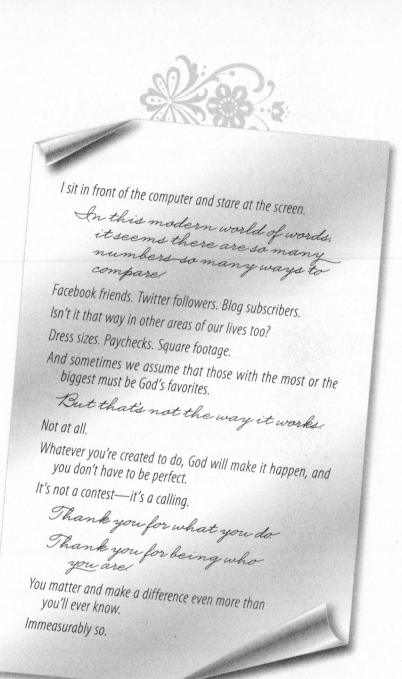

I sit in front of the computer and stare at the screen.

In this modern world of words,
it seems there are so many
numbers—so many ways to
compare!

Facebook friends. Twitter followers. Blog subscribers.

Isn't it that way in other areas of our lives too?

Dress sizes. Paychecks. Square footage.

And sometimes we assume that those with the most or the biggest must be God's favorites.

But that's not the way it works!

Not at all.

Whatever you're created to do, God will make it happen, and you don't have to be perfect.

It's not a contest—it's a calling.

Thank you for what you do.

Thank you for being who
you are!

You matter and make a difference even more than you'll ever know.

Immeasurably so.

planted a seed, a God-sized dream, that would grow in my heart and bloom."

The God-sized dream that he planted in Ashley's heart was that he was going to use her story to encourage other women in the midst of their suffering. God would use her hurt and experience to help others going through hard times too.

When Ashley first felt the reality of this God-sized dream, she pushed it aside. How could she possibly help others when she felt like she was drowning? She thought, *Lord, this just can't be true!*

She continues, "I remember when I started to feel whole again. I remember learning to trust him again. I started reading God's Word more faithfully. I developed a stronger prayer life. I started giving him my anxieties, worries, and stress. I gave him my infertility. I put it in his hands. I started to trust him no matter the outcome. I began to find healing. I felt steady again, resting in his hands."

God has been guiding Ashley beyond the valley (though still childless) for about two years. That seed, the God-sized dream, bloomed this year as she wrote about her journey and how God has led her every step.

Ashley admits, "Sharing wasn't easy. As I began to write, I felt like I was not spiritual enough, or had not experienced this trial the 'right way' (like there is a right way!), or that I had suffered too much and too deeply for good to come from sharing. Yet slowly I began rejoicing as I continued to write my story, because after I shared about my hurt, I got to share about the hope that I had found."

Even more so, Ashley is now rejoicing as women are reading her book, *How My Soul Yearns*, and finding hope in God. Hope in the midst of the valley. Hope in the midst of suffering. Hope in the midst of this sin-tainted world.

Ashley exclaims, "Only a God-sized dream can lead a hurt and wounded woman to share her story to help other hurt and wounded women! What a wonderful God we have that he uses us in these ways!"

Conclusion

God-sized dreams come in all shapes and sizes. They're not limited by geography, age, or circumstances. I could fill up thousands more pages with God-sized dreams. I hope you've enjoyed this little taste. What spoke to you most in these stories? What would you share with these women if you met them?

I'd love to hear your God-sized dream story too. You can share it with me at www.holleygerth.com.

You are part of your own beautiful story. It's being written by the Author of life, and he has more in store for you than you can even imagine. The best is yet to be for you, my friend.

············ Go Deeper Guide ············

(Download a printable version with lines for writing at www.holley gerth.com on the "Books & More" page.)

1. What are you waiting on in your life right now? Which of Kristen's tips spoke to you most?

2. Have you ever had to choose between two God-sized dreams you really wanted, like Heather? What guided you as you made that decision?

3. Keri tells us to "Do it afraid!" Describe a time in your childhood when you did so and how that impacted your life.

4. Bonnie is learning how to have joy along the path to her God-sized dreams. What have you learned about joy through your own journey?

5. Kristen's and Angie's God-sized dreams both led them to serve the poor. What's your definition of "poor"? Is it more than just financial? Who in your life can you serve?

6. Dee's dream meant expressing her creativity in a new way. What do you do to express yours? (And everyone is creative in some way—it just means the ways that God brings life into the world through you.)

7. Mela thought it might be too late for her dream. Have you ever felt that way? What's the truth instead?

8. Ashley discovered her God-sized dream in a most unlikely place—the middle of her personal desert. Have you ever found a blessing in an unexpected place or situation in your life?

— *Dream It. Do It.* —

Reading the God-sized dreams of others can encourage us in our own as well. Choose a biography, memoir, or blog of someone you admire, and spend some time reading their story this week. Perhaps the best one of all is the story of Joshua and Caleb in the Old Testament book of Numbers.

11

Commissioning **You**

The room pulsed with energy. In every corner you could hear the sounds of excitement. Over one hundred women had gathered in this place. As I stepped onto the stage, I could see smiling faces looking back at me. Each of these women had her own business as a Blessings Unlimited consultant. Each one represented a God-sized dream come true.

I could see faces of all ages and shades in the audience. Some were single, others grandmothers. From every stage and walk of life, they were here because passion for their faith and connecting with other women bound them together.

I imagine if I could see all of the readers of this book in one room, it might feel the same way. Perhaps you're reading this page on a plane, from the corner of your couch, or on the screen of an e-reader as you sit in a local park. If you look around right now, you might not even see anyone else near you.

But you, my sister, are not alone.

We are never alone in our God-sized dreams.

At the end of the session with the Blessings Unlimited women, I asked them to stand up. I commissioned them to go out into the world, to live the dreams within their hearts, to make a difference in a new and powerful way wherever they were called to be.

And I want to do the same for you.

You Are Chosen

Before your dream ever came into being, God called your name. He formed you with love in your mother's womb and intricately designed every part of who you would become. You truly are fearfully and wonderfully made—a masterpiece by the same God who spread the oceans farther than we can even see. He numbers every hair on your head. He knows every care in your heart. You belong to him.

Your journey on this path is not by coincidence. You are here because God looked out over all of history and chose you for a particular time and purpose. You could have entered the world a hundred years ago or a thousand years from now. But you are in this generation, this time, and there will never be another you or another opportunity to do what only you are chosen to complete.

Go out there in boldness knowing that you don't have to be like anyone else. You don't have to do what any other person has done. You are chosen for one life—yours.

And the wonderful news? Whatever God chooses you to do, he will equip you for. Being chosen means you will be given all you need. Being chosen means that success simply consists of obedience and God will do the rest. Being chosen means that you have a great big God as your partner every step of the way.

I remember standing on the sidelines at recess as we lined up for an impromptu game of softball. You could see on the face of every kid in that field two words: "Pick me!" We all want to be part of something greater than ourselves. We all want to know we have something to contribute. We all want to be chosen for the team.

God looks at you and says, "I pick you." And he does so with great joy.

Dare to live as someone who knows who they belong to forever.

You Are Called

When our names are called on the playground as children, we become part of a team. We have been chosen. Yet as the game begins, it's likely that at some point we'll be given a specific position. Mine always seemed to end up being picking daisies in the outfield where no ball ever made it. But in the kingdom, there aren't any wasted positions.

You're here on earth for far more than just to take up space. God doesn't want you to just "survive" until you get home to heaven where life truly begins. When we know him, eternity begins *now*. Your days are significant, and he has no intention of wasting them. We've often relegated the word *calling* to specifically spiritual vocations like being a pastor. But the reality is, we all have unique tasks we're asked to do throughout our lives.

This means that what you do every day matters. Your life has significance. God describes himself as "I am." I love that because it's present tense. It's right here and now. If God is always with us, then there are no ordinary moments in our lives. Wherever you are right now, you are standing on holy ground.

We feel a longing for "more" in our lives because God's calling always pulls us upward and onward. He doesn't let us get complacent or too comfortable. He wants to offer us new adventures with him. Yes, we are to be content. But that's very different than being passive.

As I write this, my cell phone is sitting next to me. It will ring today. It will ring again tomorrow. Being called is an ongoing process that we live out in different ways until we get home to heaven.

Your God-sized dream is an important part of the call on your life, but it's not *the* call. The ultimate calling for all of us is an intimate relationship with Jesus. It's not about the cell phone—it's about who's on the other end of the line. It's about who's saying your name in the middle of the game and asking you to take your place.

Your life matters. You have significance. You are called.

You Are Already on Your Way

Sometimes it can seem as if we're sitting by the phone and simply waiting, wondering when God will remember us and decide to give us something important to do. But that's not the way it works. God has *already* called you. You are *already* on your way to all he has for you.

You may think, "But I've taken so many detours" or "It's too late." We tend to picture God's will like a very straight line, and if we veer off at all, then we'll never get to the destination. But God can get us there in a thousand different ways. My car has a GPS system, and its favorite phrase to say to me is "recalculating." It doesn't say, "You made a wrong turn. Cancel your trip and go home." God doesn't say that to us either. He's able to "recalculate" as many times as needed to get us where he wants us in the end.

Start where you are right now. In this very moment. On this very page. Whatever has been holding you back from your God-sized dreams, drop it on the side of the road. Tell God you're ready to move forward, and he will take care of the rest. Nothing can stand in his way—or in yours when you're following him.

You Are Needed

All it takes is a few clicks through the internet and I wind up feeling inadequate. It seems everyone is off changing the world in some distant place. There are vivid pictures, inspiring stories, and leaps of faith that make my daily journey look like a walk in the park. It's easy to silently begin to believe the words "I'm not needed."

That lie has been echoing through the church since the very beginning. Paul confronted it when he said:

> Just as a body, though one, has many parts, but all its many parts form one body, so it is with Christ. For we were all baptized by one Spirit so as to form one body—whether Jews or Gentiles, slave or free—and we were all given the one Spirit to drink. Even so the body is not made up of one part but of many.
>
> Now if the foot should say, "Because I am not a hand, I do not belong to the body," it would not for that reason stop being part of the body. And if the ear should say, "Because I am not an eye, I do not belong to the body," it would not for that reason stop being part of the body. If the whole body were an eye, where would the sense of hearing be? If the whole body were an ear, where would the sense of smell be? But in fact God has placed the parts in the body, every one of them, just as he wanted them to be. If they were all one part, where would the body be? As it is, there are many parts, but one body.
>
> The eye cannot say to the hand, "I don't need you!" And the head cannot say to the feet, "I don't need you!" (1 Cor. 12:12–21)

You are irreplaceable. What other parts of the body of Christ are doing isn't better—just different. You have something to offer that no one else can, and that's *you*.

As I type these words, I'm wearing a green rubber bracelet that arrived in the mail yesterday from my friend Jessica Turner. Engraved on the bracelet are four words: "Gitzen Girl" and "Choose Joy." Gitzen Girl, whose real name is Sara Frankl, went home to Jesus a few short weeks ago after being homebound with illness for three years even though she was only in her thirties. And yet from within her home's walls, she found a way to touch thousands of lives through her words. As she got ready to head home to Jesus, stories from all over the internet poured out, and our eyes widened as we realized how impactful Sara's life had been—even more than we knew before. Knowing Sara changed me and my definition of limitations because she turned hers into opportunities.

Sara never said, "I'm not a wife. I'm not a mom. I can't leave my house. I'm not needed." Instead she shifted her focus to others and simply asked, "Who can I encourage today?" Sara's role in the body of Christ looked different than many others', and yet she beautifully and joyfully chose to fulfill it. We can all do the same.

We need each other. I need you. You need me. None of us can do it all, but we can all do (and be) our wonderful, God-chosen part.

You Are Loved

Our culture commonly opens conversations with, "What do you do?" It's a casual question with a subtle implication—that what you do defines who you are. Yet it doesn't work that way in the kingdom. God is always first about identity and then destiny.

An odd thing can happen on the way to a God-sized dream. Somewhere along the way we can begin to confuse our dream with who we are. *You are not your dream.* Yes, it's an important part of your life and calling, but it's not your identity.

That's good news for many reasons, but perhaps this is the most encouraging of all: you are not loved for your dream. And you can't stop being loved no matter how it turns out.

Whew.

Did anyone else just breathe a sigh of relief with me?

Something within us wants a measurable way to earn love. It makes us feel more secure. We believe, "If I can just do X, then it means I must be loved." But the problem with that kind of thinking is this: as soon as we mess up, we begin to doubt that we can be loved.

You are loved as you are by a God who does not change.

Nothing you do will make him love you more.

Nothing you don't do will make him love you less.

His love for you is based on who he is and who you are as his child. Your dreams and what you accomplish in your life are part of the amazing journey you will take with God—but they are not the determiner of your relationship.

You are free to risk because you are not risking what matters most of all.

No matter what you lose, you still win in the end.

Because you'll go home with love.

You're Going to Make It

There's always this moment, this space between the knowing and the coming true. It's the hardest place. It's where most people quit.

But you're not a quitter.

God says, "This Promised Land is yours." It's *ours*. But we have to go up and possess it. And that's messy. Wild. Exhausting. It

Hello, friend, getting ready to take that next step in your day

Through a door.

Into a dream.

On that hard path.

Wherever you are, I just want to let my words lean in close and whisper, "Keep going."

You can take the next step.

No matter how small.

Or how big.

Both make a difference.

And even if you're called to stand still, you can still keep going.

Going to your knees.

Going to the One who came for you.

You've got prayers behind you, the One who loves you beside you, and more than you can even imagine ahead of you too.

makes us think, "Maybe I didn't hear God right. Maybe I shouldn't go this way."

Go.

That's only the sound of fear whistling in your ears. You can do this. He can do this in you, through you. I've lived in that place. I know the way a heart can pound. Let's keep going, you and I, all the way to the place God promised . . . and farther up and into it for the rest of our lives.

You are not responsible for making sure you get where God wants you to go. You're simply asked to say yes when he asks you to take the next step. Much of the time you won't know where it leads. Even when you do, the purpose might be unclear. This isn't a journey about speed or efficiency. Instead it's about trust. It's about knowing and believing that the One guiding you is good.

Only God knows the way to your Promised Land. But you can lean on this: he's even more committed to getting you there than you are. Sometimes it feels as if God doesn't care about our dreams. But when they are truly from him, he's even more passionate about them than we are. He never stops bringing his purposes into being in this world.

I'm good at being a spiritual backseat driver. I like to tell God the equivalent of, "Um, I think you missed your turn." When I do, it sometimes feels as if he smiles knowingly at me, then looks back at the road and simply whispers to my heart, "Peace, daughter. I will get you there. You are free to enjoy the ride."

You are too.

Your Dream Is Going to Change the World

I may not know what your dream is, but I know this: it's going to make a difference. Every God-sized dream does. Your dream might feel small. It might feel bigger than a mountain. But as we talked about in the very beginning, it's not the size of the dream that counts but instead the Giver of it.

Your dream may change the world in ways that make the front page of the news. Or it might change the world in ways that only your family knows. That doesn't reflect the importance of it but rather the purpose of it.

And I can guarantee this: you will not see the full impact of your dream this side of heaven. That can be one of the hardest parts.

All day long I click, type, look through the screen at the faces of people I love who live halfway across the country or even on the other side of the world. And sometimes, in the quiet moments, I wonder if what I do really makes a difference. "You can't see it in person," hisses the enemy. "You can't touch it. How do you know it's real?"

Then I think about how I should be doing something tangible— rocking a baby, handing out food, building a house. I feel a heart hunger to know the results with my five senses. I whisper this to Jesus one morning as sunlight spills in through the open window. I ask him if I've gotten it all wrong—if I should be doing something else. A verse pops into my heart like a present left on the front porch:

> Now faith is confidence in what we hope for and assurance about what we do not see. (Heb. 11:1)

I've always thought of those words in the context of believing in God. But that morning it seemed the One who loves us whispered that part of faith is also about believing that our obedience makes a difference—even when we can't see the results.

Sure of what we hope for . . . that what we do matters in the world, that hearts out there really are encouraged, that the flicker of our shining can bring light to a life again.

Certain of what we do not see . . . that the bonds we make, the needs we meet, the prayers we lift up are as real as what's right in front of us—that the great I Am is everywhere and in all we do in his name.

I think then of a conversation I had with my friend and fellow author Ann Voskamp many months ago about much the same thing. We tossed and turned thoughts around between us until at the end we nodded, smiled, and said . . .

How can we say that the virtual doesn't matter when the Spirit is virtual?

The kingdom has always been about more than what we can sense. Oh, friends, it's more about what we know in our hearts—and about following faithfully the One who whispers to us there—believing that in all things he is working together for good.

Sometimes that good is something we can see, touch, taste, and smell.

And sometimes it's built of eternal things that we won't know until heaven.

So press on, sisters.

Keep the faith.

Do what you do, be who you are, walk in that sometimes blind, always beautiful obedience.

Yes, you really are making a difference.

Your Dream Will Change You Too

When we begin a dream, it always seems to be about where we're going. We think of the future, the finish line, the results we want to see. Yet eventually we realize that this dream isn't about where we're going at all—it's really about who we're becoming along the way.

Yes, your dream will change the world. Even more, it will change you.

You are not the same person now that you were when you began to dream.

You will not be the same person you are today later on down the road.

The adventures we share with Jesus shape us from the inside out. We change, grow, stretch.

The other night I stayed up too late, curled under my covers with a book in hand. It spoke of things that made me take deep breaths and let them out slowly with relief. It spoke of freedom and grace and whispered that I am enough. In *The Me I Want to Be*, John Ortberg says:

> Here is the good news: When you flourish, you become more you. You become more that person God had in mind when God thought you up. You don't just become holier. You become you-ier. You will change: God wants you to become "a new creation." But "new" doesn't mean completely different; instead it's like an old piece of furniture that gets restored to its intended beauty.... God wants to redeem you, not exchange you.[16]

God-sized dreams are one of the main ways this happens in our lives. We think that God is concerned about us accomplishing a lot for him. But the God who spoke the world into being doesn't have any trouble with his to-do list. What he's interested in most is relationship. He wants to see you draw closer to him, become more like Jesus, and in doing so discover who you're truly meant to be as someone made in his image.

Becoming all you're created to be is simply saying yes to God whenever he asks you to grow with him.

You'll Be Glad You Did It

As I think back over the God-sized dreams in my life, both incredibly joyful and painful moments come to mind. But they all have one thing in common: I would do them again. Life is meant to be lived. Even what seems like the most colossal of mistakes in the moment can be redeemed by God.

It has been said that we all experience pain in our lives. As we've talked about, what we get to decide is whether it's the pain of risk or regret. There isn't a way to lead a completely safe life. And sometimes doing nothing is the greatest threat of all.

No one ever gets to their last breath and says, "I wish I hadn't said yes to Jesus so often. I could have had a much more comfortable life." As Jim Elliot, who lost his life for the gospel, said, "He is no fool who gives what he cannot keep to gain that what he cannot lose."[17] It's unlikely that you will have to literally die for your faith—but you will have to die to yourself. That's the paradox of a God-sized dream. It makes you come alive and causes you to die to yourself all at once.

You have a limitless, resurrected Jesus empowering you. He created you with strengths, gifts, and a calling that no one else will ever have. He has given you everything you need for a godly life (see 2 Pet. 1:3). He looks at you with love, has promised to be with you wherever you go, and will complete the good work he began in you.

Your God-sized dream is invincible with Jesus. Does that mean it will turn out the way you imagine? Nope. But it does mean that if you say yes to what God asks of you, he will complete his purposes in and through you. The greatest risk is not failure—it's disobedience.

You are not that kind of woman. I know it. You are already saying yes to what God asks just by reading these words, just by being open to dreaming. He will show you the next steps. He will make a way even when there seems to be none. He will guide you into all that he has for you.

And it will be amazing.

The "More" That Matters Most

We started our journey together talking about how we all long for more in our lives. Finding it seems like something mysterious. We wait for "more" to come to us. But here's the reality: most of the time we discover it along the way as we're saying yes to God.

The "more" we long for isn't something we can produce—instead it's something we receive. It's not found inside our comfort zones but instead just beyond them in the wild and glorious adventures God invites us to take with him.

You won't find "more" on your couch.

You won't find it in long hours at the office.

You won't find it in the new car parked in the driveway.

You won't even find it in your friends and family.

You'll only find it in the arms of Jesus.

Behind every "more" we dream of, he is what our hearts really want most. And they will never be satisfied with settling for anything less.

Consider the God-sized dreams in your heart as invitations to a fuller life. A life with more joy, passion, and growth. A life that makes you rejoice on the good days and push through the hard days because you know it's worth it.

You only get one shot at this world. And we only get one you. Make the most of your time here. Dare to dream. Dare to do. Dare to find out just how much God has in store for you.

I've loved sharing this journey with you. I wish we could end with a real-life conversation. I'd ask you all about what your heart has heard and your God-sized dream. I'd lean in and let you tell me all about it. I'd smile, nod, and cheer you on through every word. Before we left, I would pray for you too.

And until we get to have that face-to-face chat here or in heaven, I'm going to pray for you anyway . . . starting right now, right here as I type these words.

> *Lord,*
>
> *Thank you for the one who is on this page right now. You know her name, her needs, her dreams. I thank you that she is a woman of faith and courage—a Joshua or Caleb in her generation. I thank you that even though she may feel some fear, she is saying yes to what you have placed in her heart to do.*
>
> *As she finishes this book and goes about her day, I pray that you would continue the work you've started here. Guide her into the next step of her journey with you. Show her more of what you have in store for her. Provide what she needs all along the way.*
>
> *I'm so glad you're with her the way I wish I could be today. Give her heart a hug for me. Help her with her dream. Thank you that it's going to change the world, her life, and eternity too.*
>
> *Amen.*

As we walked out the door of that little café, I'd say the four words we use in the South when we're feeling happy and want to encourage someone. Yes, here's a little send-off just for you . . .

"Go get 'em, friend!"

Go Deeper Guide

(Download a printable version with lines for writing at www.holley gerth.com on the "Books & More" page.)

1. *You are chosen.* What does God want you to do with your life—today, this week, in the future?

2. *You are already on your way.* What's one thing you can do right here, right now to make a difference and move a little closer to your God-sized dream?

3. *You're needed.* "The body is a unit, though it is made up of many parts; and though all its parts are many, they form one body" (1 Cor. 12:12 NIV 1984). What part of the body of Christ do you think you might be—heart, hands, eyes?

4. *You're loved.* What helps you hold on to God's love?

5. *You're going to make it.* What challenges are you facing right now? How will you get past them?

6. *Your dream is going to change the world.* At the end of your life, what do you want your legacy to be?

7. *Your dream will change you too.* How do you want to be different than you are right now a year from now, a decade from now, even longer? Growth is a lifelong process, and you will never stop until you're home.

— *Dream It. Do It.* —

It's time for you to close this book, my friend. And that means the most important thing you can do is to simply go out there and take the next step in your dream. What will it be? I'd like to know, and you can share it with me at www.holleygerth.com. You can also take a look at the e-coaching section of the site for one way I can partner with you in your God-sized dream.

Acknowledgments

The more I write, the more I realize it's about so much more than words on a page. It's really about a beautiful community of people joining together to birth something into the world.

Mark, thank you for helping me become the woman God created me to be and supporting my God-sized dreams. We make a great team, and I love you more every year.

My family (especially Mom, Dad, Stephen, Amber, Granny Eula, and Poppi) for showing me that words are a way of loving that can truly make a difference. You have prayed for all my dreams and cheered me on every step of the way. I'm so grateful.

Chip MacGregor, thanks for your work as my agent on this book. You're also a wise friend, a valued advisor, and one of the first who caught the vision.

Jennifer Leep, every time I think of how God gave you to me as my editor at Revell, I still get happy tears in my eyes. Your insight, friendship, and support have meant more to me than I can even express. I'm so glad we get to do this together again.

Twila Bennett, you are the queen of marketing, and I'm so thrilled to have found a fabulous friend as well as a wonderful partner on this project through you. We are like a pair of cute shoes at our favorite store (you know the one). The perfect match.

The DaySpring, Blessings Unlimited, and (in)courage teams—I am so blessed to do ministry and business with you.

The women of (in)courage—you are my extended network of sisters. If I listed all the ways each of you has blessed me, I would need to write another book! Thank you for your love, your grace, and the way you make me brave enough to go out there into the world with my words.

To my real-life girlfriends, thank you for all of the hours you spent talking with me about these things over coffee—for being my sounding board and safe place. You are a gift to me, and I thank God for you so often.

To my blog readers, thank you for sharing this journey with me. This book started with you, and you helped me grow this seed of an idea into what it is today. Your beautiful fingerprints are all over the place here.

To all the other God-sized dreamers in my life, thank you for what you've taught me about living with courage, taking leaps of faith, and being committed to growth and relationships for a lifetime.

Most of all, thank you to Jesus for being willing to use me just as I am. Let's keep dreaming together. I'm yours forever.

Notes

1. Rick Warren, *The Purpose Driven Life: What on Earth Am I Here For?* (Grand Rapids: Zondervan, 2003), 11.

2. You can read about the study at http://www.gammawomen.com.

3. "Citizenship in a Republic," speech at the Sorbonne, Paris, April 23, 1910, quoted at "In His Own Words," Theodore Roosevelt Association, http://www.theodoreroosevelt.org/life/quotes.htm.

4. Marcus Buckingham and Donald O. Clifton, *Now, Discover Your Strengths* (New York: Free Press, 2001).

5. Gretchen Rubin, *The Happiness Project: Or, Why I Spent a Year Trying to Sing in the Morning, Clean My Closets, Fight Right, Read Aristotle, and Generally Have More Fun* (New York: HarperCollins, 2009), 66–67.

6. Sharon Wooten, "I Really Need to Get Over It," (in)courage, July 21, 2001, http://www.incourage.me/2011/07/i-really-need-to-get-over-it.html.

7. Bruce Wilkinson, *The Dream Giver: Following Your God-Given Destiny* (Colorado Springs: Multnomah, 2003), 98.

8. Bonnie Gray, "A Tribute: Sara's Song & Why It's Hard to Say Goodbye," *Faith Barista* (blog), September 18, 2011, http://www.faithbarista.com/2011/09/a-tribute-sara-frankls-song-and-why-its-hard-to-say-goodbye/.

9. Laurel Mellin, *Wired for Joy* (Carlsbad, CA: Hay House, 2010), 2.

10. Timothy Ferriss, *The 4-Hour Workweek: Escape 9–5, Live Anywhere, and Join the New Rich*, expanded and updated ed. (New York: Crown, 2009), Kindle ed., 36–37.

11. Janet Kornblum, "Study: 25% of Americans Have No One to Confide In," *USA Today*, June 22, 2006, www.usatoday.com/news/nation/2006-06-22-friendship_x.htm.

12. Wilkinson, *The Dream Giver*, 110.

13. John Piper, *Don't Waste Your Life* (Wheaton: Crossway, 2003), 97.

14. Kristen Strong, "What Every Bit of Bad News Holds," *Chasing Blue Skies* (blog), November 29, 2011, http://chasingblueskies.net/?p=2685.

15. Jill Churchill, quoted in "Mother's Day Love and Appreciation," *Positive Impact*, May 8, 2012, http://www.positiveimpactmagazine.com/2012/05/08/mothers-day -love-and-appreciation/.

16. John Ortberg, *The Me I Want to Be: Becoming God's Best Version of You* (Grand Rapids: Zondervan, 2009), 16.

17. Jim Elliot, journal entry, October 28, 1949; archived at the Billy Graham Center, Wheaton, IL, http://www2.wheaton.edu/bgc/archives/faq/20.htm.

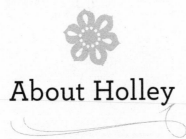

About Holley

Holley Gerth is a bestselling writer, life coach, and speaker who loves sharing God's heart with women through words. She's done so through several books, a partnership with DaySpring, and her popular blog. Holley is also a co-founder of (in)courage, a website for women that received almost a million page views in its first six months. Holley now does e-coaching for God-sized dreamers, and you can find out more about how she can partner with you at www.holleygerth.com.

Holley shares her heart and home with her husband, Mark. She lives in the South, likes to say "y'all," and would love to have coffee with you so she could hear all about you too. Until then, she hopes you'll hang out with her online at www.holleygerth.com.

Hello, friend!

Thanks again for sharing this journey with me. I truly wish I could have a cup of coffee with you today and hear about your God-sized dreams. Until then, I hope we can stay connected in some other ways!

I'd love for you to stop by and visit my place online at **www.holleygerth.com**. The e-coaching section will tell you about one way I can partner with you in your God-sized dream. And when you subscribe to my blog by email, you'll get free encouraging messages sent right to your inbox.

With Jesus you really are made for more, my friend. Keep believing that's true and dreaming like you do!

Love,

Holley Gerth

PS: Together we can help women all over the world fulfill their God-sized dreams. A portion of author proceeds from this book will go to the Compassion International Leadership Development Program. To find out more about the program, visit **www.compassion.com.**

Connect with
Holley at
HolleyGerth.com

How would your life be different if you truly believed you're loved just as you are?

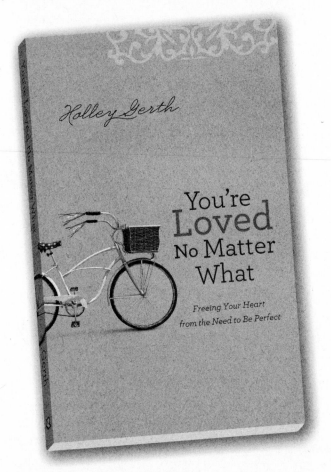

When we know we're truly loved, the response is to love in return—and that changes everything.

....

"I often say it doesn't have to be perfect to be beautiful. Holley Gerth shows women that's just as true for our hearts as it is for every other area of our lives."

—Myquillyn Smith, The Nester, author of *The Nesting Place*

Ɽ Revell
a division of Baker Publishing Group
www.RevellBooks.com

Available Wherever Books Are Sold
Also Available in Ebook Format

If your life isn't perfect . . .
If you've ever been disappointed . . .
If you feel stressed or tired . . .
This is for you.

"Holley Gerth is a fresh voice for every woman—
she echoes the voice of our Father."

—Ann Voskamp, *New York Times* bestselling
author of *One Thousand Gifts*

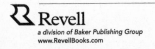

Revell
a division of Baker Publishing Group
www.RevellBooks.com

Available Wherever Books Are Sold
Also Available in Ebook Format

Discover the dreams God has given you—
and then dare to pursue them.

Ebook Only

Holley Gerth takes you by the heart and says,
"Yes! You can do this!" She guides you with insightful
questions, action plans to take the next steps, and most
of all, the loving hand of a friend.

ℛ Revell
a division of Baker Publishing Group
www.RevellBooks.com

Available Wherever Books Are Sold
Also Available in Ebook Format

Be the First to Hear about Other New Books from REVELL!

Sign up for announcements about new and upcoming titles at

RevellBooks.com/SignUp

Don't miss out on our great reads!

Revell

a division of Baker Publishing Group
www.RevellBooks.com